Disrupted Intersubjectivity

Thinking|Media

Series Editors
Bernd Herzogenrath
Patricia Pisters

Disrupted Intersubjectivity

Paralysis and Invasion in Ian McEwan's Works

Andrei Ionescu

BLOOMSBURY ACADEMIC

NEW YORK • LONDON • OXFORD • NEW DELHI • SYDNEY

BLOOMSBURY ACADEMIC
Bloomsbury Publishing Inc
1385 Broadway, New York, NY 10018, USA
50 Bedford Square, London, WC1B 3DP, UK
29 Earlsfort Terrace, Dublin 2, Ireland

BLOOMSBURY, BLOOMSBURY ACADEMIC and the Diana logo are
trademarks of Bloomsbury Publishing Plc

First published in the United States of America 2020
This paperback edition published in 2021

Cover design by Daniel Benneworth-Gray
Cover image © Paolo Sanfilippo

Library of Congress Cataloging-in-Publication Data
Names: Ionescu, Andrei, 1985- author.
Title: Disrupted intersubjectivity: paralysis and invasion in
Ian McEwan's work / Andrei Ionescu.
Description: New York: Bloomsbury Academic, 2020. |
Series: Thinking/media | Includes bibliographical references and index.
Identifiers: LCCN 2019053350 | ISBN 9781501362460 (hb) |
ISBN 9781501362446 (epdf) | ISBN 9781501362453 (ebook)
Subjects: LCSH: McEwan, Ian–Criticism and interpretation. |
Social interaction in literature.
Classification: LCC PR6063.C4 Z69 2020 | DDC 823/.914–dc23
LC record available at https://lccn.loc.gov/2019053350

ISBN: HB: 978-1-5013-6246-0
PB: 978-1-5013-9114-9
ePDF: 978-1-5013-6244-6
eBook: 978-1-5013-6245-3

Series: thinking media

Typeset by Deanta Global Publishing Services, Chennai, India

To find out more about our authors and books visit www.bloomsbury.com
and sign up for our newsletters.

In the loving memory of my deepest roots: my mother
Reli and grandmother Ana

Contents

Acknowledgments

Many thanks to Bernd Herzogenrath and Patricia Pisters, the editors of the *thinking media* series, and to Katie Gallof and Erin Duffy, publishers at Bloomsbury, for their invaluable assistance in bringing the book to its final form.

I would like to thank Barend Van Heusden and Liesbeth Korthals Altes, my professors from the University of Groningen, who played a fundamental role in both my professional and my personal development during my MA studies, and who taught me the value (but also the risks) of interdisciplinary and experimental thinking.

Annalisa Oboe, from the University of Padua, offered valuable advice on what paths my work could explore and took great care not to let me lose my way in the middle of my journey through the (often) dark woods of my research.

This book could not have existed, at least in its current form, without my discussions with Christopher Norris, an extraordinary scholar and human being, who taught me the intricacies of the unfathomable human mind, now beacon, now sea. I will be forever grateful for his support.

My gratitude goes to Ellen Spolsky, too, one of the founders of cognitive humanities, whose excellent books and articles have been fundamental for my understanding of human relations and their artistic renditions. In particular, her insightful analyses of failures of understanding in social interaction have been a great source of inspiration for this book.

I would also like to thank Marco Caracciolo, one of the keenest contemporary minds studying the relation between literature and science, for being open to discussions whenever I needed to clarify things. Many thanks to my philosopher friends, Bogdan Deznan and Mihai Ometiță, with whom I discussed more things from heaven and earth than I dreamed about in this book, often in front of a beer or two, and to Andrei Mocuța, an exceptional contemporary poet whose groundbreaking art incessantly inspired me. I would also like to express my gratitude to Martino Garonzi, a brilliant mathematician passionate about literature too, who helped me clarify many aspects of this book during our frequent meetings.

My deepest gratitude though goes to my family: my parents, Reli and Sorin, from whom I've inherited the passion for literature and who continued to nourish it for many years; my grandmothers, Ana and Lena, to whom I always ran for shelter; my cousin Vlad, whose analytical mind combined with a deep understanding of literature helped me clarify some of my arguments; and last but definitely not least, my wife, Argita—the one who basked with me in the sun but also stood by me through the darkest storms.

Parts of this book are based on two previously published articles: "A Manifesto Against Failures of Understanding: Ian McEwan's *Atonement*," published in *Critique: Studies in Contemporary Fiction*, 1 August 2017, copyright Taylor & Francis, LLC, available online: https://doi.org/10.1080/00111619.2017.1347555; and "The Success of Failure: Using Literature to Complexify Science," published by Padua University Press in the collective volume *Forma Critica: Nuove Prospettive per gli Studi Letterari dagli Anni Zero* (2018). I would like to thank Taylor & Francis and Padua University Press for their permission to draw upon these materials.

Abbreviations

At	*Atonement*
BD	*Black Dogs*
CA	*The Children Act*
CT	*The Child in Time*
EL	*Enduring Love*
H	"Homemade"
OCB	*On Chesil Beach*
Sl	*Solar*
St	*Saturday*
SG	"Solid Geometry"

Ian McEwan's Intuition Pumps

One possible and plausible, even if rather simplistic, way to characterize Ian McEwan's work is by claiming that it consists of a series of literary investigations of various forms of pathology. From his first collections of short stories written in the 1970s to his latest novel, *Machines Like Me* (2019), the reader repeatedly stumbles upon pathological cases, ranging from sexual dysfunctions including sadism, masochism, or erotomania (and occasionally verging toward psychopathy, as in the short story "Butterflies") to neurological disorders such as dementia or Huntington's disease (to give just a very brief list of examples). This recurrent and obsessive concern with madness, or to put it less strongly, with deviance, brought him the (in)famous nickname of Ian Macabre and made critics like Kiernan Ryan characterize his work as an "art of unease" (cf. Ryan 1994: 1–5).

Although no systematic and comprehensive study of pathology in McEwan's works has yet been performed, it is not the aim of my study to do this either. Instead, what I plan to focus on are cases lying somewhere in-between mental health and full-blown psychopathology. In particular, I will explore two classes of phenomena creating failures of understanding in social interaction, which I will refer to as "paralysis" and "invasion." As I will argue, both paralysis and invasion should be understood as disrupted forms of intersubjectivity, the former being characterized by a lack/deficiency of ways of relating to others, and the latter by an unnecessary surplus. One of my leading hypotheses is that paralysis and invasion are complementary both theoretically and experientially: since paralysis refers to a lack and invasion to a surplus, the two *concepts* are theoretically complementary; however, since paralytic ways of dealing with alterity often breed invasion during concrete social encounters, the two classes of *phenomena* are also experientially complementary.

By studying the literary representation of these phenomena in a selection of Ian McEwan's literary works, I will shed more light on (1) the nature and functions of literature and (2) the structure of human relationships in general. This project can be considered, theoretically and methodologically, as part of the developing field of cognitive literary studies. In contrast to most of the research done in this field until now, though, my study not only aims to use cognitive-scientific theories in order to clarify literary issues, but also aims to investigate to what extent literature itself can contribute to the process of understanding the workings of the human mind. By employing what Marco Caracciolo (2016) calls a cognitive-thematic approach to literature, that is, an investigation of the metacognitive issues staged and reflected upon in literary works, I aim to challenge and refine contemporary cognitive and philosophical approaches to intersubjectivity and give directions for further theoretical and empirical research.

In the following section, I will discuss in more detail the theoretical and methodological underpinnings of a cognitive-thematic approach and situate it within contemporary literary studies. After discussing the figure-ground relationship characterizing literary interpretation in general, where interpretations (figures) can be placed in dialogue with different sets of theoretical frameworks (grounds), I will briefly summarize the ground against which I will place my interpretations of McEwan's novels, that is, a set of developmental and philosophical accounts of intersubjectivity. I will argue that although these theories have already been used for explaining both successful cases of social interaction (e.g., empathy, emotional attunement) and highly pathological ones (e.g., autism, schizophrenia), they have not yet been employed in addressing cases lying between health and pathology, such as those I gather under the conceptual headings of "paralysis" and "invasion." In the two major chapters of this study, by analyzing how (1) sexual breakdowns and (2) clashes of worldviews are staged and reflected upon in a selection of Ian McEwan's works (the short story "Homemade" and the novels *On Chesil Beach* and *Enduring Love*), I will argue that literary works can be used as "intuition pumps" (cf. Dennett 1991, 2013) in order to shed more light on aspects of intersubjectivity contemporary cognitive science and philosophy did not yet systematically address.

Thus, I stress the epistemological potential of the literary medium by exploring how a close reading of a selection of McEwan's novels and stories can offer invaluable insights into extraliterary matters—in this case, the ubiquitous failures of understanding and disrupted ways of interaction haunting social relations. In other words, I show how literature can be said to "think" in a certain sense, sometimes even deeper and in more complex ways than science and "philosophy proper." Although I employ scientific and philosophical theories of intersubjectivity in order to shed light on forms of intersubjectivity McEwan stages and reflects upon in his works, I do not consider these theories to necessarily reflect universal truths, but rather to be open to revision. In fact, I argue that a close engagement with McEwan's multilayered rendition of intersubjective dynamics enables us to complexify contemporary scientific and philosophical accounts of social interaction. Thus, my monograph stages what I consider to be a proper form of dialogue between literature, science, and philosophy, where each of the three participants has equal status in the production of knowledge.

1.1 Theoretical and Methodological Framework

In his phenomenological investigation of the "literariness" of literature, *The Singularity of Literature* (2004), Derek Attridge criticizes what he calls literary instrumentalism, which he "crudely summarize[s]" as "the treating of a text . . . as a means to a predetermined end: coming to the object with the hope or the assumption that it can be instrumental in furthering an existing project, and responding to it in such a way as to test, or even produce, that usefulness" (7), resulting in "the diminishing of careful attention to the specificity of the literary within the textual domain, and to the uniqueness of each literary object" (10). Thus, he calls for an approach that does justice to the specificity of the literary medium and the uniqueness of individual literary works, and that tries to clarify the nature of the reading process in general as well as of particular reader responses to particular literary texts.[1]

My attitude toward Attridge's position is ambivalent. On the one hand, I admire, agree with, and see the relevance of his project: my own extensive and intensive engagement with literary works too, in both my personal and professional life, made me clearly realize the importance of paying attention to their particularity, as well as to the unique experiences of reading and reflecting upon them. And although a large amount of stylistic, narratological, and phenomenological work has already been done in order to increase our understanding of what precisely this specificity entails, I believe that as long as new events of literary writing and reading occur, our work in this area can never be considered complete. However, I would not refrain from completely banishing what he calls instrumental readings.

The main reason for this is quite simple: literature does not exist in a vacuum. Neither its writing and reading, nor its subject matter is isolated from other social and cultural practices. On the contrary, they all exist and acquire significance as parts of highly interconnected webs of meaningful activities. Attridge recognizes this when he claims that "there is no doubt that [literature] has had a role to play in significant, and frequently laudable, social changes [and that it] functions, and is made to function, as a powerful and invaluable instrument of individual and social advancement" (8), as well as when he admits that it "would be naïve to think that reading could be innocent of exterior motivations and goals" (9).

However, by repeatedly stressing the *dangers* involved in using literature instrumentally in dealing with "political, moral, historical, biographical, psychological, cognitive, or linguistic" projects (7), he becomes to a certain extent blind, in my opinion, to the *benefits* such a use could bring to the development of such projects, and shies away from a full understanding of the complexity, power, and functions of literature (and perhaps even of the precise nature of the Grail he seeks for, that is, the medium's specificity).[2] Furthermore, an obsessive focus on the specificity of *reading* experiences might also ignore how such experiences are related to other types of experiences, that is, how our involvement with literature is both influenced by and influences various other facets of our "being-in-the-world" (cf. Heidegger 1927).[3]

I believe one area in contemporary literary criticism in which instrumental readings could prove to be extremely productive is what Marco Caracciolo describes, in his article discussing the status of interpretation in the cognitive literary studies, as cognitive-thematic approaches to literature (2016: 196–202). Although literary studies have always been to a certain extent interdisciplinary, the past three decades witnessed the emergence and development of what Crane and Richardson called a "new interdisciplinarity" (1999), that is, cognitive literary studies, a field defined by Alan Richardson in 2004 as "the work of literary critics and theorists vitally interested in cognitive science" (2).[4] As Richardson acknowledges, this is a highly interdisciplinary venture, especially given the fact that cognitive science is a strongly interdisciplinary field too.[5] This is the main reason why, according to Lisa Zunshine, a "dialogic, decentralized view has shaped the trajectory of cognitive approaches to literature over the last decade," and why cognitive literary scholars do not generally feel the need either "to iron out differences among their 'potentially conflicting aims and methodologies'" (2015: 1) or to "give their differences sharper definition" (4).

Although both Richardson and Zunshine celebrate the "dynamic, relational nature" (Zunshine 2015: 1) of this field of research, together with its "openness and unpredictability" (3), and argue that its definition should not focus "on the boundaries, goals, or methods" that characterize it (1), I find such a lack of (meta-)theoretical reflection and clarity quite problematic. While I agree that in such interdisciplinary approaches theoretical and methodological eclecticism is necessary and even unavoidable, I nevertheless think that much confusion can emerge when scholars unreflectively "borrow" concepts, theories, and methods from certain academic disciplines and transfer them to other disciplines without carefully reflecting upon the differences between these disciplines and, consequently, upon the validity and relevance of their approaches.

As Jackson (2003) and Caracciolo (2016) argue, such problems emerge most pointedly when cognitive literary scholars are trying to interpret particular literary texts by using various concepts and theories from the cognitive sciences, without reflecting upon the precise relationship between hermeneutics and science, and thus, upon the validity of such interpretive "moves." In Caracciolo's opinion, "Literary interpretation is . . . a far cry from any scientific project, because it relies on argument as opposed to empirical testing, because it cannot be falsified, and because it seeks to shed light on a *specific* text or corpus of texts as opposed to some general question about the world or human psychology" (188; emphasis in original). This incommensurability between hermeneutic and scientific approaches makes Caracciolo (as well as Jackson before him) initially argue that there are other, more productive and less problematic, ways of integrating literary studies and cognitive science, such as what he calls the "processual" and the "functional" approaches to literature.

In processual approaches, the act of reading becomes the focus of attention. Instead of interpreting particular literary texts, scholars in this field investigate, often from empirical perspectives, how actual readers make sense of texts, that is, they try to discover the underlying neurological and psychological processes involved in reading literature. As Caracciolo admits, such a line of research can be seen as an extension of "classical" reader-response theories,[6] this time, however, strongly informed by current cognitive-scientific paradigms and methods and (at least potentially) open to experimental testing and validation (188).[7]

Functional approaches, on the other hand, seek "to shed light on how engaging with literary texts can play a role in broader psychological processes" (194). The main presupposition behind these approaches is that cognition and culture (including literature) are intrinsically related and that literary works can play an important role in the acquisition and development of various cognitive abilities. Reading is understood as a "cognitive workout" (194) that can increase the readers' capacity of organizing their present and past experiences, of "fine-tuning" their social skills through enhancing their capacity of ascribing complex mental states to others, and even of refining their moral frameworks.[8]

Both the processual and the functional approaches are seen by Caracciolo as highly important and productive ventures within cognitive literary studies, where "literary study and scientific investigation may find a genuine, and potentially *mutually* advantageous, point of convergence" (195; my emphasis), and open thus pathways toward more appropriate, that is, *bi*-directional, interdisciplinary exchange.[9] Whether the focus is on the reading experience (in processual approaches) or on the interplay between cognition and culture (in functional approaches), Caracciolo believes that "literary scholars can bring to the table of these projects a unique sensitivity to the nuances of texts and contexts that may lead to new hypotheses and, possibly, enrich scientific understanding" (195).

However, as he further argues, one aspect of these approaches that might appear problematic to literary scholars is that there is a strong tendency to marginalize, or even sidestep completely, what in literary studies has generally been seen as highly important and central—"a key component of literary study as a profession and institution" (195), that is, interpretation. "Should we conclude that cognitive approaches to literature prefigure a different model of literary scholarship," Caracciolo asks, "one where interpretation is marginalized and ultimately supplanted by empirical methods lifted from the mind sciences" (196)? The two cognitive literary approaches discussed above would certainly point toward an affirmative answer to this question. However, despite the skepticism regarding the status, relevance, and even validity of interpretation engendered by these approaches, Caracciolo maintains his hope and optimism that "there are important payoffs to practicing interpretation," with the caveat that interpretive practices should nevertheless "be accompanied by full awareness of [their] own epistemological limitations" (196).

To clarify his position, Caracciolo discusses two other cognitive approaches to literature, which he calls "analogical" and "cognitive-thematic." In both of these approaches, interpretation plays a central role. Before addressing them in more detail, however, he makes a more general claim regarding the nature of the interpretive process. Drawing upon analyses of perception from Gestalt psychology, he describes interpretation as having a "figure-ground" structure: for a literary text to acquire meaning ("the figure"), it must be projected against an aspect of the interpreter's worldview ("the ground"). "The figure or interpretive meaning," Caracciolo claims, "always emerges from a ground, and different grounds will lead interpreters to focus on a different figure" (189). This feature of interpretation can be used to explain the existence of multiple readings of the same literary text: since there are many grounds the text can be put in dialogue with, different meanings will emerge with every different ground.[10] Furthermore, there are different ways in which the relationship between figure and ground can be realized (8). Different interpretations (i.e., figures) can thus emerge even from placing the same text against the same ground *in different ways*. In cognitive literary studies, for example, cognitive science plays the role of the interpretive ground. However, the use of this ground differs in analogical and thematic approaches.

The analogical approach starts with the assumption that there is a basic affinity between actual and fictional minds. Literature is therefore seen as representing the workings of human psychology and particular literary works are used to exemplify the ways in which the human mind functions in general. Since fictional characters are understood as being to a certain degree analogical to real people, scholars working in this subfield believe that analyses of these fictional "minds" and their behavior within story worlds can shed more light upon how real minds operate.[11]

There are at least two main problems with this approach. On the one hand, as Caracciolo argues in another article (2014a), drawing mainly upon research from a subfield of contemporary narrative theory called "unnatural narratology,"[12] the assumptions that fictional and actual minds are analogous and that we make sense of fictional characters in much the same way as we make sense of real people can be challenged by (1) taking into account the specificity of the literary medium, that is, by paying attention to the ways in which fictional minds are mediated through language, stylistic, and narrative devices, and so on and (2) acknowledging the power of literature to construct "unnatural" minds, that is, characters whose cognitive functioning diverges to a large extent from that of actual people.

Secondly, there is a dangerous tendency in analogical approaches to use what I would call *rigid* interpretive grounds, which often gives rise to strongly evaluative forms of criticism. In other words, certain theories from cognitive science are taken as ground and are considered by interpreters as expressing universal and unchallengeable truths about the human mind. Consequently, literary works will be evaluated as successful or not according to how much they "reflect" the taken-for-granted cognitive-scientific theories. As Eugene Goodheart argues in his critique of literary Darwinism, such forms of criticism encourage readers "to find confirmation of what evolutionary psychology determines to be psychological truth" (2008: 182) and when they do not find it, "it is literature that is at fault" (184).[13]

This is a highly problematic attitude, however, because it tends to foreclose any possibility for a bi-directional knowledge transfer between literary studies and cognitive science. In the conclusion of his article from 2002, Jackson claims that knowledge production "in whatever academic context involves at least the following three aspects: it combines a *theory* with some more (in the sciences) and less (in the humanities) *formalized method* to drive a *practice*" (176; his emphases). The important thing here is, for Jackson, "the dialectical relationship between the theory and practice." In other words, "the theory determines the investigative practice, but the practice can, at least in principle, recursively affect the theory" (176). This cannot happen, he claims, when using cognitive theories in the study of literature. "The originating theory cannot," he argues, "even in principle, be recursively affected by the investigation [even if an] application of that theory to literature may well change something of our understanding of literature" (177). Research done within the analogical "camp" would seem to reinforce Jackson's conclusions and his consequent negative outlook regarding the utility of this new form of interdisciplinarity. However, the last approach Caracciolo identifies and discusses, the thematic one, seems to offer some hope that, *pace* Jackson, a bi-directional knowledge transfer could emerge and that interpretation could find a relevant place within the cognitive literary studies.

Caracciolo is careful to argue though that a "given reading of a literary work cannot contribute to a scientific project *as is*" (2016: 192; emphasis in original). Although such a reading "can serve as application or illustration of a scientific theory," as usually happens within analogical approaches, "one cannot find evidence for a particular view of the mind in a literary text, because textual evidence is different from scientific evidence, and the criteria and methods of scientific investigation are different from those of literary interpretation" (192–93). Nevertheless, he claims that in cognitive-thematic approaches to literature, interpretation can contribute to scientific knowledge *heuristically*, "serving not to straightforwardly advance but to inspire and stimulate cognitive-scientific research," by raising questions and considering possibilities "that may later be taken up and assessed in scientific research" (196).

Whereas in analogical approaches, literary works were understood as *representing* the workings of human psychology, in thematic ones they are also seen as *interrogating*, at the thematic level, the functioning of the mind, a feature which can prompt interpreters to "connect literary texts to metacognitive questions (i.e., questions about the functioning of our own cognitive apparatus)" (196). And although, from a cognitive-thematic angle, interpreters use as ground cognitive scientific theories (as in analogical approaches), in this case, these theories are "always projected against a larger background of metacognitive concerns" (199).

This is why, Caracciolo concludes, the heuristic aspect of these interpretive practices "arises from the dialogue—or in some cases the clash—between the cognitive-scientific model that is brought to bear on the text and the transhistorical set of metacognitive questions[14] that the interpreter has in common with the text's author and previous interpretive communities" (199). Seen from this angle, Caracciolo claims, "literature becomes a repertoire of historically patterned engagements with metacognitive problems" (199), and literary interpretations are conceptualized as "intuition pumps"[15] asking us "to experience cognitive realities by way of imaginative engagements" (197). For Dennett, intuition pumps are "fiendishly clever devices" (1991: 282), and are "more art than science," helping us to "conceive of new possibilities, which we can then confirm by more systematic methods" (440).

Caracciolo identifies three steps characterizing a cognitive-thematic approach. Initially, the metacognitive questions arising from literary texts prompt readers to take as ground for interpretation a set of theories from contemporary cognitive science (step 1). The interpretations that are produced in this way not only attempt to answer the metacognitive questions (step 2), but also, most importantly, can make interpreters "become aware of the historical gap between cognitive-scientific models and the conceptions of the mind embedded in literary texts," a feature which can have the effect of revealing the limitations of current scientific knowledge (step 3). The frequent tendency, which characterizes the analogical approach, to see the cognitive-scientific models that serve as ground for interpretation as ultimate "truths" or "facts" about the mind is therefore problematized in the thematic ones. As Caracciolo argues, interpretations from a cognitive-thematic angle point to "the inherently provisional nature of any attempt at understanding mental phenomena—including cognitive science itself" (201).

In Derek Attridge's view, both analogical and cognitive-thematic approaches would consist of instrumental readings, and thus be probably dismissed. However, if in analogical approaches, literary texts are used to *exemplify* cognitive-scientific theories (whose truthfulness is taken for granted) and thus reinforce the unidirectionality of knowledge transfer haunting cognitive literary studies, in cognitive-thematic approaches, texts can be used in order to *challenge* and *refine* cognitive-scientific models, thus opening the possibility of a more powerful and relevant form of interdisciplinarity, where literature and interpretation can heuristically affect scientific knowledge. As I will argue in my study, a cognitive-thematic approach to Ian McEwan's works can shed more light on the nature of intersubjectivity and help clarify some of the contemporary cognitive-scientific debates regarding this topic. In the next section, I will identify and briefly discuss a set of scientific and philosophical theories that can be used as a ground for my interpretations of McEwan's works, that is, the developmental and phenomenological critiques of the theory of mind debates from contemporary philosophy of mind and cognitive science.

1.2 Forms of Intersubjectivity

In this section I will provide a brief overview of developmental and phenomenological critiques of scientific and philosophical conceptualizations of intersubjectivity as being inherently structured by observational, inferential, and theoretical processes. In contrast, both empirical studies of child development and phenomenological analyses of lived experience point toward the fact that interpersonal understanding develops gradually during ontogeny, passing through several phases—primary intersubjectivity (dyadic embodied and affective interactions), secondary intersubjectivity (joint attention and action, culminating in the development of capacities for narrative sense-making), and tertiary intersubjectivity (the acquisition of a self-other meta-perspective). As I will argue toward the end of this section, these different types of social interaction are characterized by different types of social perspectives—implicit and explicit first-person perspectives (1PP), second-person perspectives (2PP), and third-person perspectives (3PP).

1.2.1 The Theory of Mind Debates

A useful ground against which an interpretation of McEwan's works can be placed consists of the developmental and phenomenological alternatives to the "theory of mind (ToM) debates" from contemporary philosophy of mind and cognitive science. If one looks into the contemporary ToM debates, interpersonal understanding appears to be a very complicated issue. According to Gallagher and Zahavi, theory of mind is our capacity to attribute mental states to ourselves and others and to interpret, predict, and explain behavior in terms of mental states such as beliefs, desires, and intentions (2008: 171). Whereas some scholars claim that our understanding of people is theoretical, inferential, and quasi-scientific in nature,[16] others argue that we initially simulate the others' behavior in order to infer their mental states.[17] In both its abovementioned varieties (TT and ST), our relationship with alterity is understood as being characterized by an immense gap. A fundamental asymmetry, and ultimately disconnectedness between the self and the other is postulated to exist in each instance of social interaction. As Mrs. Dalloway bitterly reflects, "Here was one room; there another. Did religion solve that, or love?" (Woolf 1996 [1925]: 141). Whereas self-experience appears to have a quality of immediacy, transparency, and deep, personal inwardness,[18] the mental states of others seem to be hidden from our senses (cf. Leslie 1987: 139). In Tooby's and Cosmides's words, "No human has ever seen a thought, a belief, or an intention" (cited in Baron-Cohen 1995: xvii).

From the assumption that the mental states of others cannot be directly perceived, it naturally follows that they can only be inferred from their external manifestations (in facial expressions, gestures, or patterns of behavior). Following Woolf's spatial metaphor, there are neither doors nor windows directly connecting the two separated rooms that could offer the possibility of directly perceiving from one room what happens in the other. Not even through a glass, darkly, can the self gain access to another's inwardness. Interpersonal understanding becomes a detective game, a struggle for interpretation. Indirect signals must be deciphered in order to solve the mystery of otherness.[19]

In the context of such a Heraclitean understanding of otherness in terms of concealment,[20] two main strategies of interpersonal interpretation have been proposed. In the "theory theory of mind (TT)," philosophers of mind and cognitive scientists claim that in order to understand the other's mental states, a theoretical, quasi-scientific stance must be adopted, grounded in an already existent and internalized (yet ever-expanding) folk psychology, that is, in a set of expectations we develop during ontogeny regarding how people behave and why they behave as they do.[21] The quasi-scientific nature of such a form of grasping alterity has a role in objectifying the living other, in turning him or her into a distinct and distant entity which we contemplate and reflect upon. No traces of genuine *conversation* between the embodied self and the embodied other remain when thinking in these terms. The other is turned into a distant star seen through a telescope or into a close-to-invisible germ captured under the microscope.

It is also a very complex form of dealing with alterity. Developmental psychologists argue that such capacities for mind reading emerge only later in ontogeny. Children younger than four, as well as autistic children, repeatedly fail the so-called false-belief tests.[22] The conclusion the scientists draw from such experiments is that such children are not (yet) able to appreciate the distinction between the external world and their own minds, between reality and their beliefs about reality (Gallagher and Zahavi 2008: 173–74). These experiments do not show, of course, that young or autistic children do not have beliefs, intentions, or desires. However, they do show they do not have beliefs *about* beliefs and other mental states. In other words, they have not yet developed a *theory* of mental states, that is, a folk psychology. Naturally, such an account leaves open the following question: If one understands mind reading in such complex terms, how can one make sense of the nature of social interaction in younger children?

Before returning to this question and trying to provide an answer, a few words must also be said about the other side of the debate, namely the "simulation theory of mind (ST)." Having its roots in the classical "argument from analogy,"[23] ST claims that instead on drawing on theoretical- or folk-psychological inferences during processes of interpersonal understanding, we initially simulate the others' behavior in order to infer their mental states. Our understanding of others is thus rooted in our ability to imaginatively project ourselves into their situation (Goldman 2005: 80–81). Consequently, such a form of projection does not mainly exploit our theoretical abilities but rather our motivational and emotional resources (cf. Gallagher and Zahavi 2008: 174). By placing ourselves into the other's "mental shoes," by pretending to face a similar situation to his or hers, we attempt to simulate his/her reasons for action and emotions.

There is an internal division within ST regarding the question whether such simulations are explicit or implicit. In other words, whether we are conscious of each step we take in simulating the other's behavior, or whether many of these steps remain beyond the threshold of awareness. As Gallagher and Zahavi claim, there are significant problems with explicit accounts of ST (e.g., Goldman's) since there is no phenomenological, that is, experiential evidence that conscious imaginative and introspective simulation routines occur during instances of social interaction (2008: 176). Implicit versions of ST, which claim that our simulation of the other seems to be "immediate, automatic, and almost reflex like" (Gallese 2005: 102), look more credible. Furthermore, the discovery of resonance systems in the brain appears to provide scientific support to such theories.[24] However, as Gallagher and Zahavi argue, this neuroscientific data could also be open to an alternative, more parsimonious, kind of interpretation. Instead of claiming that neuronal resonance processes are part of a process of implicit *simulation*, one could also argue that they underlie intersubjective *perception* (2008: 178).[25] In such a view, the actions, intentions, and emotions of the other become much more transparent, much closer to the surface, closing or, at least, reducing the gap between selfhood and alterity. "Look into someone else's face," Wittgenstein wrote, "and see the consciousness in it, and a particular shade of consciousness. You see on it, in it, joy, indifference, interest, excitement, torpor, and so on. . . . Do you look within *yourself*, in order to recognize the fury in *his* face?" (1980: § 927; emphases in original).

Mental states appear to be thus much more "visible" than either TT or ST scholars are ready to acknowledge. This does not mean, of course, that they are *always* visible. As Wittgenstein remarks elsewhere, "One can say 'He is hiding his feelings.' But that means that it is not *a priori* they are always hidden" (1992: 35e; emphasis in original). Indeed, many instances of social interaction can be described in terms of lying, deception, or dissimulation. But such phenomena are possible *precisely* because there are also cases where beliefs, intentions, and emotions can be directly perceived in bodily expression and do not need to be inferred through the use of either folk psychology or simulation processes. Therefore, TT and ST accounts, although correct in particular cases, fail to do full justice to the complexity of interpersonal understanding.

A much more comprehensive picture emerges from a combination of developmental psychology, neuroscience, and phenomenology. By analyzing developmental processes during ontogeny (and backing them up with neuroscientific data) as well as phenomenological accounts of the lived experience of alterity, the so-called interaction theory of mind (IT) (cf. Gallagher and Jacobson 2012) is a powerful critique of the reductionist tendencies inherent in both TT and ST.[26] As already mentioned, such approaches acknowledge the existence of instances of social interaction where complex, inferential types of understanding are needed in order to deal with alterity. However, they try to ground them in more fundamental forms of intersubjectivity, where the relationship between the self and the other does not seem to be haunted by such huge gaps and problems. Three important precursors to a fully developed "theory of mind" are identified and discussed: primary intersubjectivity, secondary intersubjectivity (cf. Trevarthen 1980), and narrative competency/practice (cf. Gallagher and Hutto 2008).

1.2.2 Primary Intersubjectivity

In developmental terms, primary intersubjectivity is considered the first to emerge in ontogeny. It is a direct, sensorimotor, emotional, perceptual, and nonconceptual form of social interaction, characterized by a common bodily intentionality shared across the self and the other (Gallagher and Zahavi 2008: 187–89). Almost immediately after birth, infants are able to distinguish between animate and inanimate objects and have a strong tendency to imitate *human* facial expressions (cf. Melzoff and Moore 1977).[27] Furthermore, they are able to see bodily movement as goal-directed intentional movement and to perceive others as agents (cf. Gallagher and Jacobson 2012: 220). An affective coordination between the gestures and the expressions of the infant and those of other persons is established, giving rise to a *perception-based* form of understanding that requires neither theoretical nor simulative inferences.

Consequently, long before we have the capacity to ask ourselves what others believe or desire, we already have an embodied, perceptual understanding of how they feel, whether they are attending to us or not, or whether their intentions are friendly or not (Gallagher and Hutto 2008: 22). Gestures, expressions, intonations, and actions are thus initially transparent and full of meaning, without requiring inferences to hidden mental states. At this stage, others are not seen as objects in need of explanation that we encounter cognitively as passive observers, but rather as partners in embodied/affective interactions.

1.2.3 Secondary Intersubjectivity

What is still missing at this point is an understanding of the others' directionality toward the world. In the first year of life, infants are not yet capable of conceptualizing the others (and themselves) as agents situated and acting in pragmatic contexts. Around the age of one year, however, a "Copernican revolution" occurs in development, giving rise to what Trevarthen calls secondary forms of intersubjectivity. Following the emergence of capacities such as gaze following and pointing (and consequently joint/shared attention toward aspects of the environment and situations in which the self and other are co-involved; cf. Tomasello 1999; Eilan et al. 2005), the affective dyadic relation with the other characteristic of primary intersubjectivity explodes into the world.

Children enter into contexts of shared attention and situations in which they learn what things mean and what they are for (Gallagher and Zahavi 2008: 189).[28] As Merleau-Ponty argues, "In so far as I have sensory functions . . . I am already in communication with others. . . . No sooner has my gaze fallen upon a living body in process of acting than the objects surrounding it immediately take on a fresh layer of significance; they are no longer simply what I myself could make out of them, they are what this other pattern of behavior is about to make of them" (1962: 353). Thus, by interacting with others in pragmatic contexts, we not only gain a more complex understanding of their intentions and actions, but also start to be able to make sense of the world together (cf. Gallagher and Jacobson 2012: 222).[29] The relationship between selfhood and alterity is characterized, at this point, by a "shared engagement in a common world" (Gallagher and Zahavi 2008: 190). Nor in this case can the other be considered an object reflected upon by the self, but rather a partner in *cooperative* projects.[30]

1.2.4 Narrative Sense-Making

Yet, neither the embodied and affective face-to-face interaction with others nor our later involvement in contexts of shared attention and cooperative projects with them can explain more complex forms of interaction, when the others' reasons for action are not directly expressed in bodily behavior or world directedness. Our understanding of the other as an animate being or an intentional agent developed in contexts of primary and secondary intersubjectivity does not yet explain our capacity to see the other as a *mental* agent, that is, as a possessor of mental states such as beliefs and intentions which are not clearly transparent in bodily expression or pragmatic action.[31] However, a much more fundamental capacity than either theoretical or simulative inferences can shed more light on such developments.

Once our linguistic capacities reach a certain degree of sophistication (around the age of two; cf. Gallagher and Zahavi 2008: 193), a competency for comprehending as well as producing narratives also emerges. As Salman

Rushdie claims in his memoir, "Man was the storytelling animal, the only creature on earth that told itself stories to understand what kind of creature it was" (2013: 19). Thus, from an early age, children are repeatedly exposed to stories about characters acting for various reasons.

The previously developed capacities for joint attention are now employed in a more complex manner: instead of focusing together with his or her caregivers solely on aspects of the physical and social environment, the child's attention is also drawn to certain narratives (both fictional and nonfictional) which help him/her develop a certain understanding of "what actions are acceptable and in what circumstances, what sort of events are important and noteworthy, what can account for action, and what kind of explanations constitute the giving of good reasons" (Gallagher and Hutto 2008: 31). Such training in narrative practices teaches children both what others can expect from them and what they can expect from others (31).[32]

Furthermore, the use of narrative competency in interpersonal understanding does not start from the premise that other persons are autonomous entities, disconnected from the world, and therefore characterized solely by a hidden inwardness which must be deciphered, as TT and ST presuppose. On the contrary, the others' "attitudes and responses as whole situated persons" (Gallagher and Zahavi 2008: 193) constantly interacting with the (social) environment and caught up "in the middle of something that has a beginning and that is going somewhere" (193) are taken into account.

1.2.5 Tertiary Intersubjectivity

Soon after children develop narrative competency, they are finally ready to engage in forms of interaction that include the ones discussed in the theory of mind debates, that is, in what scholars such as Bråten and Trevarthen call "tertiary intersubjectivity" (2007) and which according to them develops in two stages: first-order and second-order tertiary intersubjectivity. First-order tertiary intersubjectivity emerges around eighteen months of age and is characterized by the development of conversational and narrative speech, as well as by predication (around two years of age),[33] the emergence of a sense of a verbal self (around two years of age), and narrative self (around three years of age), together with the capacity to understand others too in terms of their verbal and narrative selves (cf. Bråten and Trevarthen 2007: 23; Bråten 2009: 72–73).[34] This form of intersubjectivity also entails pretend play with peers, engagement with invisible companions, and inner dialogues (Bråten 2009: xvii, 209–44). Moreover, at this stage, new types of "self-other conscious emotions" such as shame, embarrassment, or guilt emerge (cf. Fuchs 2013:

676–77; Zahavi 2014: 197–241), which, according to Zahavi, testify to the self's "exposure, vulnerability, and visibility" (2014: 235).

"Second-order tertiary intersubjectivity" emerges around three years of age and is described by Bråten and Trevarthen in terms of a "meta-understanding of other's understanding entailing *second-order* mental understanding of thoughts and emotions in self and other in virtue of recursive mental simulation of mental processes in others" (2007: 26; emphasis in original). In Bråten's and Trevarthen's opinions, it begins with the emergence of capacities for deceiving/discerning deception in others and for attributing false beliefs, as well as with the development of children's abilities to engage together with others in "co-narrative fictional constructions." At this stage, children listening to stories are also able, besides just following the story lines, to take the point of view of fictional characters (26). This capacity develops concurrently with that of being able to complete their interlocutors' aborted statements during conversations "as if being virtual co-authors" (Bråten 2009: 59; cf. also Bråten 2002). In other words, as Thomas Fuchs argues, the "hallmark of [second-order] tertiary intersubjectivity" (2013: 678) is the development of children's capacity to arrive at a self-other meta-perspective.

Thus, interpersonal understanding emerges during ontogeny in several phases: primary intersubjectivity, characterized by an embodied and affective face-to-face interaction with the other; secondary intersubjectivity, in which the self and the other are involved in contexts of shared attention and are able to collaborate in pragmatic projects; narrative sense-making, where the other is grasped as situated in temporally extended situations, which can be made sense of through the use of storytelling; and tertiary intersubjectivity, characterized by the emergence of a verbal and narrative self and the development of a self-other meta-perspective.

Obviously, more complex forms of intersubjectivity build upon simpler ones in a cumulative process. The development of capacities for joint attention is grounded in prior embodied and affective exchanges between the child and caregivers (cf. Gallagher and Hutto 2008: 23–26; Gallagher and Zahavi 2008: 189). Similarly, the emergence of narrative competency strongly depends upon both our cooperative abilities and our embodied and affective understanding of alterity and our capacity for imaginative and emotional identifications (Gallagher and Hutto 2008: 32). Furthermore, all intersubjective capacities, once acquired in development, remain active throughout our entire life. Developmentally primary forms of understanding are not superseded but remain and operate in parallel with more complex ones. They strongly underpin later practices that might involve explaining or predicting mental states, in cases such as the ones described in TT or ST accounts (22).

In the following section, I will discuss Fuchs's account of the development of social perspectives, and explain how they are related to the forms of intersubjectivity I summarized above.

1.2.6 The Development of Social Perspectives

In his article "The Phenomenology and Development of Social Perspectives," Fuchs discusses what he calls the 1PP, 2PP, and 3PP in social cognition research and advocates the foundational role of second-person interactions for the development of social perspectives. For Fuchs, the term "perspective" denotes a specific form of experiential access to oneself and to others. Thus, he defines the 1PP as "the subjective or experiencing perspective"; the 2PP as "the intersubjective, participant or co-experiencing perspective, referring to situations of reciprocal interaction that are characterized by some form of mutual relatedness and coupling of the partners"; and the 3PP as "the observer perspective, referring to situations of one-way, remote observation of others or to situations of talking or thinking about absent persons" (2012: 658). He further argues that children, through triangular interactions with persons and objects, and thus through processes pertaining to secondary intersubjectivity, expand their understanding of perspectives and arrive at a self-other meta-perspective, which, as already mentioned, he calls the "hallmark of tertiary intersubjectivity" (2012: 678). As Fuchs claims, this allows children "to grasp the other's as well as their own perspective as such, which is equivalent to an explicit third person perspective and to an explicit first person perspective" (655).

At the beginning of his arguments, Fuchs distinguishes theory theory of mind (TT), simulation theory of mind (ST), and interaction theory (IT) according to what perspective they prioritize, or, as he puts it, what kind of access we use in understanding other persons, according to each of these theories. Whereas TT is grounded in an observational, 3PP and ST in a first-person model, IT prioritizes the second-person route, which is, in his opinion, the correct way of understanding in developmental and phenomenological terms the ways in which social interactions are structured in primary and secondary intersubjectivity (656).

As he stresses, however, although the 2PP is the primordial one from which the others emerge and develop, all three perspectives have a particular role to play in certain instances of social encounters. At some point in their development, he claims, children become able to take the others' perspectives and to transpose themselves into the others' point of view, that is, they are sometimes using their first-person experience in order to understand others, imagining what one would feel like in their situation.[35]

Other times, they also attempt to infer another's mental states, such as his/her intentions, beliefs, or desires, from a 3PP, especially when the other is absent and verbal communication is thus impossible. Nevertheless, he argues, these more "sophisticated, explicit forms of understanding others" are not only grounded in second-person interactions, but also continue to "display an inherently intersubjective, dialogical structure" (657).

He also distinguishes within each of the three perspectives between an implicit level, a pre-reflective awareness of self and other, and an explicit level of understanding the perspective *as such*. In his view, adopting an explicit perspective, or a self-other meta-perspective, hence "taking a step back" and examining the social interaction from a certain "distance," usually occurs when an irritation, misunderstanding, or disturbance destabilizes the smooth functioning of the social encounter, and we are forced to explicitly reflect upon the status of our relationship with the other. Adopting such a self-other meta-perspective may include deliberately taking the other's perspective (explicit 3PP), reflecting on oneself (explicit 1PP; 659), or reflecting upon the whole social interaction (explicit 2PP).

In Fuchs's view, the explicit 1PP, or the first-person meta-perspective, already evident with the development of cognitive, reflective, and narrative consciousness (cf. Nelson 2005), is constituted through our intersubjective encounters, since "it presupposes that I have realized and adopted the other's gaze on me, or that I have learnt to see myself in others' eyes." Thus, reflective thinking, self-consciousness, and even conscience "may be regarded as an internalized dialogue which is originally derived from the interaction with the other" (Fuchs 2012: 664).

As I argued in the previous section, the emergence of an explicit 1PP is a fundamental characteristic of first-order tertiary intersubjectivity. However, the acquisition of an explicit 3PP and 2PP, or a self-other meta-perspective, occurs later in ontogeny (between four and five years of age), and is the main feature which differentiates second-order from first-order tertiary intersubjectivity. In order to explain the emergence of an explicit 3PP and 2PP, Fuchs distinguishes between *sharing* perspectives, an ability developing in the context of joint attention; *taking* perspectives (recognizing another's point of view when it differs from one's own), an ability developing around two and a half years of age during interactions pertaining to first-order tertiary intersubjectivity; and *understanding* perspectives, a much more sophisticated capacity, which entails, as he puts it, an understanding that "people may not only see different things but see things differently" (669). Fuchs argues that understanding perspectives develops through (1) collaborative interactions, in which children become aware of what adults are attending to, and thus learn to "grasp the other's state of knowledge" (671); (2) pretend play, which implies "distancing oneself from the immediacy of perception and action" (672); and (3) verbal interactions, which train children's "understanding not only of the reversibility, but also of the generality of possible viewpoints" (673). In his view, only when children develop this capacity of understanding perspectives and are consequently able to be aware of different perspectives simultaneously and to flexibly shift among them (670), can we claim that they have entered the tertiary level of intersubjectivity.

In the following section I will argue that although these theories have been useful for explaining both successful and pathological forms of interaction, they have nevertheless not yet taken into account intermediary cases, such as those I describe though the concepts of "paralysis" and "invasion."

1.3 Blindness and Insight in Contemporary Cognitive-Scientific and Philosophical Accounts of Intersubjectivity

1.3.1 Insight into Extremes: Health and Pathology

As argued before, intersubjectivity should be better understood as a multilayered, rather than a unitary, phenomenon. Regardless of what ToM scholars believe, there is no *single* capacity that could comprehensively account for the richness and complexity of our interpersonal encounters. Various processes and capacities are at play in any social interaction. However, as it became clear, at least in ontogeny, a certain "logic" of development appears to characterize the interplay between selfhood and alterity. As I have shown, various psychologists and philosophers analyzed the ways in which intersubjectivity develops over time in terms of a gradual progression from embodied and affective dyadic forms of interaction (primary intersubjectivity) to similarly embodied and affective triadic interactions (secondary intersubjectivity), and, finally, to highly complex, linguistically and culturally mediated tertiary forms of sociality, featuring new capacities such as that of shifting between various perspectives, or of acquiring a self-other meta-perspective.

As I repeatedly stressed, this development follows a "staircase logic": (1) newly emergent forms of intersubjectivity build upon the previous ones, and (2) the previous forms *remain* functional even when more sophisticated ones emerge. Therefore, in adulthood, *all* forms of intersubjectivity usually function in tandem, although, in certain instances of interactions, some forms are prioritized over others. Thus, ToM scholars' assumption that, when dealing with other persons, we are *always* trying to infer their mental states is strongly reductive. Although, admittedly, in some cases we are definitely doing this, in many others we employ highly different "methods." In sexuality, for example, as I will argue more systematically later, capacities, which develop within the context of primary intersubjectivity, such as those of kinetically and affectively attuning our bodies, seem to be predominant. More generally, (smoothly functioning) romantic relationships or friendships are characterized by a similar focus on affective sharing, emotional attunement, and empathic engagement. In embodied collaborative activities, on the other hand, such as carrying or building something together, capacities of joint attention and action, emerging during secondary intersubjectivity, play a fundamental role. In neither of these examples is any form of "mind reading" needed. On the contrary, as I will discuss in more detail later, when such abstract ways of dealing with alterity happen to interfere with the more basic and concrete ones, there is a significant risk of breakdowns in the smooth functioning of the interactions/relationships.

Thus, the developmental accounts I sketched above seem particularly well suited for providing systematic explanations of various *successful* forms of social interaction from adulthood. "Healthy" sexual and romantic relationships, as well as (accident-free) embodied collaborative forms of interaction can be described as structured by capacities developing in the context of primary and secondary intersubjectivity.

Furthermore, these theories can also play a crucial explanatory role for how social interactions are structured in pathological conditions such as autism or schizophrenia. Whereas ToM scholars tend to describe these pathologies as involving deficits in mind-reading abilities, Thomas Fuchs, for instance, describes autistic and schizophrenic patients as suffering from basic disturbances of being-with-others which they try to compensate by explicit inferences and hypotheses about others (2015: 191). In autism, significant disturbances of capacities pertaining to primary intersubjectivity, such as sensory-motor integration, imitation, affect attunement, or holistic perception, have clear negative effects on social interactions (195–98). Autistic persons' lack of "a primary *sensus communis* or a sense of bodily being-with-others" (198) forces them to employ strategies seen as fundamental by ToM scholars, such as explicit mentalizing and inferring from social cues, in order to compensate for their deficit in primary intersubjective capacities.[36] More recently, Allan Schore (who provides some of the most detailed descriptions of the neurobiological underpinnings of primary intersubjectivity as located in the right brain hemisphere), defines autism as an attachment disorder, "a severe impairment of the right-lateralized cortical-subcortical implicit self-system that acts unconsciously, beneath levels of conscious awareness"

(2019: 81), and as a "developmental neuropathology and developmental psychopathology of the early developing right hemisphere, which for the rest of the life span is dominant for the *implicit* nonverbal, holistic processing of rapidly communicated information and *spontaneous* social interactions" (80; emphasis in original).

Schizophrenia too appears to be characterized by disturbances in primary intersubjectivity, such as a weakening of the basic sense of self, a disruption of implicit bodily functioning, and a disconnection from the intercorporeality with others: "the basic sense of being-with-others is replaced by a sense of detachment that may pass over into threatening alienation" (199). Schizophrenic patients tend to observe the others' behaviors from a distant, 3PP instead of entering second-person embodied interactions, and, thus, their managing of interpersonal relations becomes a very complicated, and mostly unsuccessful, affair (200).

Furthermore, Fuchs argues that certain symptoms of schizophrenia, such as loss of ego-boundaries or delusions, can be explained in terms of disturbances in tertiary intersubjectivity. Due to deficits in experiencing a primary, embodied sense of self, schizophrenic patients also develop significant problems in more advanced ways of dealing with others pertaining to tertiary intersubjectivity. As Fuchs puts it, "Becoming aware of others as being aware of oneself will become precarious" (201–02), and thus, in instances when schizophrenics are grasping the other's perspective, they are often no longer able to maintain their own embodied center, their ego-boundaries: "The perspectives of self and other are confused instead of being integrated from a self-other meta-perspective, resulting in a sense of being invaded and overpowered by the other" (202).

Fuchs also explains delusions in terms of disturbances in tertiary intersubjectivity. Due to the initial lack of affective attunement, the sense of trust which, in healthy individuals, develops during the passage through the three intersubjective stages and the gradual accumulation of a history of interactions, is severely disrupted in schizophrenia: the faces, the gazes, and the behavior of others are seen as increasingly ambiguous, causing the co-constitution of a shared world to fail and to be "replaced by the new, idiosyncratic coherence of delusion" (206–07). Although schizophrenics are able to take the others' (supposed) perspective, sometimes even excessively, they lack an independent position from which they could compare their own and another's point of view (a self-other meta-perspective), and, thus, once paranoid delusions start to emerge, all the others' perspectives seem to be threateningly directed toward themselves.

Thus, the developmental theories which I have sketched in the previous section appear extremely useful in explaining a vast range of social interactions characterizing adulthood too. However, as I have shown, the types of interactions that have been discussed until now in the light of these theories tend to fall into two distinct and opposite categories: either highly transparent, successful interactions, or highly pathological ones. As I will argue in the following section, though, many human interactions fall *in-between* these extremes.

1.3.2 Blindness to Intermediary Cases: The Ubiquity of Failures of Understanding and Some Preliminary Remarks on Paralysis and Invasion

In *A Pitch of Philosophy: Autobiographical Exercises*, philosopher Stanley Cavell asks what does it say "about human actions that they can be done unintentionally, involuntarily, insincerely, unthinkingly, inadvertently, heedlessly, carelessly, under duress, under the influence, out of contempt, out of pity, by mistake, by accident" (1994: 87). Such a question points toward the fact that human actions and interactions are not always smooth processes, and they can be many times haunted by rather severe problems. Just a little recollection and self-reflection on our daily interactions can certainly prove the existence of what Ellen Spolsky calls "the ordinariness of human failures of understanding" (2015a: 131). Often, none of our capacities for embodied and affective attunement, for jointly attending and acting with others, for taking the others' perspectives, or for understanding perspectivity as such can help us avoid more or less severe failures in our social interactions.

However, contemporary cognitive science and philosophy seem to be focused mainly on explaining the extremes of the intersubjective spectrum: either unmistakable success, or utter, pathological failure. Even if scholars such as Fuchs and Bråten mention and briefly discuss, from their developmental perspectives, breakdowns in interpersonal understanding that could be situated between health and pathology, they do not offer any systematic account of such phenomena.

The aim of my study is to open a path toward beginning to address these problems in a scientifically and philosophically informed manner. My question is not only how the theories of intersubjectivity I have sketched above can be used in order to understand some of the failures of understanding haunting social relations, but also how thinking about these phenomena from *other* perspectives (in my case, literature) could make us reassess the validity and relevance of some of these scientific and philosophical theories of intersubjectivity.

More specifically, I will identify and extensively discuss two groups of phenomena, which I call paralysis and invasion and which can be seen as breeding failures of understanding in social interactions. My hypothesis is that careful investigations of several of Ian McEwan's works can be of crucial help in discovering the structure and various experiential manifestations of these phenomena. Although I will only be able to provide a comprehensive description of paralysis and invasion *through* my interpretation of McEwan's "intuition pumps," some preliminary remarks concerning these classes of phenomena are in place.

As I have repeatedly mentioned, intersubjectivity develops in several steps or stages, each newly emergent stage building upon the previous ones. But what happens if in certain moments the vital connection with the more primary stages is intentionally or unintentionally, voluntarily or involuntarily, sincerely or insincerely, thinkingly or unthinkingly, advertently or inadvertently broken, forgotten, or ignored? What happens if the embodied and affective connection to the others is sidestepped in our interactions with them and we are left somehow "hanging in the air," lost in abstraction, in our attempts to make sense of alterity? Such a "blockage" within abstract ways of sense-making, such a forgetfulness of the "essentials," and such a tearing apart of our basic embodied roots are what characterize (one form of) paralysis.

As I will discuss at length later, certain forms of paralysis are characterized by a solipsistic attitude toward (social) reality, an utter ignorance of the others' living body and bodily expressiveness, or an obsessive, monomaniac way of interpreting the others' behaviors through projecting upon them ready-made structures/frameworks derived from abstract domains such as science, religion, or aesthetics. My detailed analyses of the ways in which McEwan stages and reflects upon instances of paralysis in several of his works will hopefully shed more light on an experientially recurrent, yet scientifically and philosophically ignored, phenomenon.

Furthermore, what happens when a social encounter, (ideally) pertaining to primary or secondary intersubjectivity, is suddenly de-structured and destabilized by various external and contextual factors, such as language and culture, or by ways of sense-making pertaining to tertiary forms of intersubjectivity? What happens, for example, when what should be a kinetically and affectively synchronized interaction, filled with feeling yet ideally devoid of thought, such as a sexual encounter, ends up in failure when the context in which the interaction is embedded forces itself with centripetal violence upon the scene, implodes *within* the relationship, breaking it apart? What happens when our memories, our traumas, our historical context, our words, and our silences creep within our beds and wreak havoc in what should be an ecstatic form of blood-knowledge?

Or, to give another example, what happens when a similar context impinges upon an embodied collaborative activity, an instance of joint action, whose success depends *precisely* on its simplicity, on its capacity of sheltering itself against external influences? What happens when I try to carry a heavy couch up the stairs with someone, and instead of focusing on the activity itself, I endlessly try to think about what the other is thinking about me? Will I not perhaps drop the couch and break both of our legs? Such violent impingement of external forces upon primary or secondary forms of social interaction characterizes what I call invasion.

In the following chapter, I will analyze two works of McEwan dealing with sexual failures—the short story "Homemade" and the novel *On Chesil Beach*. I will argue that by staging the ways in which sexual encounters are (de) structured by forms of interaction pertaining to tertiary intersubjectivity, as well as by various linguistic, historical, and cultural forces, McEwan builds a strong critique of (1) D. H. Lawrence's view of sexuality as a form of "blood-knowledge," that is, as a "pure," embodied and affective form of interaction, devoid of mental processes, and (2) contemporary cognitive-scientific and philosophical explanations of sexuality in terms of processes pertaining to primary intersubjectivity, that is, intercorporeality, interaffectivity, and attachment.

2

Sexual Breakdowns

2.1 A Brief Look at Sexuality in Ian McEwan's and D. H. Lawrence's Works

Many critics have tended to see sexuality as a central aspect in Ian McEwan's works.[1] This is not surprising, since concerns with sexuality and the myriad problems it engenders can be found in most of McEwan's works. From his early stories to his latest novels, McEwan appears to be fascinated by the complex ways in which sexual relations operate between individuals and within larger social and historical contexts.

The stories collected in McEwan's first two published volumes, *First Love, Last Rites* (1975) and *In Between the Sheets* (1978), prefigure many of the troubling aspects of sexuality the author will struggle with and try to express in more depth throughout his entire career. The theme of sexual initiation, of the passage beyond what McEwan, following Joseph Conrad, calls "the shadow-line" between childhood and adulthood,[2] together with many of the problems it entails—touched upon, for example, in "Homemade," "Last Day of Summer," "First Love, Last Rites," or "In Between the Sheets"—is further developed in his first novel, *The Cement Garden* (1978), and later in *The Innocent* (1990), *On Chesil Beach* (2007), and *The Children Act* (2014). On many levels and in different ways, all these works struggle to find an answer to the questions of what is gained and what is lost during this transition from (an alleged) innocence to (sexual) knowledge. Furthermore, as I will discuss in greater depth later in this chapter, they also attempt to build a typology of the various forces (e.g., linguistic, cultural, historical) which interfere with the characters' first experiences of embodied and affective sexual acts.

Although it is beyond the scope and aims of my chapter and book to discuss it at length, another theme which almost obsessively recurs within McEwan's works concerns the ways in which power relations structure sexuality. The intricate interplay between sadism and masochism, together with the troubling relation between these sexual pathologies and gender stories like "Solid Geometry," "Pornography," or "Psychopolis" stage, is later on expanded in novels such as *The Comfort of Strangers* (1981), *The Child in Time* (1987), and, again, *The Innocent*.[3] Furthermore, the fluidity and inherent theatricality/performativity characterizing gender, which feminist and queer theorists like Judith Butler reflected upon in a more systematic vein,[4] are foregrounded in works such as "Disguises" and *The Cement Garden*, pointing toward the fact that masculinity and femininity are less stable categories than usually claimed by essentialist theorists of sexuality. Finally, instances of incestuous relationships,[5] pedophilia,[6] fetishism,[7] or bestiality[8] also figure prominently throughout McEwan's career, pointing toward the deep relationship between violence and sexuality, as well as toward an understanding of sexuality as a force that can dissolve the boundaries between various domains usually seen as separate, such as childhood and adulthood, life and matter, or human and animal.

Yet, McEwan is far from being solely a diagnostician of the pathological aspects of sexuality. Novels like *The Child in Time* or *Atonement* (2001) powerfully portray instances of what could be called, albeit in a normative way, "healthy" or "successful" sexual interactions.[9] Although there are significant differences between the couples in *The Child in Time* and *Atonement*, in terms of age, previous sexual experience, and the general nature and history of their respective relationships,[10] the way in which their sexual encounters are described is highly similar. Stephen and Julie, during their first sexual encounter after a long separation, "had to do no more than remove their clothes and look at one another to be set free and assume the uncomplicated roles in which they could not deny their mutual understanding" (*CT*: 67–68) and joyfully affirmed "what biology, existence, matter itself had dreamed . . . for its own pleasure and perpetuity" (68). Similarly, Robbie and Cecilia, "too selfless . . . to be embarrassed . . . clearly knew their own needs" and acted upon them until "there was nothing but obliterating sensation, thrilling and swelling" (*At*: 136) during their sexual initiation in the library from Cecilia's house.

Words such as "biology," "matter itself," "pleasure," or "sensation" all point to an understanding of sexuality as a strongly *affective* phenomenon, deeply rooted in the *body*, as something "good and simple" (*CT*: 68) and "fundamental, as fundamentally biological as birth" (*At*: 137). Furthermore, the "mutual understanding" between Stephen and Julie, as well as Robbie's and Cecilia's "knowledge" of their own needs, clearly refers to nonlinguistic/ conceptual, embodied, and affective forms of understanding similar to those I will discuss as paradigmatic of primary intersubjectivity.

McEwan's indebtedness to D. H. Lawrence in portraying sexuality in these ways is unmistakable.[11] Discussing the book of Genesis from the Bible in his *Studies in Classic American Literature*, Lawrence writes:

> In the first place, Adam knew Eve as a wild animal knows its mate, momentaneously, but vitally, in blood-knowledge. Blood-knowledge,

not mind-knowledge. Blood knowledge, that seems utterly to forget, but doesn't. Blood-knowledge, instinct, intuition, all the vast vital flux of knowing that goes on in the dark, antecedent to the mind. (1923: 90)

As scholars like Dalewski (1965), Kermode (1973) or, more recently, Doherty (2001) forcefully argued, although there are endless tensions between Lawrence's literary output and his more theoretical and critical projects, the view of sexuality as a pre-reflective natural force, escaping the confines of the abstract, mental sphere that is threatening to destroy, in Lawrence's view, Western civilization, is a pervasive theme in both his fictional and philosophical works. Compare, for example, Lawrence's celebratory view of sexuality as involving a "resurrection of the body" and a "democracy of touch" rooted in a "blood-consciousness" clean of any traces of mental life from his work of literary criticism *Studies in Classic American Literature* (1923: 89–90)[12] with the aesthetic staging in his novel *The Rainbow* (1915) of the sexual relation between Ursula Brangwen and Anton Skrebensky in terms such as: "the life of the running blood" (1995 [1915]: 266), "compact of . . . flesh" (276), and "dark, blind, eager wave urging blindly forward, dark with the same homogeneous desire" (415). In fact, in 1915, Lawrence expressed similar views in a letter to Bernard Russell too, where he describes the differences between blood and mental consciousness:

> Now I am convinced of what I believed when I was about twenty—that there is another seat of consciousness than the brain and the nerve system: there is a blood-consciousness which exists in us independently of the ordinary mental-consciousness, which depends on the eye as its source or connector. There is the blood-consciousness, with the sexual connection, holding the same relation as the eye, in seeing, holds to the mental consciousness. One lives, knows, and has one's being in the blood, without any reference to nerves and brain. This is one half of life, belonging to the darkness. And the tragedy of this our life, and of your life, is that the mental and nerve consciousness exerts a tyranny over the blood-consciousness, and that your will has gone completely over to the mental consciousness, and is engaged in the destruction of your blood-being or blood-consciousness, the final liberating of the one, which is only death in result. (Lawrence 1981 [1915]: 470)

As Doherty discusses in great depth in his study, Lawrence's powerful critiques of "mentalized sex" (Doherty 2001: 54) and his project of describing and, perhaps, living sexuality as a "non-verbal Enlightenment" (120), of expressing and experiencing "the direct sensation of the thing-in-itself before thought-constructions take over" (129), bear a strong resemblance to Tantric doctrines and practices, aiming toward "a certain detachment and impersonality, a freedom from ego-constraints, the abolition of conventional space/time parameters, and the access to non-verbal forms of communication" (99). These views also resonate with Michel Foucault's discussion of the Eastern (e.g., Chinese, Japanese, Indian, or Arabic) practice of *ars erotica* which he contrasts with what he calls *scientia sexualis*. Although both *ars erotica* and *scientia sexualis* are seen by Foucault as techniques of producing the "truth about sex," in the case of the former, knowledge is drawn from pleasure itself, not from abstract discourses about it (as in the latter case), usually under the guidance of a master. Moreover, this pleasure is evaluated and further used to shape sexual practice (cf. Foucault 1978 [1976]: 57–58).[13] Drawing upon these Eastern traditions, Lawrence constructs sexuality as "presymbolic, presocial—anterior to cultural enmeshment in the intricate coils of the verbal . . . an ecstatic mind-shattering *puissance* that abolishes the ego" (Doherty 2001: 7, 12; emphasis in original) and aims to "destroy those fixed thought-constructions . . . that intervene between perception and the sensual reality of the thing-in-itself—to recover pristine sensation, stripped of its symbolic and cultural aggregations" (29).

As I will argue in the following section, the conceptualizations of sexuality offered by McEwan in *The Child in Time* and *Atonement* and by Lawrence in most of his fictional and theoretical works, with their emphasis on preverbal, pre-reflexive, embodied, and affective forces stripped of mental, symbolic, and cultural aggregations, find a rather surprising parallel in how developmental psychologists and philosophers describe primary intersubjectivity, that is, the forms of interaction of infants and caregivers in the first months after birth.

2.2 Blood-Knowledge as a Vestigial Form of Primary Intersubjectivity

2.2.1 Primary Intersubjectivity

In this section, I will provide an overview of theories of what Trevarthen calls primary intersubjectivity (Trevarthen 1979, 1980)—our embodied and affective interactions with others that emerge from the beginning of life, develop during the first year, and remain crucial in all our subsequent social interactions.

Most of the critics of the theory of mind approaches to social cognition stress the fact that long before children reach the age of four (the supposed age for acquiring a theory of mind), several sensorimotor, perceptual, emotional, and nonconceptual *embodied* practices, which constitute our primary access for understanding others, are already well developed (Gallagher and Zahavi 2008: 187; Gallagher and Hutto 2008: 20). These practices include (among others) imitation, the parsing of perceived intentions, and affective interchange (Gallagher and Hutto 2008: 20) or, as Thomas Fuchs puts it in a recent study, a set of "intercorporeal and interaffective relationships" (Fuchs 2018: 177).

In contrast to scholars claiming that intentions, beliefs, and desires are always internal and must therefore be inferred, Gallagher and Zahavi, adopting insights from the phenomenological tradition, claim that in most of our social interactions we have a direct understanding of another person's intentions because they are explicitly expressed in their embodied actions and expressive behaviors. Such an understanding does not require of us to postulate or infer believes or desires hidden in the other person's mind (2008: 187), but can rather be explained as "a common bodily intentionality that is shared across the perceiving subject and the perceived other" (188).

In other words, before we are in a position to think about what other persons believe or desire, we already have specific perceptual understandings of what they feel, whether they are attending to us or not, or whether their intentions are friendly or not (188). Thus, before theorizing, simulating, explaining, or predicting the others' mental states, we can already interact with them and understand them in terms of their expressions, gestures, intentions, and emotions, as well as from how they act toward ourselves and others (189). As Gallagher and Zahavi further argue, such understanding does not require highly developed cognitive abilities; it is rather a "fast, automatic, irresistible and highly stimulus-driven" perceptual and embodied capacity (Scholl and Tremoulet 2000: 299; cited in Gallagher and Zahavi 2008: 188). In the following section I will discuss the notion of embodiment and its fundamental role in the development of cognition.

The Embodiment of Cognition

The role of the body in cognition was practically ignored in classical (cognitivist and connectionist) cognitive sciences. In the cognitivist paradigm (1950s–70s) the mind was conceptualized in purely mechanistic/computational terms, as an information-processing device or a symbol-manipulating machine. The brain transformed sensory input into abstract symbols which were internally processed and subsequently generated motor output, in a linear process. Mental activities were therefore understood as non-conscious symbolic computations, a view which made cognitivists ignore not only the embodiment of the organism but also its subjective, conscious experiences.

In another computer-based metaphor, the hardware of the mind—the biological constitution of the brain and organism—was seen as irrelevant, all the focus being placed upon the software—the manipulation of abstract symbols (Thompson 2007: 5). Since cognition was mainly understood as the solving of abstract problems, the focus of the cognitivists' research agenda was primarily on higher-level processes such as deductive reasoning and linguistic cognition.

The 1980s witnessed the emergence of a second paradigm in the development of the cognitive sciences called *connectionism*. Here, the central metaphor of the mind is not the computer, but the artificial neural network, a virtual system run on a computer and composed of layers of neuron-like units linked by numerically weighted connections, whose strengths change according to implemented learning rules, as well as due to the system's history of activity (9). Although this approach does not completely disregard the view of the mind as a symbol-processing device, it nevertheless strives to understand what the symbols discussed by cognitivists actually consist of in the brain. Therefore, inquiries into the nature of the brain's hardware seem to gain more prominence in connectionist accounts. For connectionists, cognition is still seen as computation, but at a sub-symbolic rather than symbolic level. Regarding the cognitive processes which were being studied, we can also observe a shift in focus. While the cognitivists were strongly interested in abstract deductive reasoning, which they saw as the paradigm for intelligence, connectionists were more interested in simpler, more concrete cognitive processes, such as perceptual pattern recognition (9). Furthermore, the importance of the relation between the cognitive systems and the environments in which they are embedded starts gaining more visibility in connectionist accounts. Yet, even if a sense of the dynamics of the interaction between the organism and the world slowly starts to emerge, the role of the body in cognition continued to be ignored.

Only in the early 1990s, the body was (re)discovered and its importance started to be systematically addressed from biological, psychological, and phenomenological standpoints. Most of the scholars trying to understand this neglect blame Descartes and the long-lasting influence of his dualist philosophy on European thinking (e.g., Gallagher and Zahavi 2008; Gibbs 2005).[14] Descartes's distinction between *res extensa* and *res cogitans* opened up an understanding of human beings as divided between a physical, visible body and an ethereal, invisible mind "mysteriously infused into the body" (Gibbs 2005: 4).

In the phenomenological tradition, however, the significance of the body was generally acknowledged from the very start. Edmund Husserl, the founder of phenomenology, discusses for instance the constitutional role of the body in human subjectivity, as a perspectival zero-point grounding all experience (be it perceptual, imaginative, etc.). He also addresses the primordiality of bodily movement (kinaesthesis) in perception and makes the famous and crucial distinction between the physical, spatiotemporal body as object, or as seen from the outside (*Körper*), and the body as subject, that is, as lived ([*Leib*]; cf. Zahavi 2003: 98–109).

Husserl's student, and later famous existentialist thinker, Martin Heidegger, is often accused of overlooking the embodied nature of subjectivity and of focusing instead solely on the latter's embeddedness into the world ([*in-der-Welt-sein*]; cf. Thompson 2007: 379–80). However, one can provide a philosophical account of *embodiment* (i.e., the implications of the fact of *having* a body) without accounting for the *body as such* (i.e., stature, skin, sexuality, etc.). For this reason, many scholars questioned such accusations, claiming that, even if not explicitly thematized, the body is (always) implicitly present in Heidegger's accounts (e.g., Glendinning 1998).

Nevertheless, probably the most important phenomenologist to discuss the body was the French phenomenologist Merleau-Ponty. In his groundbreaking work from 1945, *The Phenomenology of Perception*, the philosopher clearly underlines the fundamental primordiality of the body. "My body," he writes, "is the fabric into which all objects are woven, and it is, at least in relation to the perceived world, the general instrument of my 'comprehension'" (1962 [1945]: 235). His reflections, in the wake of Husserl, on the close interconnection between perception and kinaesthesis, come close to enactive accounts of perception as (being also) a motor phenomenon (e.g., Hurley 1998; Noë 2004). Merleau-Ponty also integrates Husserl's distinction between *Leib* and *Körper* into his philosophy, underlining the experiential transparency of the lived body (*corps propre* or *corps vécu*): "I observe external objects with my body, I handle them, examine them, walk around them, but as for my body, I do not observe it itself: in order to do so, I should need the use of a second body which itself would be unobservable" (1962 [1945]: 91). This transparency of the lived body in action is also noticed later by Sartre, who claims that when I reach to grasp something, "my hand has vanished; it is lost in the complex system of instrumentality in order that this system may exist" (1956 [1943]: 324).

In order to understand this phenomenon of the invisibility of that which is the closest to us, our body, the distinction made in the recent cognitive sciences between *body schema* and *body image* is helpful. Our body schema is the fundamental, pre-reflective, and proprioceptive awareness of our bodily action, whereas our body image consists of our perceptual experience, conceptual understanding, and emotional attitude toward our bodies (cf. Gallagher and Zahavi 2008: 147). It becomes clear, thus, that the transparency discussed by Merleau-Ponty and Sartre has to do with our basic body-schematic processes, with moments when our attention is directed outside into the world rather than toward our own bodies. But as the abovementioned distinction shows, the body need not always be transparent and can, from time to time, rise to awareness, in quite different ways than the objectifying one discussed by Husserl through his concept of *Körper*.

This brief incursion into the phenomenology of the body[15] foregrounded the primordiality of embodiment in human subjective experience. Starting with the 1990s, phenomenological analyses of lived experience have been incorporated in cognitive science, causing a major paradigm shift with the development of enactivism (cf. Varela, Thompson, and Rosch 1991), a cognitive-scientific paradigm focused on the fundamental embodied, embedded, and affective character of cognition, and aiming to provide careful descriptions, analyses, and interpretations of lived experience.[16]

Experience, as I argued, is centered around the body, the latter providing the former the ground from which to arise. Yet, the fact that we have (or, more appropriately, *are*) bodies is not significant only for our basic perceptual capacities. Our bodies are also the ground from which higher forms of cognition arise. A clear example why this is so can be provided by a discussion of the implications of one of the defining and distinctive features of human corporeality—the fact that we stand upright.

Gallagher and Zahavi (2008: 132–33) point out that the specificity of our anatomy and skeletal structure can have far-reaching consequences for our cognitive make-up. First, in evolutionary terms, the upright posture influences the anatomical structure of other parts of our bodies as well, such as our shoulders, arms, hands, skull, or face. Our general anatomical constitution further defines our capacities to interact with the environment and, thus, single out from the world the elements which have meaning for us.[17] Although these processes are initially sensorimotor, they extend to the most abstract and rational capacities for cognition, such as counting and the development of mathematics (Gallagher and Zahavi 2008: 132).

Secondly, in developmental terms, the achievement of the upright posture is delayed in humans. This means that in the first months of his life, the young infant must continuously struggle with gravity and must therefore be in a state of wakefulness. This striving to be awake and attentive has crucial consequences for the development of cognition. Once the upright posture is acquired, human beings achieve a certain distance from the world, their range of vision being extended, and, therefore, the environmental horizon widened and the capacities for perception and action redefined. The hands are freed from basic motor concerns and a new range of activities, such as reaching, grasping, manipulating, carrying, using tools, or pointing, becomes possible. These changes have profound impact on the development of cognition, leading finally to the emergence of rational thought.

Because of the upright posture, the visual sense becomes fundamental in human cognition, in contrast with the olfactory one, which is primary in most other mammals. The ability to see at distance opens up capacities for planning, while the shrinking in importance of the olfactory sense causes anatomical changes in the facial structure as well, enabling the development of the vocal chords, and ultimately the emergence of speech. "And if you ask Aristotle," Gallagher and Zahavi write, "he'll tell you that this means the development of both politics and rationality" (2008: 133).

After this brief overview of the phenomenologically fueled "discovery" of the body within contemporary cognitive science, I will now go back to primary intersubjectivity and describe in more detail some of its basic features—intercorporeality, interaffectivity, and attachment.

Intercorporeality

Intercorporeality is a phenomenological notion coined by Merleau-Ponty (1960) in order to describe the fact that face-to-face interactions are fundamentally structured by an embodied, preverbal, and pre-reflexive form of understanding—an intercorporeal resonance connecting the persons involved in interaction by reciprocal movements and sensations (Fuchs 2018: 178). This intercorporeality manifests initially through imitation.

More than two millennia ago, Aristotle claimed that "imitating is co-natural with human beings from childhood, and in this they differ from the other animals because they are the most imitative and produce their first acts of understanding by means of imitation" (Aristotle 2006 [c. 335 B.C.]: 10). These insights already began to be backed-up by psychological and neuroscientific research a few decades ago. Various empirical studies (e.g., Meltzoff and Moore 1977; Field et al. 1982) had shown, in contrast to previous research by scholars such as Jean Piaget who argued that children begin to imitate only a few months after birth, that spontaneous instances of imitation can be observed even a few *minutes* after birth. According to Meltzoff and Moore (1977), very young infants are already able to differentiate between animate and inanimate objects and have a tendency to imitate human facial expressions.[18]

Although these findings could be seen as evidence that the capacity for imitation is innate, most of the scholars accepting this view still stress, along with Aristotle, the fact that our imitative capacities sharply differentiate us from other animals. As Merlin Donald claims in his account of human evolution, children routinely re-enact past events and imitate the actions of their caregivers and siblings—an element largely absent from the behavior of apes (1991: 172).

A neuroscientific explanation of this seemingly innate[19] capacity for imitation started to emerge in the 1990s, after the accidental discovery, at the University of Parma, of the existence of "resonance systems" in the brain,[20] that is, clusters of so-called mirror neurons in the pre-motor cortex and Broca's area which are activated both when we engage in specific motor actions and when we see other people performing the same actions. In Gallagher and Zahavi's terms, "One's motor system reverberates or resonates in one's encounters with others" (2008: 177). This discovery proved crucial for understanding not only the interconnectedness of perceptual and motor processes, but also phenomena such as imitation.[21] According to Gallagher and Zahavi, an intermodal tie between a proprioceptive sense of one's body and the face that one sees is already functioning at birth. For the infant, the other person's body presents opportunities for action and expressive behavior which it can pursue through imitation (188).

However, as scholars such as Colwyn Trevarthen, Philippe Rochat, Claudia Passos-Ferreira, and Pedro Salem argue, understanding the nature of imitation solely in terms of the operation of innate resonance systems, what Trevarthen (2006) calls "innate intersubjectivity," is highly reductive and insufficient to address what makes *human* imitation different from, for example, instances of mimicry found in other animal species.[22] As he claims in a later article, studies of neonatal imitation have gone beyond proving that an action can be copied, or that infants can match forms of movement between their own body and another person's by intermodal equivalence. Infants appear to be capable of actively seeking and engaging with other human beings in sympathetic *dialogues*, having an active role in the development of such interactions (2011: 83). Evidences of the infants' need for such sympathetic dialogue come, in Trevarthen's opinion, from the fact that they are not just imitating in order to acquire a form of expression in which their movements match those of adults, but are also *seeking to be imitated in return* (82).

Trevarthen's insights are further developed by Rochat and Passos-Ferreira (2009) and Rochat, Passos-Fereira, and Salem (2009) through their concepts of "reciprocation" and "mutual recognition," which they consider "trademarks of human sociality" (Rochat, Passos-Fereira, and Salem 2009: 175). About two months after birth,[23] mirroring, imitation, and other contagious emotional responses tend to become more subtly attuned to interactive others and to be supplemented by an open system of reciprocation (174). Infants start to engage in face-to-face proto-conversations, where imitation continues to play a fundamental role, but is nevertheless becoming a more complex process than the previously automatic responses unconsciously elicited by the brain's resonance systems. The infants' active search not only to imitate, but also to be imitated in return discussed by Trevarthen, for example, points toward the emergence of radically different forms of social connection than before. Reviewing empirical research from the 1970s, Trevarthen concludes that, in their second and third month, infants are already capable of joining with their caregivers in an intimate coordination of rhythms of movement, moods, and expectations by means of facial, vocal, and gestural expressions, anticipating one another's behavior (2011: 86). Furthermore, from a series of videotaped experiments, it became obvious that infants responded to their caregivers' greetings with appropriate timing and changing emotions. One example of a proto-conversation between a mother and her nine-week-old daughter is described by Mary Catherine Benson: "The study of timing and sequencing showed that certainly the mother and probably the infant, in addition to conforming in general to a regular pattern, were acting to sustain it and restore it when it faltered, waiting for the expected vocalization from the other and then after a pause resuming vocalization, as if to elicit a response that had not been forthcoming" (Bateson 1979: 2; cited in Trevarthen 2011: 86).

Other more recent empirical studies documenting another type of proto-conversation characteristic of primary intersubjectivity were performed by psychologist Vasudevi Reddy and her colleagues. In their investigations of infants' anticipation of others' actions directed toward the infant, they discovered that when caregivers approach infants (aged two to four months) in order to pick them up, the latter were making specific adjustments of their bodies, such as extending or stiffening the legs, lifting their arms, or raising the chin, all of which enhanced body rigidity and therefore assisted in the smoothness of the pick-up (Reddy 2013: 31). Reddy concludes that such studies show that the goal directedness of others' actions toward infants are directly relevant to the infant, and they arouse bodily and emotional responses, that is, appropriate *responsive* acts rather than just matching "motor resonances" (32).[24]

Rochat, Passos-Ferreira, and Salem's concept of "reciprocation" gives more theoretical nuance to these empirical findings and stresses the fundamental role of these basic social interactions in cognitive development. In their opinion, the type of imitation developing after two months of age is not only a copying capacity, but also a source of innovation and learning (2009: 178; cf. also Rochat and Passos-Ferreira 2009: 197–98). As they put it, "If imitation in the strict sense is a source of vicarious experiences that give individuals the opportunity to get 'into the shoes of others' and possibly empathize with them, it is also a source of discovery and learning. New skills

can be learned by imitation following periods of discovery and learning"
(Rochat and Passos-Ferreira 2009: 197). In order for such learning to be possible, they claim, there must be some
sort of reciprocation in the context of the interaction between "the expert"
and "the novice"—a mutual, reciprocal willingness on the part of the novice
to observe and imitate the expert and on the part of the expert to be observed
by, and model for the novice (198).[25] Although the brain's resonance systems
are indeed a prerequisite for such a process to function, more complex
capacities, such as that for mutual attention and intention, are also needed.

Moreover, Rochat and Passos-Ferreira argue, recognition is also grounded
in a capacity for "mutual recognition" (2009: 199–201), that is, "the reciprocal
acknowledgement of each other" (200–01). As they put it, imitation not only
provides a basic sense of social connectedness and mutual acknowledgment
of existing with others that are "like me" (191), but also opens the path to
more complex instances of interactions, in which the participants are able "to
measure the regards others have for the self and to what extent there is some
equivalence between these regards, whether they are mutual and represent a
comparable value; in other words, whether they tend to 'mirror each other'
and express a two-way, *mutual recognition*" (200; emphasis in original).

As evidence of the importance of reciprocation and mutual recognition in
the context of proto-conversations characteristic of primary intersubjectivity,
Rochat and Passos-Ferreira cite as support the famous "still-face experimental
paradigm"—a series of studies in social psychology showing that infants are
seriously disturbed when their interactive partner suddenly freezes while
staring at them, and begin manifesting clear negative effects such as frowning,
suppressing bouts of smiling, looking away, and sometimes even crying (201;
e.g., Tronick et al. 1978). These experiments are interpreted by Rochat and
Passos-Ferreira as showing that infants develop social expectations regarding
what should happen next or what should happen while interacting with
others (202). Furthermore, they also point to the fact that very young infants
do not only possess a basic understanding of reciprocation, but they also
expect it during social interactions.

What I believe has already become obvious in my discussion of imitation
and proto-conversation is the highly affective character of social interactions
pertaining to primary intersubjectivity. In the next section I will discuss in
more detail the fundamental role emotions play in early social interactions.

Interaffectivity

In their article "Embodied Affectivity: On Moving and Being Moved" (2014),
Thomas Fuchs and Sabine Koch claim that emotions can be considered some

of the most complex phenomena of subjective experience, and that, therefore, there is still a lack of consensus regarding how exactly to define and describe them (2014: 1). After critically reviewing two of the main conflicting theories of emotion,[26] they define emotions as "affective responses to certain kinds of events of concern to a subject, implying conspicuous bodily changes and motivating a specific behavior" (2). Thus, they proceed in describing emotions along several dimensions, such as affective intentionality (what emotions are "about"), bodily resonance (how our bodily states are changed by certain affective qualities or affordances of a given situation), or action tendencies (how our bodies react while experiencing different emotions; 3). Furthermore, discussing the function and significance of emotions, Fuchs and Koch argue that they "interrupt the ongoing course of life in order to inform us, warn us, tell us what is important and what we have to react upon. They (re)structure the field of relevance and values [and] they provide a basic *orientation* about what really matters to us; they contribute to defining our goals and priorities [and] they make us *ready to act*. . . . Emotion may thus be regarded as a bodily felt transformation of the subject's world, which solicits the lived body to action." Finally, they claim that emotions, by indicating the individual's state and possible action to others, also serve a communicative/expressive function in social life (4).[27]

In ontogeny, emotions seem to structure behavior since the very beginning of life, if not even from before birth. Trevarthen, reviewing empirical studies of the face movements of newborn infants, concludes that these movements show a multitude of complex expressions, for example, an attentive relaxed mouth, cries, frowns, pouts, and smiles, all indicating changes of emotion and states of arousal and interest, and further claims that such expressions also appear from midgestation in fetuses (2011: 82). These highly developed capacities for expressivity and responsiveness of infants are, in Trevarthen's view, powerful factors in the establishment of an affectionate bond with caregivers, and "a natural interpersonal system for regulation of the infant's motive states and physiological well-being or homeostasis" (84). In a more recent study, Schore also argues that the "significant increase in current knowledge in early human *relationships* clearly demonstrate that from the very beginning, the developing human is *emotionally* relating with the *social environment*, moving the emphasis from cognitive to emotional development" (2019: 156; emphases in original).

By discussing the still-face experiments in the previous section, I argued that adults' lack of reciprocation during proto-conversations with infants gives rise in the latter to powerful negative emotions. However, reciprocation itself has a powerful affective dimension. As Fuchs and De Jaegher stress, even bodily mimesis, through the activation of resonance systems, generally gives rise to corresponding emotions in infant and adult, and "a mutual *affective resonance* gradually develops within the dyad" (2009: 478; emphasis in original). They further argue that with the emergence of proto-conversations, the affective resonance increases and the dyad "exhibits a finely tuned coordination of movements, rhythmic synchrony and mirroring of affective expressions that has often been compared to a couple dance" (478).

In the second part of the article I discussed above, Fuchs and Koch call this affective resonance *interaffectivity*[28] or *interbodily resonance/ intercorporeality*. "Our body is affected by the other's expression," they write, "and we experience the kinetics and intensity of his emotions through our own bodily kinaesthesia and sensation" (2014: 5).[29] In his later article on pathologies of intersubjectivity (2015), Fuchs similarly claims that being affected by each other's expressive behavior results in shared states of bodily feelings and affects, and further argues that already from the first months of life, infants store in their implicit or procedural memory familiar patterns of interaction and affect attunement. Through repeatedly interacting with their caregivers, infants learn how to share pleasure, elicit attention, avoid overstimulation, and re-establish contact (193).

In their discussion of empathy and sharing from phenomenological and developmental perspectives (2015), Zahavi and Rochat also stress the fundamental role played by emotions in early ontogeny. They define primary intersubjectivity (perhaps a bit reductively) as the "first active sharing of affects in proto-conversations" and describe this sharing in terms of "rhythmical turn taking" (a phenomenon strongly similar to what Rochat, Passos-Fereira, and Salem call "reciprocation") and "two way shared mutual gaze." Whereas the gaze of newborns remains often inattentive and difficult to capture, Zahavi and Rochat argue that by six to eight weeks after birth the gaze becomes "unmistakably *shared and mutual*, inaugurating a proto-conversational space of genuinely open-ended exchanges made of turn taking and a novel sensitivity." These proto-conversations structured by affective sharing have, according to Zahavi and Rochat, a very important function in development: they help infants "gauge their social situation," in other words, understand their own limits and possibilities as agents in their environment in terms of "the impact they have on others" (e.g., how much attention they are able to generate and receive from others; cf. Zahavi and Rochat 2015: 546; emphasis in original).

Attachment and the Tactile and Olfactory Senses

The intercorporeal and interaffective relationship between infants and caregivers has been described in the 1950s by Bowlby as being regulated by a biologically grounded attachment system, which has a fundamental role in developing the infants' sense of trust and security. According to Bowlby, mother-infant interactions are "accompanied by the strongest of feelings and emotions, and occur within the context of facial expression, posture, tone of voice" (1969: 120).[30] As Fuchs argues, the attachment system comprises important phylogenetically rooted signals, including searching, calling, looking at, crying, clinging, or protest in case of separation (2018: 183), and helps the infant develop physiological and psychic regulatory mechanisms, thus regulating homeostatic processes (184). In Schore's view, "During attachment episodes of *visual-facial, auditory-prosodic, and tactile-gestural* affective communications, the primary caregiver regulates the infant's internal states of peripheral and central arousal" (2019: 160; emphasis in original).

The tactile and olfactory senses appear to be fundamental in attachment. As Fuchs argues, during primary intersubjectivity, infants try to establish as much physical contact as possible for experiencing pleasant sensations of warmth, smell, and touch (2018: 200). At around three months of age, a tactile form of communication establishes between infants and caregivers, the former being able to respond with an intentional affectionate touch to the latter's affectionate touch (Schore 2019: 194). This interpersonal tactile communication has an important role in regulating emotional information and in facilitating healthy brain development (231). As Paterson argues, touch is a nonverbal, receptive, and expressive form of social communication, which "can cement an empathic or affective bond, opening an entirely new channel of communication" (2007: 3). Similarly, Wyschogrod argues that empathy and sympathy are "phenomena of proximity" and can only be understood as "feeling-acts of a tactile rather than visual subject" (1981: 32). Moreover, touch has a therapeutic function, lowering stress levels and calming and promoting neural activity in children (Shaffer and Kipp 2014: 143).

The sense of smell is also highly important for the development and maintenance of attachment. Many studies have argued that olfaction, a "highly emotive sense" (Wilson and Stevenson 2006: 139), contributes fundamentally to the formation of a secure attachment between mother and infant (e.g., Wilson and Stevenson 2006: 139; Good and Kopala 2006: 197), and that new mothers have an increased response in areas of the brain associated with care behaviors when exposed to the smell of their own child (Moore 2016: 82). In fact, as Gilbert claims, not only mothers can identify the smell of their own babies, but also the babies can pick out the scent of their mother's breasts (2008: 73). Similarly, Pelosi argues that olfactory cues are extremely important for initiating the process of breastfeeding and attracting newborns to their mothers' lactating breasts (2016: 134).

In the following section, I will return to the discussion of sexuality and argue that, according to contemporary cognitive science, sexual interaction appears to be structured by processes similar to those characterizing primary intersubjectivity, that is, intercorporeality, interaffectivity, and attachment.

2.2.2 Sexuality and Primary Intersubjectivity

In contemporary cognitive sciences sexuality is understood as a biological universal and is analyzed at great length, particularly in evolutionary accounts of the phylogenetic development of human (and other animal) species.[31] But although evolutionary theorists acknowledge the complexity of sexual *choice*, that is, the process through which we select a sexual partner, and discuss in detail the occasional failures caused by incompatibilities in mating strategies, the phenomenology of the sexual *act* itself is largely ignored in this paradigm. However, neurobiological and psychological approaches find striking parallels between sexuality and processes that I discussed above under the heading of primary intersubjectivity, that is, intercorporeality, interaffectivity, and attachment.

In an article from 1915, Freud claims that "every earlier stage of development persists alongside the later stage which has arisen from it . . . the primitive stages can always be re- established; the primitive mind is, in the fullest meaning of the word, imperishable" (1957 [1915]: 285). As I have repeatedly emphasized, similar views characterize the developmental accounts of intersubjectivity. Schore, for example, argues that the attachment dynamic characterizing primary intersubjectivity continues throughout the entire life span "as an unconscious mechanism that mediates the interpersonal and intrapsychic events of all relationships, especially *intimate relationships*" (2019: 17; my emphasis). Drawing upon the developmental accounts of intersubjectivity proposed by Daniel Stern, Ammaniti and Gallese find close parallels between the mother-child relationship and adult intimate relationships:

> Mother and child behavior overlaps with the behavior of two lovers. For example, mother and child look at each other without speaking, hold a physical closeness with faces and bodies in constant contact, display alterations in vocal expressions or synchrony of movements, and perform particular gestures like kissing each other, hugging, touching, and taking the face or the hands of the other . . . . When parents speak to their child, or lovers talk with one another . . . they emphasize the musicality of the words instead of the meaning, they use baby talk, and they express a wide range of nonverbal vocalizations. . . . Facial expressions assume a

special register also, altering and emphasizing the facial mimic. There is also a choreography in the movements of mother and baby, like those of two lovers; they move in synchrony, getting closer and more distant on the basis of a common rhythm. (Ammaniti and Gallese 2014: 110–11)

Moreover, neurobiological and psychological accounts of sexuality also consider the tactile and olfactory senses as fundamental in sexual interaction. Hatfield, for example, argues that the expression of most of our sexuality occurs through touch (1994: 581) and Crooks and Bauer claim that touch tends to predominate during sexual intimacy through the stimulation of erogenous zones (2013: 150–51). In the words of Lawrence's Connie Chatterley, sex is "really only touch, the closest of all touch" (1959: 346). However, the recent discovery of human sex pheromones, that is, chemicals produced by the body and transmitted through smell which have a role in increasing sexual attraction and arousal (Wyatt 2003: 270–301; Rako and Frielby 2004), also emphasize the importance of the olfactory sense in sexual interaction.

Such neurobiological and psychological approaches to sexuality stress its pre-linguistic, embodied, and affective character, and its apparent freedom from thought processes, resembling not only Lawrence's discussions of blood-knowledge, but also phenomena pertaining to primary intersubjectivity. Moreover, earlier phenomenological and hermeneutic approaches to sexuality also foreground similar aspects. As Merleau-Ponty argues in his chapter about sexuality from *The Phenomenology of Perception*, there "is an erotic 'comprehension' not of the order of understanding, since understanding subsumes an experience, once perceived, under some idea, while desire comprehends blindly by linking body to body" (Merleau-Ponty 1962 [1945]: 139). Such a conceptualization of sexuality as a preverbal and pre-reflexive act unencumbered by mental processes also characterizes Ricoeur's hermeneutical thought. As he puts it, "When two beings embrace, they don't know what they are doing, they don't know what they want, they don't know what they are looking for, they don't know what they are finding" (1994: 141).

However, in the two literary works I will discuss in this chapter, McEwan shows that sexuality is sometimes far from being a direct, bodily form of what Lawrence called "blood-knowledge," that is, "instinct, intuition, all the vast vital flux of knowing that goes on in the dark, antecedent to the mind" (1923: 90). On the contrary, as I will argue with the help of "Homemade" and *On Chesil Beach*, sexuality seems to be in some cases (de)structured by various psychological, social, cultural-linguistic, and historical forces.

What needs to be made clear from the very start, though, is that McEwan rarely deals with relationships structured *solely* by sexuality. In all of his works, the sexual elements are almost always incorporated into larger patterns of interpersonal interaction, where an enormous variety of emotions are negotiated and from which different forms of understanding and misunderstanding emerge.

For the purpose of this chapter, though, I will bracket most of the complexity of social interaction that we can find in McEwan's stories and novels, and focus on two works where, in my opinion, sexuality and its discontents are indeed foregrounded and harshly analyzed, that is, his first published short story, "Homemade" (1971), and one of his latest novels, *On Chesil Beach* (2007).[32] I am choosing these works because, as will become clear later, they offer powerful examples of the phenomena of paralysis and invasion.

2.3 One of the Most Desolate Couplings Known to Copulating Humanity: Homemade Sexual Initiation

In an interview with Ian Hamilton in 1978, McEwan describes "Homemade," the first piece of writing he ever published (when he was twenty-four years old), as "a story about *total* sexual failure" (17–18; emphasis in original). "I know it's fairly common for writers to write 'my first fuck' stories," he continues, "but I wanted to write a first fuck story where the actual fuck would be abysmally useless and yet its narrator would foolishly still derive huge satisfaction from it" (18).[33] Reflecting in this section upon why the sexual initiation staged in this story was "abysmally useless" and why the narrator derived such a "huge satisfaction" from it will shed more light on some crucial aspects characterizing sexuality, more specifically in this case, the *initiation* into what the anonymous narrator calls "the dawn of my sexual day" (*H*: 26).

H is a short yet very complex first-person retrospective narrative. Its complexity emerges both from its subject matter, that is, the intricate process of entering the world of sexuality, and from the various stylistic and narrative devices McEwan uses in the literary staging of the story's thematic concerns. Dominic Head compares this story's narrator with James Joyce's narrators in *Dubliners* (1914): "an older narrator reviewing an episode from his past [when he was fourteen-years old] using a sophisticated mode of expression that is inconsistent with his earlier self" (2007: 35).

In Thomas Fuchs's terminology, this narrator can be described as someone who has definitely acquired a strong, explicit 1PP—a first-person meta-perspective, a self-conscious, evaluative distance between (his) present and past (selves)—and a similarly strong, explicit 2PP—an explicit awareness of and, consequently, distance from his (past) social interactions. However, as it will become clear later, these explicit 1PP and 2PP are capacities not *only* the older narrator possesses, but his younger self seems to possess them too, and to make use of them *excessively* during his social interactions, at the expense of other ways of sense-making.

The inconsistency and distance between the telling and the told is already foregrounded in the first paragraph of the story and adds a strong metafictional twist to this narrative. As is clear from the very start, *H* is not only a story about sexual initiation but also a story about ways of telling stories about sexual initiation. In other words, *H* can be described as a narrative about narrative sense-making. As Lynda Broughton argues, "There are ironizing devices within the text which turn it back on itself; or rather, they produce an internal distancing effect [and the] narrative constantly operates on this double level, recounting the events which constitute the hero's progress from innocence to experience with the detached, adult literariness of the narrator" (1991: 139–40). Here is the beginning:

> I can see now our cramped, overlit bathroom and Connie with a towel draped round her shoulders, sitting on the edge of the bath weeping, while I filled the sink with warm water and whistled—such was my elation—"Teddy Bear" by Elvis Presley, I can remember, I have always been able to remember, fluff from the candlewick bedspread swirling on the surface of the water, but only lately have I fully realized that if this was the *end* of a particular episode, in so far as real-life episodes may be said to have an end, it was Raymond who occupied, so to speak, the beginning and middle, and if in human affairs there are no such things as episodes then I should really insist that this story is about Raymond and not about virginity, coitus, incest and self-abuse. (23)

This very long first sentence contains a compact but quite elaborate meditation on the relationship between life and narrative, foregrounding not only the unreliability of this particular narrator and his narrative act, but also the unreliability of narrative in general as a way of sense-making. As suggested here, episodes in life might not follow the Aristotelian tripartite structure of narratives, that is, they might not have, or even if they have, it might not be so easy to identify, beginnings, middles, and ends. However, as with many other things, *H*'s narrator remains agnostic regarding the ultimate truth about the connections between real-life events and narrative episodes: they might or might not be similar.[34]

Furthermore, this passage also foregrounds what I earlier called the adult narrator's use of an explicit 2PP in order to make sense of his previous social interactions: his past encounter with Connie is seen from a "bird's eye," panoramic perspective. Whereas this is perhaps a necessary, unavoidable sense-making strategy in cases of remembering past events, it nevertheless, as I will argue later, sets the stage for close to pathological employments of explicit 1PP and 2PP by the narrator's younger self (which I will discuss as important aspects of one variety of paralysis).

Before discussing these issues in more detail though, it is worthwhile to briefly return to the narrator's "metafictional agnosticism" I mentioned earlier. Its main effect, of course, is to strongly destabilize the very core of the story he tells. Not only is the reliability of the teller and of the act of telling put in question, but it is not even clear what the story is *about*. Two hypothetical scenarios emerge: if, on the one hand, episodes in real life have a narrative structure, then this story might be read as being about "virginity, coitus, incest, and self-abuse." If not, the story becomes a portrait of a character, Raymond. But even in the first case, according to the narrator, the importance of Raymond should not be underestimated: if the climax (or, in this case, as we will see, the anticlimax), the end of the story, deals with the narrator's sexual initiation, Raymond still occupies the beginning and the middle. So, who is this Raymond, and why is he so important?

Toward the end of the first paragraph, the narrator, addressing the reader directly, while at the same time starting to build the suspense and curiosity fundamental to narratives in general,[35] claims that "it was ironic, for reasons which will become apparent only very much later—and you must be patient— it was ironic that Raymond of all people should want to make me aware of my virginity" (23). Later in the text, an image of Raymond slowly starts to crystallize, an image teeming with paradox and contradiction. "Raymond was fifteen then," the narrator recounts, "a year older than I was, and though I counted myself his intellectual superior . . . it was Raymond who *knew* things, it was Raymond who conducted my education" (24; emphasis in original).

Indeed, it was Raymond who taught the narrator how to smoke (both cigarettes and marijuana) and drink, who introduced him to horror movies as well as to "the thrills of shoplifting" (25), and "acquainted [him] with the dubious pleasures of masturbation" (26), helping him acquire, "by the age of fourteen . . . a variety of pleasures which [he] rightly associated with the adult world." Ironically though, Raymond seems not to be able to fully experience and enjoy what he himself is teaching: "he was a clumsy Virgil to my Dante," the narrator confesses, "showing me the way to a Paradiso where he himself could not tread. He could not smoke because it made him cough, the whiskey made him ill, the films frightened or bored him, the cannabis did not affect him, and while I made stalactites on the ceiling of the bomb-site cellar, he made nothing at all" (27). Although Raymond appeared to "[know] the world well enough, [the world] did not want to know him" (24). The previously mentioned narrative distance between the telling and the told is thus also mirrored in the construction of this character. In Raymond's case, there is always an insurmountable gap between theory and practice and between abstract knowledge and the experiential living of such knowledge.

Such traits are highly similar to aspects of certain manifestations of what I called paralysis, that is, a disrupted form of intersubjectivity, characterized by a lack/deficiency of ways of relating to others. As it will become increasingly clear when I will discuss in more detail the narrator's relationship with other characters (as well as other instances of social interaction from McEwan's works), the concept "paralysis" subsumes various types of social interaction in which one form of intersubjectivity is obsessively employed while dealing with alterity, at the expense of all the others.

It is extremely important to notice from the very start that, although the cases of paralysis McEwan usually stages and on which I will mainly focus in this thesis are characterized by the employment of tertiary forms of intersubjectivity at the expense of primary or secondary ones, this *need not* always be the case: there could be instances of paralysis where, for example, primary or secondary forms of intersubjectivity are predominant. To give a literary example staging a prioritization of primary forms: In the life of Philip Roth's character Mickey Sabbath (from his 1995 novel *Sabbath's Theater*), sexuality, as Merleau-Ponty once put it, "spreads forth like an odor or like a sound" (1962 [1945]: 140), deeply structuring most of Sabbath's interactions with women ("You have the body of an old man, the life of an old man, the past of an old man, and the instinctive force of a two-year-old" (Roth 2007 [1995]: 335), one of his women diagnoses him). His sexual obsessions make him repeatedly view his wives and lovers only in terms of their bodies and the (sexual) affordances their bodies offer, and stop him from trying to connect with them in different ways, a tendency which ultimately destroys most of his relationships.

Sabbath's fate is similar in some ways to that of McEwan's character Michael Beard from *Solar* (2010). Although he is introduced in the first page of the novel as "a man of narrowed mental condition, anhedonic, monothematic, stricken" (3), Beard is nevertheless many times so powerfully engulfed in and enslaved by his bodily sensations that all traces of (abstract) thought are forgotten. His relationships with women, all pursued "in predatory mode" (339), can thus be characterized in terms of paralysis within primary intersubjectivity. Here is, for example, how his relationship with Darlene, "a woman of fifty-one, whose body was as slack and tired and inflated, as scribbled on by varicose veins, as his own" (340) is described: "For Beard the affair was an unexpected sexual renaissance, with piercing sensory pleasure, much like that near-inversion of agony he remembered from his twenties. A lifetime had swept by since he last shouted out involuntarily like a madman at the moment of orgasm. He never would have believed he would be experiencing such extremities of sensation with [Darlene]" (339–40). Although this looks, at first sight, like a successful way of dealing with a (sexual) relationship, the demands put on Beard by Darlene (exceeding by far an indulgence in primary forms of intersubjectivity), make his behavior amenable to be described in terms of paralysis.

But to go back to "Homemade," the narrator's distant, observational stance toward himself and others, characterized by a combination of *explicit* 1PP, 2PP, and 3PP, sidestepping any *implicit* 1PP (i.e., pre-reflective self-awareness) or 2PP (i.e., pre-reflective self-other awareness, based on embodied interaction) is prefigured through Raymond's general being-in-the-world. However, whereas paralysis is a concept dealing specifically with forms of *inter*subjectivity, Raymond's problems appear to have a higher degree of generality: his *overall* connection with the world (of which the social sphere is only one part) and, thus, his entire range of experiences are haunted by an unbearable distance between knowing and being/doing and between theoretical and practical knowledge.

Although the narrator appears much more skilled in practicing and living the activities Raymond teaches him, when it comes to sex, he becomes strangely similar to Raymond. His first sexual encounter (with his younger sister, Connie) uncannily resembles Raymond's distanced, abstract, "second-hand" experiences mentioned before, thus giving the readers a clue why this story might be considered "about Raymond," as the narrator claims in the first paragraph. If Raymond's connection, or, better, *lack* of connection with the experiential world, is mirrored in the narrator's distance from the experience of sexuality, the story could indeed be read as being about Raymond, in the sense that it can be seen as staging and reflecting upon types of experiential being-in-the-world for which Raymond is the main prototype.

But in contrast with the comic atmosphere surrounding Raymond's failures, the narrator's bleak entry into sexuality leans more toward the grotesque. If "Fortuna played practical jokes on Raymond, perhaps she even kicked sand in his eyes," the narrator admits, "she never spat in his face or trod deliberately on his existential corns—Raymond's mistakings, losses, betrayals and injuries were all, in the final estimate, comic rather than tragic" (33). On the other hand, as we will see, the narrator's discovery of the "'fleshly grail' of adult [*sic*] knowledges" (Broughton 1991: 139) is, if not utterly tragic, at least tragi-comic.

The narrator's shocking decision to "rape [his] sister" (*H*: 37), and thus gain entrance in the last "fur-lined chamber of that vast, gloomy and delectable mansion, adulthood" (27) is once more influenced by Raymond, who tells the narrator that, for only a shilling, he could have "a glimpse at the incommunicable, the heart of mystery's mystery, the Fleshly Grail, Dinky Lulu's pussy" (32). Lulu Smith, a girl from their school "whose physical enormity was matched only by the enormity of her reputed sexual appetite and prowess, her grossness only by the grossness she inspired, the legend only by the reality," is described not only in hyperbolic terms, as in the previous quote, but also in quasi-mythical ones. A veritable urban legend, "who—so fame had it—had laid a trail across north London of frothing idiots, a desolation row of broken minds and pricks spanning Shepherds Bush to Holloway, Ongar to Islington," is described by the narrator as a "heaving, steaming leg-load of schoolgirl flesh who had, so reputation insisted, had it with a giraffe, a humming-bird, a man in an iron lung (who had subsequently died), a yak, Cassius Clay, a marmoset, a Mars Bar and the gear stick of her grandfather's Morris Minor (and subsequently a traffic warden)" (28).

This hyperbolization, mythologization, and idealization of the sexuality embodied by Lulu marks the narrator's general ways of conceptualizing sexuality as well as his virginity. Speaking of sexual initiation, for example, after claiming that he "resented" his virginity, he declares with a combination of confidence and shame: "I knew it to be the last room in the mansion, I knew it to be for certain the most luxurious, its furnishings more elaborate than in any other room, its attractions more deadly, and the fact that I had never had it, made it, done it, was a total anathema, my malodorous albatross" (29). The mythical way in which sexuality is understood arises not only from his recurrent use of spatial metaphors for conceptualizing temporal relations, where the abstract passage to adulthood is mapped metaphorically into a more concrete journey through space, but also through describing his virginity as a curse, an anathema that keeps him separated from the social sphere.[36]

The powerful influence of society in shaping the narrator's conceptualization of sexuality and of his relation with it is recognized and discussed at length by Dominic Head. The "dilemma of the story," Head argues, "is predicated on social and peer-pressure concerning sexual experience. . . . In desperately seeking experience he is also an innocent suffering from the pressure to conform, and in ways that suppress his emotional being" (2007: 36).

According to Zahavi and Rochat (2015), group identification begins in ontogeny with the emergence of "self-other related emotions" such as shame, pride, or envy, which can be seen as evidence of children's awareness of being constantly evaluated by others. This developing awareness starts to significantly shape their social and affective lives, that is, they start to care about their image and reputation in relation to others, and they also begin to conceal their intentions or feelings, consciously manipulating what parts of themselves they expose in front of others. Furthermore, they also become sensitive to the others' approbation or disapprobation and are thus "constantly gauging and promoting their own social affiliation" (547). As Zahavi and Rochat argue, such developments mark the beginning of a sensitivity to group norms and affiliation as well as to its counterpart— the possibility of being socially excluded. Entering institutions outside their family environment, such as kindergartens or pre-schools, children become aware of "the institutional or consensual collective order that transcends and ultimately governs personal wants and inclinations," and gradually immerse themselves in forms of "group-based we-experience": they start identifying with the group, showing in-group biases, and endorsing the views and preferences of the group. Their self-esteem and self-worth is increasingly derived from group membership and group status. Moreover, already since four years of age, they start to manifest out-group gender and racial stereotypes,[37] as well as other implicit group attitude biases toward persons not belonging to their group. Finally, from seven years on, "the self and social identity begins to be conceptualized on the basis of combined social affiliation and exclusion processes," and they consequently begin to manifest active ostracism and social rejection of persons outside their group in order to affirm their own group affiliation and identity (547).

However, what McEwan's story adds to these theoretical reflections is how the pressure to identify with a social group can sometimes have powerful negative effects on one's emotions (particularly the self-other conscious ones such as shame, pride, or guilt) and, thus, also on one's concrete, embodied, and affective connections to others. But although Head mentions "the broader, distorting social forces" that influence the narrator's "sense of personal failure and inadequacy" (2007: 36), he does not stress enough the extent to which society, language, and culture structure his understanding of sexuality *before* his direct sexual experience. He learns about sex not only from Raymond, but also from a whole array of workers in a café in which he spends much time, listening "transfixed" to stories of

> cunts, bits, skirt, of strokings, beatings, fuckings, suckings, of arses and tits, behind, above, below, in front, with, without, of scratching and tearing, licking and shitting, of juiced cunts streaming, warm and infinite, of others cold and dry but worth a try, of pricks old and limp, or young and ebullient, of coming, too soon, too late or not at all, of how many times a day, of attendant diseases, of pus and swellings, cankers and regrets, of poisoned ovaries and destitute testicles; we listened to who and how the dustmen fucked, how the Co-op milkmen fitted it in,

what the coalmen could hump, what the carpet-fitter could lay, what
the builders could erect, what the meter man could inspect, what the
bread man could deliver, the gas man sniff out, the plumber plumb, the
electrician connect, the doctor inject, the lawyer solicit, the furniture
man install—and so on, in an unreal complex of timeworn puns and
innuendo, formulas, slogans, folklore and bravado. (29–30)

As testified by this comic and almost delirious passage, the narrator is
utterly flooded by linguistic, oral descriptions of sex, including a rich array
of metaphors and metonymies connected to various sociolects, giving
rise to a huge polyphonic discourse on sexuality, reflected through and
tainted by the voices of myriad subcultures and social groups. "I listened
without understanding," the narrator confesses, "remembering and filling
away anecdotes which I could one day use myself, putting by histories of
perversions and sexual manners—in fact a whole sexual morality, so then
when finally I began to understand, from my own experience, what it was
all about, I had on tap a complete education which, augmented by a quick
reading of Havelock Ellis and Henry Miller, earned me the reputation of
being the juvenile connoisseur of coitus [. . . and] all this after one fuck—
the subject of this story" (30). But why, in the end, does this "one fuck"
turn out to be "one of the most desolate couplings known to copulating
mankind" (43)?[38]

   In an article from 1991, Lynda Broughton gives a very interesting, yet,
in my view, problematic linguistic analysis of the name of the narrator's
sister, "Connie." Her general argument in this article revolves around the
idea that McEwan creates his main character as a parody of the hero from
the tradition of high romance, who is usually an introspective character,
"singular, complete, unified," celebrating "his separation from the society
in which he finds himself" (Broughton 1991: 139).[39] In Broughton's view,
McEwan's complex use of a "narrative voice which is consistently aware of the
ironic spaces in its discourse" (139) and thus tells "an entirely self-referencing
[story], signposting its own construction" (143) subverts the traditional
heroic narratives and ironizes "the hero," who, although he finds the "fleshly
grail" he was looking for at the end of the story, discovers it in a strongly
anticlimactic scene: after his sexual encounter with his sister, he "did not want
to see a naked girl, or a naked anything for a while yet" (*H*: 43).

   Connie's name is a "translinguistic pun," in Broughton's opinion.
Knowledge, in French, is *connaissance*. And since she considers the hero's
quest to be in search of knowledge, she reads Connie allegorically, as a
symbol standing for the abstract concept of "knowledge." But, since "con/
naissance is both knowledge, and birth (*naissance*) through knowledge,"

and furthermore, Broughton argues, "*con* is [not only] French for cunt,"[40] but also, in English "to 'con' is both to learn and to trick someone by supplying them with false meanings, as in 'con-man'" (Broughton 1991: 141), the name Connie becomes a very complex signifier, an almost purely linguistic creation, strongly disconnected from any nonlinguistic, experiential dimensions. However, this is, in my opinion, a problematic interpretation since it tends to repeat what in the story turned out to be a huge mistake.[41] Instead of approaching sexuality with a trust in its nonlinguistic, embodied, and affective dimensions, our hero tends to continuously project language upon nature, in a frenzy caused both by his anger that he does not yet know the phenomenon of sexuality intimately, through experience, and by the unbearable anticipation of finally acquiring such knowledge:

> Raymond promised to confront the divine Lulu Smith with our proposition the following day after school, and since I was pledged to look after my sister that evening while my parents were at the Walthamstow dog track, I said goodbye to Raymond there at the café. All the way home I thought about cunt. I saw it in the smile of the conductress, I heard it in the roar of the traffic, I smelled it in the fumes from the shoe-polish factory, conjectured it beneath the skirts of passing housewives, felt it at my fingertips, sensed it in the air, drew it in my mind and at supper, which was toad-in-the-hole, I devoured, as in an unspeakable rite, genitalia of batter and sausage. And for all this I still did not know what a cunt was. (35)

As Head argues, the retrospective narrator "reinterpret[s] his adolescent obsession with all things sexual, adding a new layer of descriptive intensity . . . to revivify earlier sensations" (2007: 35).[42] He repeatedly and deliriously projects upon his whole environment what for the fourteen-year old character was still just an abstract name, a concept, and his seemingly *perceptual* access to *it* ("I saw it," "heard it," "smell it," etc.) is, ironically, nothing more than an imaginative access to a linguistically mediated *representation* of it. When it comes to sexuality, the narrator is still blocked at the level of the abstract, fleshless signifier, without any access to the fleshly signified. And as we will see, when the narrator finally encounters the "thing-in-itself," in his bodily interaction with his sister Connie, the concreteness of his sexual encounter, which should have better remained, in such a case, as close as possible to a pure form of embodied and affective primary intersubjectivity (an interaction grounded in and structured by an implicit 2PP), is *invaded* by more complex forms of intersubjectivity (steeped in explicit 1PP, 2PP, and 3PP) reliant upon the various social, linguistic, and cultural forces which until then have structured his understanding of such phenomena.

Such a normative description of sexuality, that is, as *better* remaining as close as possible to a pure form of primary intersubjectivity, raises an important question regarding the nature of paralysis: Can the kinds of pure sexual encounter idealized and fought for by Lawrence, for example, the Tantric traditions, be described as instances of paralysis? After all, such views of sexuality aim to keep the sexual act "clean" of all conceptual, linguistic, or mentalistic "impurities" and thus to "block" it within *one* form of intersubjectivity—the primary one. But can such sexual encounters be characterized by a *lack/deficiency* of ways of relating to the other? In my view, absolutely not: the very terms "lack" and "deficiency" imply the *absence* of something which *should not* be absent. Take Mickey Sabbath's case again: his excessive libido blocks him repeatedly within primary forms of intersubjectivity *when* other ways of relating to his women *are necessary*. Only because of this can Sabbath's behavior be described in terms of paralysis within primary intersubjectivity. On the contrary, when other forms of intersubjectivity besides the primary one are *not* needed/necessary during the sexual act (which I believe to be the case most of the times), I think it would be quite wrong to describe the encounter in terms of paralysis.

Ironically enough, Sabbath himself provides at one point a powerful critique of instances of paralysis where tertiary forms of intersubjectivity predominate. Kathy, one of his many young students he seduced, tells him: "I love. . . I love your mind. I love how you expose your mind when you talk." Hearing such a confession, Sabbath replies enraged and full of his usual bitterness and cynicism: "My mind? Well, this is quite a revelation. *I* thought you loved my ancient penis. My *mind*? This is quite a shock for a man of my years. Where you really only in it for my mind? Oh no. All the time I was talking about fucking, you were watching me expose my mind! Paying unwanted attention to my *mind*! You dared to introduce a mental element into a setting where it has no place" (Roth 2007 [1995]: 244; emphases in original).

But what happens when, during a sexual act in which other forms of intersubjectivity besides the primary one are not needed but are nevertheless used, as in the case of the narrator's intercourse with Connie? Such a type of social interaction, that is, an unnecessary employment of a *surplus* of forms of intersubjectivity, is what I would characterize as invasion. McEwan's portrayal of invasion in this story is built upon a critical intertextual engagement with Lawrence.

Relying on her complex linguistic analyses, Broughton misses in my view the more direct intertextual connection McEwan establishes by naming the narrator's sister Connie. Lawrence's heroine Connie Chatterley can be seen as a prototypical embodiment of Lawrence's idealization of sexuality as a form of "blood-knowledge," a much more powerful and truthful form of knowledge than what he calls "mind-knowledge," that is, a relation with the other strongly structured by social, linguistic, and cultural codes and forces. In my reading, by ironically naming his character Connie, McEwan builds a harsh critique of Lawrence's idealism regarding the purity of sexuality. By foregrounding the invasive forces structuring even sexual *initiations*, McEwan strongly challenges Lawrence's soteriological project. But let us finally have a look now at the narrator and Connie's sexual encounter.

Connie pops into the narrator's mind shortly after Raymond tells him about Lulu. His excitement for seeing Lulu's "fleshly grail" brings into his mind his mother and Connie, the only women he has ever seen naked: "my mother was vast and grotesque, the skin hanging from her like toad-hides, and my ten-year-old sister was an ugly bat whom as a child I could hardly bring myself to look at, let alone share the bath-tub with" (31). And yet, a few pages later, when he arrives home after his surreal walk home while constantly thinking "about cunt," he starts changing his evaluation regarding his sister:

> I eyed my sister across the table.[43] I exaggerated a little just now when I said she was an ugly bat—I was beginning to think that perhaps she was not so bad-looking after all. . . . So it was not surprising that I came to be thinking . . . that with some cajoling and perhaps a little honest deceit Connie could be persuaded to think of herself, if only for a few minutes, as something more than a sister, as, let us say, a beautiful young lady, a film star and maybe, Connie, we could slip into bed here and try out this rather moving scene, now you get out of these clumsy pajamas while I see to the light. . . . And armed with this comfortably gained knowledge I could face the awesome Lulu with zeal and abandon. (35)

It is interesting to notice here how, from the very beginning, the narrator is unable to approach Connie directly, for the sake of the interaction itself.[44] Instead of relying on perception, he is still lost in imagination. Not only is he fantasizing about intercourse with his sister as *just* training for his future encounter with Lulu, but he also anticipatively projects a film script over the interaction. Instead of trusting his senses, he uses frames from popular culture to structure his approach. Again, to put it in Fuchs's terms, he uses an explicit 2PP, complicated by his projection of frames taken from popular culture, instead of an implicit 2PP, which would be definitely more suited for such a type of interaction. This aspect is foregrounded also in his strategies of deceiving Connie to have sex with him: he convinces her to play games with him—first, hide-and-seek and later on "Mommies and Daddies." Various semiotic layers interfere in an interaction that should be, according to Lawrence, a primary, embodied, and affective, form of intersubjectivity.

When they are finally in bed and the narrator tells Connie that they still have to do "one of the most important things that Mommies and Daddies do together," and when Connie asks what this is, his answer pushes their interaction once more into the linguistic sphere. "They fuck together, Connie" he says, "surely you know about that." When Connie immediately repeats the word in puzzlement, a strong feeling of defamiliarization descends upon the narrator: "On her lips the word sounded strangely meaningless, which in a way I suppose it was, as far as I was concerned. The whole idea was to give it some meaning" (39). What the narrator does not realize though is that precisely his struggle for giving it *meaning*, caused by his obsessive reliance on tertiary forms of intersubjectivity (i.e., his paralysis), will ruin the encounter and transform it into a case of invasion. His mythical anticipative *conceptualization* of the sexual act completely destroys its perceptual and affective character:

> I searched her tiny crevice without the least notion of what I was looking for, but half expecting all the same to be transformed at any moment into a human whirlwind of sensation. I think perhaps I had in mind a warm fleshy chamber, but as I prodded and foraged, jabbed and wheedled, I found nothing other than tight, resisting skin. . . . My supporting arm was seared by pins and needles, I was feeling raw and yet still I poked and pushed, in a mood of growing despair (41).

When finally, with Connie's guidance, he is able to penetrate her, instead of enjoying the bodily sensations caused by the act and immersing himself in a thoughtless form of physical interaction, he is once more, and probably stronger than ever, flooded by *thought* processes. The insurmountable distance between the telling and the told is once more mirrored by the gap and feeling of dissociation lying at the core of our fourteen-year-old hero's self. Immediately after the penetration, a deep lust for exhibitionism invades him. "I wished Raymond could have seen me. . . . I wish Dinky Lulu could have seen me," he rambles, "in fact if my wishes had been granted I would have had all my friends, all the people I knew, file through the bedroom to catch me in my splendorous pose" (42–43). The reason such strange desires invade him is that

> more than sensation, more than any explosion behind my eyes, spears through my stomach, searings in my groin or rackings in my soul—more

> than any of these things, *none of which I felt anyway*, more then than even
> the thought of these things, I felt proud, proud to be fucking . . . proud in
> advance of being able to say "I have fucked," of belonging intimately and
> irrevocably to that superior half of humanity who had known coitus, and
> fertilized the world with it. . . . I moved gently backwards and forwards,
> just a few times, and came in a miserable, *played-out, barely pleasurable*
> way. (43; my emphases)

What should remain an implicit 2PP, underlying primary forms of
intersubjectivity, becomes once more a highly complex mixture of an explicit
1PP (the narrator's highly self-conscious perspective upon himself and his
[changing] relationship with the social group he wants to become a part of,
that is, those who have experienced sexuality "first-hand," evident from his
self-other conscious emotion of pride) and 2PP (his observational, distant
view of his interaction with Connie). Blind to perception and sensation;
largely anhedonic; invaded and enslaved by a myriad of social, linguistic, and
cultural forces, it is no wonder that he is utterly unable to experience the
soteriological powers of sexual initiation some of Lawrence's characters so
intensely live.

To conclude, this short story stages some of the intricate ways in which the
phenomena of paralysis and invasion operate and interact with each other in
the context of sexuality. Paralysis—a phenomenon which I defined in terms
of ways of relating to others characterized by a lack/deficiency of forms of
intersubjectivity—is clearly visible in the narrator's "methods" of dealing
with alterity. Due to his obsessive employment of complex intersubjective
strategies pertaining to tertiary intersubjectivity, such as approaching the
others from explicit 1PP, 2PP, and 3PP, and his failure to engage in the pre-
reflective self-awareness and self-other awareness (implicit 1PP and 2PP)
characterizing primary intersubjectivity, he is unable to understand and
experience the *diversity* of ways in which he could interact with others.

Paradoxically though, the very same problem (i.e., his paralysis) appears
to be the main cause of a powerful instance of invasion—a phenomenon
which I defined in terms of ways of relating to others characterized by
an unnecessary surplus of forms of intersubjectivity—during his sexual
initiation. His excessive employment of sense-making strategies pertaining
to tertiary intersubjectivity *during* an act which should ideally remain within
the bounds of primary intersubjectivity, turns his intensely anticipated
discovery of the "fleshly grail" into "one of the most desolate couplings
known to copulating humanity."

This paradoxical nature of the interaction between paralysis and invasion[45]
points to a paradox at the heart of sexuality itself, which I will discuss in

greater detail in the next section focused on McEwan's more recent novel, *On Chesil Beach*: the fact that the initiation into a form of interaction which, in order to function smoothly, should remain a concrete, nonlinguistic/ conceptual intermingling of bodies and affects, is *necessarily* and *unavoidably* structured by complex linguistic, conceptual, cultural, and historical forces.

2.4 Always Bound by Our History and Our Guilty Natures: Sexual Failure on Chesil Beach

Published in 2007, thirty-five years after *H, OCB* is a study of sexual initiation too. But if *H* dealt extensively with the dangers linguistic excess posed to sexuality, *OCB* is a more elaborate meditation on how both language (oral and written) *and* silence can threaten sexual interactions. The cases of invasion and paralysis portrayed by McEwan here are more complex than in his first story. As we will see, the forces that de-structure and destabilize Edward and Florence's first sexual encounter come from various directions and take different forms. And if in *H* the retrospective narrator was the ultimate judge of the *meaning* of his younger self's sexual initiation, authoritatively calling it "one of the most desolate couplings known to copulating humanity" (*H*: 43), in *OCB* the multiplicity of timescales structuring the characters' sexual initiation, together with the intricate play of perspectives from which the meaning of their sexual act is evaluated, ultimately complicates any attempt of thinking in rigid binary oppositions such as success/failure or right/wrong.[46]

As in the case of *H*, the first sentences of *OCB* succinctly yet comprehensively express the main themes McEwan will expand upon later. As he put it in an interview with David Remnick, "These lines offered a whole story, waiting to be unpacked" (Roberts 2010: 174). The main characters of this short novel, or novella,[47] Edward Mayhew and Florence Ponting, are introduced as being "young, educated, and both virgins on this, their wedding night" (*OCB*: 3). In the same first sentence, the heterodiegetic narrator[48] further claims that "they lived in a time when a conversation about sexual difficulties was plainly impossible," pointing immediately to the importance not only silence in itself, but a silence *structured* by historical forces will acquire in the economy of the plot. Yet, as Lynn Wells observes, although the retrospective narrator initially creates a sense of historical distance between Edward and Florence's world (the novel is set in 1962) and contemporaneity, the next sentence ("But it is never easy") already problematizes a widespread understanding of the "sexual revolution" of the 1960s as marking a fundamental turning point in the social, cultural, and political attitudes toward sexuality (Wells 2010: 93).

OCB is set in 1962, one year before what poet Philip Larkin called the "annus mirabilis." Published in 1974 in the poetry collection *High Windows*, and originally written in 1967, Larkin's poem "Annus Mirabilis" is apparently a radical acknowledgment and celebration of the sexual revolution of the 1960s. I am saying radical because Larkin's poem draws a hyperbolic picture of the historical developments in Britain which at first sight, at least, does not leave any room for doubt that, indeed, a truly revolutionary change regarding the attitudes toward sexuality occurred in those years, or more precisely, according to Larkin, in 1963.[49]

Of course, this poem could also be read ironically, as a satirical critique of the alleged radicalism of the developments in the 1960s. But whether we read it ironically or not, I believe the poem foregrounds a widespread attitude within the social, political, and cultural discourses related to sexuality that gradually emerged after this period. As Stephen Garton argues in his *Histories of Sexuality*, "One of the most popular cultural narratives of the late twentieth century has seen the 1960s and the 1970s as an age of "sexual revolution"" (2004: 210). Even if not so radical as Larkin in locating the origins of the revolutionary change in a particular year, many scholars as well as people outside academia from all social spheres seem to be convinced that something fundamental changed in how sexuality was conceptualized, regulated, *and* lived beginning with the 1960s.

Such a view appears to be shared by Edward too, close to the end of the novel, when he reflects on Florence's proposal to continue to live together in a platonic relationship, with him having full freedom to satisfy his sexual needs elsewhere (a proposal he refuses with indignation): "Towards the end of that celebrated decade, when his life came under pressure from all the new excitements and freedoms and fashions, as well as from the chaos of numerous love affairs—he became at last reasonably competent—he often thought of her strange proposal, and it no longer seemed quite so ridiculous, and certainly not disgusting or insulting. In the new circumstances of the day, it appeared liberated, and far ahead of its time, innocently generous, an act of self-sacrifice that he had quite failed to understand" (160–61; my emphases).

Whereas how sexuality was lived in a certain period is always difficult to understand and reconstruct due to the scarcity of available empirical data, how it was conceptualized and, especially, regulated seem to be more directly available for historical reconstruction. The regulation of sexual conduct, for example, leaves clear traces in legal and political archives. Changes in laws regarding sexuality are indeed visible in the post-1960s period. Jeffrey Weeks argues that a liberal strategy of regulation has gained the upper hand in this period, replacing to a large degree the previously dominant absolutist strategy

(2010: 117–24). Weeks argues that the way legal systems regulate sexuality is caused by how sexuality is generally understood. Thus, he differentiates between three different perspectives giving rise to three different strategies of regulation. In the first one, sex is regarded "as dangerous, disruptive and fundamentally antisocial," in the second one, "the powers of desire" are seen as "basically benign, life-enhancing and liberating," and in the third one, "it is perhaps less certain . . . whether sex in itself is good or bad." The first position gives rise to absolutist strategies, which "propose tight, authoritarian regulation," the second one to libertarian strategies that are "liable to adopt a relaxed, even radical set of values" (2010: 118), and the third one to liberal strategies which are more pragmatic, trying to achieve "an appropriate balance between private and public spheres" (121).

As an example of a liberal strategy, he refers to the Wolfendon Committee Report on prostitution and male homosexuality, published in Great Britain in 1957, which provided the framework for further reforms in the laws on obscenity, homosexuality, abortion, censorship, and divorce (2010: 121; cf. also Weeks 1989 [1981]: Ch. 13). According to Weeks, the Wolfendon Report made clear that the duty of the law is to regulate the public sphere, thus to maintain common standards of public decency, without interfering in and trying to regulate the private sphere (2010: 121). In Weeks's opinion, this change in the state's attitudes toward sexual conduct stems from the development of a moral agnosticism characterizing liberal strategies, that is, an understanding that there is no universal ethical framework to decide the morality or immorality of sexual behavior. And whereas both absolutist and libertarian strategies stem, according to Weeks, from essentialist conceptualizations of sexuality, liberal ones are grounded in social constructionist views, which seems to be a fundamental cause of the moral agnosticism characterizing such strategies (2010: 120; see also 18–23).

Besides these changes in juridical and political policies, many other developments occurred in society and culture at large that influenced to some degree attitudes toward sexuality. To give just a few examples, the emergence of the civil rights movement, aiming at ending the racial segregation and discrimination against black Americans; the women's rights movement, led by the desire to bring equality between genders; and the protests against the war in Vietnam, contributed, even if sometimes indirectly, to the ongoing debates around sexuality. Developments in popular culture too, such as the emergence of rock-and-roll music, closely connected to the drug-fueled hippy culture (with its climax at the Woodstock festival in 1969), as well as the publication and immense success of popular magazines such as *Playboy* and *Cosmopolitan* also had a strong impact on how sexuality was conceptualized and understood. Furthermore, the founding of organizations such as the

Sexual Freedom League and the establishment of resorts like the Sandstone retreat had a more direct influence in changing not only how sexuality was legalized and conceptualized, but also how it was lived.

It is important to notice, however, that the sexual revolution was far from being a unified movement or phenomenon. It can be better understood as a bundle of sometimes divergent phenomena and mutually criticizing movements, or, as historian Angus McLaren puts it, as "an emergence and clash of a variety of different sexual agendas and cultures" (1999: 166–67; cf. also Allyn 2000: 3–9).[50] Furthermore, as Garton acknowledges, several historians tend to place the 1960s and 1970s developments into a larger context of sexual revolutions, considering the 1920s as the period of a first sexual revolution (Garton 2004: 211; cf. also Szreter and Fisher 2010).

However, whether the revolution is located in the first or second part of the twentieth century, until Michel Foucault's first volume of *The History of Sexuality* was published in 1976, historians generally considered the attitudes toward sexuality characterizing this century as being in stark contrast with those underlying the so-called Victorian period.[51] In popular culture, as well as in the pioneering historical studies of this period,[52] and in the medical theories of influential doctors and sexual reformers from the end of the nineteenth century and the early twentieth century, such as Havelock Ellis, Sigmund Freud, or Richard von Kraft-Ebing, Victorianism is generally seen as an era of "excessive sexual austerity, repression . . . prudery [and] Puritan moralism" (Garton 2004: 101). It is also considered by some scholars, though, as an age of hypocrisy. Steven Marcus (1966), for example, famously argued that, while social conventions forbid any public discussion about sexual issues, at the same time, pornography and prostitution flourished, creating what Garton calls "a split in Victorian culture" (101). The hypothesis that sexuality was severely repressed during the Victorian period led, under the influence of psychoanalytic theories, to the idea that it had to find various outlets, such as those discussed by Marcus.

However, Marcus's "repressive hypothesis" has been strongly challenged in Michel Foucault seminal work *The Will to Knowledge* (1978 [1976]).[53] Foucault criticizes Marcus's idea that silence regarding sexual issues was publicly imposed by Victorian culture. In contrast, he claims that the Victorian era witnessed an enormous proliferation of discourses about sexuality, in a variety of contexts such as the family, school, work, clinic, asylum, or prison (Foucault 1978 [1976]: 1–50). And whereas Marcus praises psychoanalysis, with its tendency to encourage talking about (repressed) sexual issues and bringing them from the unconscious to the "surface," and considers it a crucial turning point in the passage from Victorianism to contemporaneity, Foucault places psychoanalysis in the same context as previous confessional techniques practiced in churches and argues that their aim was to discover "the truth about sex," that is, to develop a *scientia sexualis* (51–74).

Indeed, the Victorian period witnessed the rise of various sciences dealing with sexuality in increasingly complex ways. Medicine (including psychiatry), pedagogy, demography, criminology, or epidemiology, instead of repressing sexuality, all struggled to develop a large number of theories about sex and sexual desire, and through such operations, in Foucault's view, *produced* rather than discovered various sexual categories[54] that have been later understood in essentialist terms. In other words, Victorian discourses *created* various subjects and (sexual) identities. The ultimate outcome of such a view is to consider sexuality itself as a social-historical construct rather than a biological given. As I will argue later though, *OCB* challenges both social constructivist and essentialist views of sexuality.

Where McEwan's novel clearly resonates with Foucault's theories, however, is in its deconstruction of any clear binary opposition between Victorianism and the contemporaneity. In contrast with many reviewers and academic critics tending to read the novel as dealing with a historical turning point,[55] Peter Mathews, following Foucault, argues that "the critical consensus that *On Chesil Beach* is an affirmation of sexual liberation from the values of the Victorian era . . . has a suspiciously ideological ring to it" and advises to rather "see the story of Florence and Edward as a qualified continuation of the Victorian trajectory rather than a break" (Mathews 2012: 90). To back up his argument, Mathews relies not only on Foucault but also on fiction writers dealings with the same issues such as John Fowles (in his novel *The French Lieutenant's Woman* from 1969) and A. S. Byatt (in her novel *Possession* from 1990). Furthermore, he discusses other novels by McEwan where the very notion of a "turning point" is challenged. A pertinent example he gives is the following fragment from *Black Dogs*: "Turning points are the inventions of storytellers and dramatists, a necessary mechanism when a life is reduced to, traduced by a plot, when a morality must be distilled from a sequence of actions, when an audience must be sent home with something unforgettable to mark a character's growth. Seeing the light, the moment of truth, the turning point—surely we borrow these from Hollywood or the Bible to make retroactive sense of an overcrowded memory" (McEwan 1999 [1992]: 27; cited in Mathews 2012: 89).[56]

Indeed, the Victorian proliferation of discourses trying to regulate sexuality is clearly visible in the novel and strongly structures both Florence's and Edward's attitudes, in quite similar ways to how oral and written narratives about sexuality structured the attitudes of *H*'s narrator. The "visceral dread [and] helpless disgust as palpable as seasickness" Florence feels is augmented by her reading of "a modern, forward-looking handbook that was supposed to be helpful to young brides, with its cheery tones and exclamation marks and numbered illustrations" (*OCB*: 7), where she read "certain phrases or words that almost made her gag: *mucous membrane*, and the sinister and glistening *glans*. Other phrases offended her intelligence, particularly those concerning entrances: *Not long before he enters her* . . . or, *now at last he enters her*, and, *happily, soon after he entered her*. Almost as frequent was a word that suggested to her nothing but pain, flesh parted before a knife: *penetration*" (7–8; emphases in original). Such language makes her ponder whether "she [was] obliged on the night to transform herself for Edward into a kind of portal or drawing room through which he might process" (8).[57]

Edward's attitudes toward sexuality are also structured, in a "second-hand" manner, by various discourses he is exposed too. Although he is not reading the same "modern, forward-looking handbooks" like Florence, he is nevertheless also bombarded with discourses about sexuality, which appear to be coming, in large part, from his peers at University College, London, from popular culture, and from his engagement with pornographic materials. For example, in the first pages of the novel, his "specific worry" about his sexual initiation is identified as regarding "over-excitement . . . what he had heard someone describe as 'arriving too soon'" (7) but, regardless of such worries, "indulged constantly in what one enlightened authority called 'self-pleasuring'" (20). Furthermore, the

> blues he had heard at the Hundred club[58] suggested to Edward that all round him, just out of sight, men of his age were leading explosive, untiring sex lives, rich with gratifications of every kind. Pop music was bland, still coy on the matter, films were a little more explicit, but in Edward's circle the men had to be content with telling dirty jokes, uneasy sexual boasting and boisterous camaraderie driven by furious drinking. (39–40)

Thus, just like in the case of *H*'s narrator, both Florence's and Edward's relations to sexuality before their first sexual encounter is an obsessively distant/observational rather than participative one, structured by the myriad discourses surrounding them. Such an excessive exposure to discourses *about* sexuality is, as it will become clear later, one of the important causes of their incapacity to successfully engage with each other bodily and affectively, to smoothly coordinate their movements, expressions, and emotions during their sexual encounter. As in *H*, the characters' paralyses and their inability to fully open themselves to the rich variety of ways of connecting to each other will ultimately structure a tragi-comic[59] event of invasion, that is, the emergence of a chaotic, unnecessary surplus of ways of relating to each other during their futile attempt to consummate their marriage, completely sidestepping the only necessary ingredients for a successful night—their bodily synchronization and affective attunement. However, in *OCB*, McEwan tries much more extensively than in *H* to identify and meditate upon the variety of forces causing and structuring the phenomena of paralysis and invasion portrayed.

The tremendous power of discourses to infiltrate and interfere with embodied experience and even to shape identity is foregrounded later in the novel, this time in a more general vein, without a direct connection with sexuality.[60] In his youth, Edward experiences a powerful epiphany regarding how categorization can shape identity. According to Ellen Spolsky, categorization is an innate ability which humans share with even the simplest life-forms, which are able, for example, to distinguish between food and nonfood (2015a: xxiv). She defines categorization as a multipurpose cognitive apparatus (22), grounded in an ability to abstract from token to type (15), and to organize these abstractions into ascending levels of generalization (33). As Mervis and Rosch put it, a "category exists whenever two or more distinguishable objects or events are treated equivalently" (1981: 45; cited in Spolsky 2015a: 45). Furthermore, Spolsky argues, this process of categorization is both flexible enough to be adaptive to change and stable enough to be useful in most everyday thinking (35).[61]

In Edward's case, not only his but also his mother's identities are at stake and are influenced by his ability to categorize. In the years after being hit on the head by the door of a train, "with sufficient force to fracture her skull, and dislocate in an instant her personality, intelligence and memory" (70), Edward's mother "kept herself content with the notion, an elaborate fairy tale in fact, that she was a devoted wife and mother, that the house ran smoothly thanks to all her work, and that she deserved a little time to herself when her duties were done," while her family, "in order to keep the bad moments to a minimum, and not alarm that scrap of her former consciousness . . . colluded in the make-believe" (67).[62] In fact, she was "a ghostly figure, who drifted about the house as she drifted through their childhoods, sometimes communicative and even affectionate, at others remote," although Edward did not "fully understand that there was something wrong with [her] until he was fourteen" (65).

What makes Edward understand his mother's condition is his father's labeling/categorizing her as "brain-damaged." Although he considered the term "an insult, a blasphemous invitation to disloyalty" (69), Edward, "with the adaptability of his years, continued to make the quiet transition from shock to recognition" (72). Since, as we will see, Edward's thoughts on these issues not only prefigure Florence's later attitude toward the label he brutally attaches to her during their final discussion on the beach, but are also a powerful meditation upon the ways in which language can structure (inter) subjectivity, it is worthwhile to quote them at length:

> Of course, he had always known. He had been maintained in a state of innocence by the absence of a term for her condition. He had never even thought of her as having a condition, and at the same time had always accepted that she was different. The contradiction was now resolved by this simple naming, by the power of words to make the unseen visible. *Brain-damaged.* The term dissolved intimacy, it coolly measured his mother by a public standard that everyone could understand. A sudden space began to open out, not only between Edward and his mother, but also between himself and his immediate circumstances, and he felt his own being, the buried core of it he had never attended to before, come to a sudden, hard-edged existence, a glowing pinpoint that he wanted no one else to know about. She was brain-damaged, and he was not. (72; emphasis in original)

There is a pointed ambiguity in this passage regarding the connection between language and identity/subjectivity that occurs later in the novel too and problematizes any clear interpretation. It would be a forced if not completely ludicrous move, of course, to claim that the label Edward's father attaches to his wife *constitutes* her identity. In this case, it rather seems that the labeling *discloses*[63] (for Edward, at least) something that has already been there, that is, her medical problems. The claim that "the power of words" lies in making "the unseen visible" clearly points toward such an interpretation. In other words, language here works as a hermeneutic tool, helping Edward make sense of his mother's condition. On the other hand, the very hermeneutic *act* Edward performs has marked effects on the development and crystallization of his identity. Although describing his "being" in terms of a "buried core" initially invites the reader to interpret his relation with language also as disclosing or unearthing something already existent, the fact that this core "come[s] to a sudden, hard-edged existence" points to an opposite interpretive direction: Edward's identity appears to be to a large degree constituted by his father's speech act.[64]

Furthermore, the claim that the employment of the term "brain-damaged" in describing his mother's condition "dissolved intimacy" and "coolly measured [her] by a public standard that everyone could understand," opening thus a gap between Edward and his immediate circumstances, is crucial for understanding important aspects of paralysis and invasion. Although theorists of categorization such as Spolsky praise this ability, considering it fundamental for the survival and reproduction of the human animal (and not only), they nevertheless fail to acknowledge and describe the negative effects an *excessive* employment of this capacity can give rise to.

In *OCB*, the intimacy between Edward and his mother, an immediate, embodied, and affective connection underlying primary intersubjectivity, is shattered through an act pertaining to tertiary intersubjectivity, that is, the brutal labeling/categorization suddenly attached to his mother. Edward's subsequent incapacity to relate to her otherwise than through the lens of an abstract, medical category, can certainly be described in terms of paralysis.[65] Moreover, in such conditions, concrete interactions with her which should be better structured solely by affectivity, and thus remain within the sphere of primary intersubjectivity, will constantly be invaded by an unnecessary surplus of forms of intersubjectivity: in this case, tertiary forms structured by categorization. Once more, McEwan powerfully stages the intricate and troubling connection between paralysis and invasion.

Toward the end of the novel, we experience a similar scene when the characters are on the beach, bitterly discussing their sexual failure. "I know failure when I see it" (144), Florence cruelly tells Edward, to which he later retorts: "You tricked me. Actually, you're a fraud. And I know exactly what else you are. Do you know what you are? You're frigid, that's what. Completely frigid. But you thought you needed a husband, and I was the first bloody idiot who came along" (156). If before, "what troubled her was unutterable, and she could barely frame it for herself" (7), immediately after his accusations, Florence reflects: "Frigid, that terrible word—she understood how it applied to her. *She was exactly what the word meant*" (157; my emphasis). The same ambiguity discussed before emerges here too. Through Edward's labeling, Florence's sexual identity appears either to be disclosed or, as in the cases discussed by Foucault (see footnote 45), actually constituted through linguistic practices. Here, Edward's paralysis has a powerful effect not only on his interaction with Florence, manifested in the emergence of an event of invasion breaking apart a social connection which should have better remained within the bounds of primary intersubjectivity, but also on Florence's self-understanding and, thus, her identity: in her opinion, she *was* exactly what the world meant.

However, Florence's ways of relating to alterity too could be characterized in terms of paralysis. A certain distance between Florence and her experiences, similar to that between the characters from *H* and their world, is repeatedly foregrounded in the novel. "Had it taken her this long to discover that she lacked some simple mental trick that everyone else had," she ponders, "a mechanism so ordinary that no one ever mentioned it, *an immediate sensual connection* to people and events, and to her own needs and desires? All these

years she had lived in isolation within herself and, strangely, from herself"
(61; my emphasis). The lack of "an immediate sensual connection" to people
is, indeed, an extremely appropriate way of describing a certain variety of
paralysis—that in which tertiary forms of intersubjectivity are excessively
used at the expense of primary or secondary ones. In this novel, however,
McEwan is not only trying to describe his characters' paralyses. By studying
the characters' life histories, he is also attempting to identify the etiology of
their inadequate ways of relating to others.

In the same scene on the beach, Florence tells Edward a "brave little joke
she had thought of earlier [:] Perhaps I should be psychoanalysed. Perhaps
what I really need to do is kill my mother and marry my father" (153). Yet,
although her tone is ironical, the reader suspects, due to various previous
hints in the novel, that perhaps her remarks are less of a joke than she claims
them to be. Indeed, her relationship with both of her parents is far from
being unproblematic. Her father, for example, "aroused in her conflicting
emotions. There were times when she found him physically repellent and
she could hardly bear the sight of him. . . . But sometimes, in a surge of
protective feeling and guilty love, she would come up behind him where he
sat and entwine her arms around his neck and kiss the top of his head and
nuzzle him, liking his clean scent. She would do all this, then loath herself
for it later" (49–50). Several hints are scattered throughout the novel that
these conflicting emotions, as well as her subsequent disgust with sex, might
have arisen from her father sexually abusing her during their trips in his
boat when she was twelve and thirteen, trips about which they "never talked"
afterward (50).

In their hotel room, for example, when Edward begins to undress, the
"smell of the sea . . . summoned . . . the indistinct past," when "her father was
moving about the dim cramped cabin, undressing, like Edward now," during
which Florence's "only task was to keep her eyes closed and to think of a tune
she liked" (99). And a bit later, after Edward ejaculates on her "in vigorous
but diminishing quantities, filling her navel, coating her belly, thighs, and
even a portion of her chin and kneecap in tepid, viscous fluid" (105), long
before anything resembling penetrative sex occurs between them, Florence
is suddenly flooded by "memories she had long ago decided were not really
hers," dragging with them "the stench of a shameful secret locked in musty
confinement" (105–06).[66] Thus, traumatic sexual abuses during childhood
appear to be, in cases such as this one, important causes for the development
and intensification of paralytic ways of relating to others sexually during
adulthood.

Florence's mother, Violet, seems to play an important (negative) role too
in her development. A "physically distant" philosophy professor, Violet "had

never kissed or embraced Florence, even when she was small" (55). Besides this lack of physical contact that might have proven highly detrimental to Florence's emotional and sexual development, her mother is also "too intellectual, too brittle" for Florence to be able to talk to her and share her problems: "Whenever [Violet] confronted an intimate problem, she tended to adopt the public manner of the lecture hall, and use longer and longer words, and make references to books she thought everyone should have read" (10). Instead of engaging in primary, embodied, and affective forms of intersubjectivity with her children and thus paving their way toward future healthy relationships,[67] Violet remains paralyzed within much too complex forms of dealing with others, structured by abstract, philosophical discourses[68]—an attitude that can also be considered an important cause of Florence's pathological reliance on language and various abstract discursive strategies for dealing with bodily practices.

However, it is not only Florence's development that ruins their first and last sexual encounter and their relationship. Edward's life history plays a crucial role too. Besides his lack of understanding that linguistic labeling/categorization might sometimes fail to do justice to the complexity and fluidity of experience which I have already discussed above, Edward's personality makes him "capable of behaving stupidly, even explosively":

He was known to his university friends as one of those quiet types, prone to the occasional violent eruption. According to his father, his very early childhood had been marked by spectacular tantrums. Through his school years and into his time at college he was drawn now and then by the wild freedom of a fist fight. From schoolyard scraps round which savagely chanting kids formed a spectator ring, to a solemn rendezvous in a woodland clearing near the edge of the village, to shameless brawls outside central London pubs, Edward found in fighting a thrilling unpredictability, and discovered a spontaneous, decisive self that eluded him in the rest of his tranquil existence. (91)

This predisposition toward anger and violence, together with the "state of excitement, ignorance and indecision" (91) he experiences during his wedding night, make Edward "not trust himself [and] not be certain that the tunnel vision and selective deafness would never descend again, enveloping him like a wintry mist on Turville Heath, obscuring his more recent, sophisticated self" (95). His fears of the violent behavior he might be capable of, emerging from his life history, together with his sexual ignorance, cause Edward to continuously "misread the signs" (90), that is, mistake Florence's fear and disgust for lust, and her first and brief "beginnings of desire" (87) for a simple muscular spasm. Inspired by the phenomenological tradition and by Wittgenstein's philosophy, contemporary cognitive scientists claim that in non-pathological cases, basic emotions can be perceived directly in facial and bodily expressions. "Look into someone else's face," Wittgenstein wrote, "and see the consciousness in it, and a particular shade of consciousness. You see on it, in it, joy, indifference, interest, excitement, torpor, and so on . . . Do you look within yourself, in order to recognize the fury in his face?" (1980: § 927). In contrast, by staging Edward's recurrent misreading of Florence's emotions, McEwan's novel shows the haunting opacity of emotional expression that sometimes characterizes social interaction.[69]

Although *OCB*'s narrator claims that it "is shaming sometimes, how the body will not, or cannot lie about emotions" (86),[70] the pathetic attempt of sexual interaction between Edward and Florence clearly shows that emotional expression can certainly be misinterpreted. The newlyweds' deficient ways of connecting to each other, their incapacity for understanding each other's bodily expressions and affective states, and, thus, of coordinating their movements and emotions in an ecstatic form of primary intersubjectivity[71] (in other words, their paralyses structured by their troubled life histories) give rise to a powerful instance of invasion during their sexual encounter. Their obsessive employment of explicit 1PP, 2PP, and 3PP, instead of their implicit counterparts during their wedding night and their relentless (yet futile) attempts to get to *know* what the other is *thinking*, instead of trying to build and maintain the intercorporeality and interaffectivity so much needed for the success of their encounter, unavoidably invade their embodied experience, de-structuring and destabilizing their sexual act. Just like in *H*, lack paradoxically breeds an unnecessary surplus in this novel too.

Moreover, following his premature ejaculation and Florence's disgusted reactions toward it, Edward can barely "hold back the advance of an element that initially he did not care to admit, the beginnings of a darkening of mood, a darker reckoning, a trace of poison that even now was branching through his being," that is, anger, the "demon he had kept down earlier when he thought his patience was about to break" (133). His incapacity to contain his anger makes him insensitive to Florence's attempts at reconciliation on the beach and destroys their relationship completely.

Thus, both Florence's and Edward's life histories have a crucial role in de-structuring their sexual encounter. The hints that Florence was sexually abused by her father, together with Edward's history of aggressive behavior, show that sexuality is not only driven by the instinct to reproduce, as evolutionary theorists would have it, but also by complex and varied ontogenetic processes, which, in some circumstances, can wreak havoc in sexual development.

As Dominic Head argues, these characters can be understood as "emotional oddities" (2013: 121) and, therefore, in his view (and in contrast with the opinion of other critics and even of McEwan himself),[72] *un*representative of their historical context (118). However, it would be reductive to read their failure solely in terms of the influence of their life histories on their personalities and to ignore the role of the larger social, cultural, and historical context in which their interactions are embedded. At one point, the novel's heterodiegetic narrator bitterly and ironically reflects: "What stood between them? Their personalities and pasts, their ignorance and fear, timidity, squeamishness, lack of entitlement or experience or easy manners, then the tail end of a religious prohibition, their Englishness and class, and history itself. Nothing much at all" (96).

History in fact figures as a predominant theme in the novel, particularly in the construction of the character Edward. A historian by profession with a degree from University College, London, Edward takes a position against his university tutor, in whose view, "History, properly capitalized, was driven forward by ineluctable forces toward inevitable, necessary ends," and who believes that "soon the subject would be understood as a science." In contrast, Edward believes that "forceful individuals could shape national destiny . . . a wayward conclusion [in his supervisor's opinion] that earned him a B minus" (13).

As Mathews argues, Edward's view integrates perfectly with the Victorian understanding of history, and the latter's "special study of the 'great man' theory of history" (*OCB*: 13) has "an obvious precedent in Lytton Strachey . . . a member of the Bloomsbury Group [who] pioneered a new form of biography that combines historical narrative with ironic psychological observations about his subject's motivations" (Mathews 2012: 84).[73] For Strachey, Mathews claims, the Victorian era constitutes "a turning point in the struggle between historical circumstance and human will [and] produced a final crop of great men and women who, in attempting to change the world, shipwrecked themselves in the process" (86).

Precisely this tension between historical circumstances and human will is one of the recurrent motifs McEwan plays with in this novel. Although the characters' sexual failure is to a certain extent caused by their deviant personalities, the historical context strongly mediates their encounter too. Before having their dinner, for example, it "was, in theory, open to them to abandon their plates, seize the wine bottle by the neck and run down to the shore and kick their shoes off and exult in their liberty." However, "the times held them," and even when they "were alone, a thousand unacknowledged rules still applied" (*OCB*: 18).

Although, as we have seen, the proliferation of discourses about sexuality Foucault identified in the Victorian era structures the characters' understanding of (what is expected from) their relationship, there is also a certain degree of silence imposed by society (including, of course, their families), which does not allow them to speak about their problems, to share their troubled life histories, and perhaps have a chance to start this relationship on a better, more honest, and open ground. As the narrator puts it, when trying to diagnose their break-up on the beach, "They barely knew each other, and never could because of the blanket of companionable near-silence that smothered their differences and blinded them as much as it bound them" (148). In the first pages of the novel too, the fundamental presence of silence between them, as well as the powerful role external forces had in imposing this silence from the very beginnings of their relationship, is pondered upon:

> Their courtship had been a pavane, a stately unfolding, bound by protocols never agreed or voiced, but generally observed. Nothing was ever discussed—nor did they feel the lack of intimate talk. These were manners beyond words, beyond definition. The language and practice of therapy, the currency of feeling diligently shared, mutually analysed, were not yet in general circulation. While one heard of wealthier people going in for psychoanalysis, it was not yet customary to regard oneself in everyday terms as an enigma, as an exercise in narrative history, or as a problem waiting to be solved. (21)

In this passage, the crucial influence of class is also foregrounded. By contrasting the upper classes that were "going in for psychoanalysis" and were thus more ready to acknowledge and discuss their problems, with the ethos of silence characterizing the middle classes to which Edward and Florence belonged, McEwan comes close to Marcus's discussion of the spread of puritanism (tinged with hypocrisy) within these latter classes (cf. Garton 2004: 101). Therefore, by engaging both with Foucault's analyses of the pervasiveness of discourses dealing with and regulating sexuality and with Marcus's arguments regarding the silence toward sexual issues pervading the middle classes, McEwan's novel could be a good starting point for arguing that perhaps Foucault's and Marcus's accounts should not be seen as contradictory (as Foucault would claim), but rather complementary.

Their lack of communication, structured by their identification with a social group (the British Victorian puritans) and its underlying ethical stance,[74] not only opens a propitious context for invasion to emerge during Edward and Florence's sexual encounter, but also strongly influences their subsequent separation. Going to look for Edward on the beach, Florence is convinced that "there were no words to name what happened, there existed no shared language in which two sane adults could describe such events to each other" (139). A bit later, her anger rises too and she starts to feel "a little cheated. If he had an unusual condition," she ponders, "why had he not told her, in confidence" (140–41)? And yet, she remembers that she was also incapable of sharing her own problems, and quickly admits to herself that "she understood perfectly why he could not. . . . How could he have begun to broach the matter of his own particular deformity, what could have been his opening words? They did not exist. Such a language had yet to be invented" (141).

This admission on Florence's part that the fault for their disastrous attempt at intercourse might lie in external forces that they cannot quite control could open the way toward their reconciliation. Indeed, after the spiteful exchange of accusations I discussed earlier, Florence attempts to build a compromise and finally breaks the silence regarding her disgust toward sex. Yet her proposal that they remain together as husband and wife, with Edward free to pursue his sexual desires elsewhere, only intensifies Edward's anger and makes him label her as frigid, releasing her from the shackles of silence only to trap her even more brutally into the prison house of language. After his angry outburst, Florence departs, leaving him once more standing "in cold and righteous silence in the summer's dusk, watching her hurry along the shore, the sound of her progress lost to the breaking of small waves" (166). Bound by history and their guilty natures, crippled by their paralyses, invaded by both language and silence, Edward and Florence tragically fail in their quest for blood-knowledge.

2.5 The Success of Failure or the Heuristic Potential of McEwan's Works in Understanding Sexuality

In this chapter I focused on the theme of sexual initiation and its connection to paralysis and invasion in two of Ian McEwan's works, "Homemade" and *On Chesil Beach*. A close reading of these literary works clearly points toward the close-to-unfathomable complexity of human sexuality, a phenomenon continuously structured and de-structured by an unstable combination of biological-evolutionary, psychological-developmental, and social-historical contexts. McEwan's intricate intertextual engagement with a variety of scientific,[75] philosophical,[76] and literary sources[77] could certainly open further debates regarding the ambiguous nature of sexuality and its relation to other human behaviors.

McEwan's position regarding Lawrence's idealization of sexuality as a pure form of primary intersubjectivity is clear: regardless of how desirable it would be for sex to remain an act that is free from thought processes, rooted in the body, and structured solely by affective forces, experience shows that, sadly, this is rarely the case. Sexual encounters are often far from remaining within the bounds of primary forms of intersubjectivity and should better be characterized by a constant interplay between various forms of intersubjectivity.

In ontogeny, *before* our first sexual interactions, we are continuously bombarded by a great variety of discourses *about* sexuality, and we run thus the risk of approaching our sexual partners in distant, observational ways (explicit 1PP, 2PP, and 3PP), often sidestepping the *implicit* 1PP and 2PP so necessary for a smooth intermingling of bodies and affects. This lack/deficiency of ways of relating to the other, which I called paralysis, frequently engenders an unnecessary surplus of forms of intersubjectivity *during* concrete sexual encounters (i.e., invasion). Such a reading of McEwan's novels in terms of paralysis and invasion has both the hermeneutic potential of enriching our understanding of his complex artworks *and* the heuristic potential of providing directions for theoretical and empirical research in the cognitive sciences and philosophy. To paraphrase Ellen Spolsky, literary representations of instances of intersubjectivity lying in-between health and pathology can occasionally be caught in the act of responding to the failure of cognitive scientists and philosophers to take into account the enormous variety in which humans relate to one another and could thus disrupt habit and open a space for learning (Spolsky 2015b: 34).

Clashes of Worldviews

In the previous chapter, I studied the phenomena of paralysis and invasion and their intricate interplay in the context of sexuality. By analyzing two cases of sexual initiation in "Homemade" and *On Chesil Beach*, a preliminary sketch of invasion and paralysis gradually emerged. I have shown the ways in which primary, embodied, and affective forms of intersubjectivity can be severely de-structured and destabilized through the employment of an unnecessary surplus of forms of intersubjectivity in contexts where a coordination of movements and affects would be sufficient for a smooth, successful interaction. Furthermore, I have argued that deficient ways of relating to others, in which processes and abilities belonging to tertiary intersubjectivity are excessively used for making sense of alterity, at the expense of sense-making strategies pertaining to primary or secondary intersubjectivity, can strongly disrupt social interactions too.

What already became clear is that invasion and paralysis are far from being simple, unitary phenomena, and can take different forms even if we restrict our analyses to sexuality. In this chapter, I will show that the boundaries of what we understand through these concepts can be even further expanded and will argue that secondary forms of intersubjectivity, such as joint attention and action, can also fail due to the influence of various other phenomena emerging from the contexts in which these cooperative and world-oriented forms of interactions are embedded. Moreover, I will also describe in terms of paralysis the ways of relating to others engendered by monomaniac worldviews[1] and structured by discursive domains such as science, religion, or art. My case study will be *Enduring Love*, published in 1997. Before discussing this novel though, I will provide a brief overview of other works by McEwan dealing with similar themes.

3.1 Science versus Religion versus Art in McEwan's Works

Already in an early, surreal short story, "Solid Geometry," originally published in 1973, McEwan started exploring the problems that clashes of different worldviews create in social interaction. The narrator's highly rational, mathematically driven perspectives on the world or, as Jack Slay puts it, his obsessive beliefs in "the achingly rational" (1996: 27) are set against his wife's equally obsessive spirituality (cf. also Head 2007: 37;[2] McEwan 1982 [1981]: 12),[3] which the narrator describes pejoratively as "sentimental Buddhism . . . junk-shop mysticism, joss-stick therapy, magazine astrology" (*SG*: 8).

In many later novels, such as *The Child in Time*, *Black Dogs*, *Enduring Love*, *Saturday*, *Solar* or *The Children Act*,[4] McEwan expands upon this theme, staging more elaborate reflections on the unstable and uneasy relation between rationality and affectivity, materiality and spirituality, and sense and sensibility. Through creating characters like the quantum physicist Thelma Drake (*CT*), the amateur entomologist Bernard Tremaine (*BD*), the physicist/ science writer Joe Rose (*EL*), the neurosurgeon Henry Perowne (*St*), or the theoretical physicist Michael Beard (*Sl*), McEwan relentlessly explores the ways in which scientific worldviews structure not only his characters' personal experience, but also their relationship with others and with larger social, historical, and cultural contexts.

As in "Solid Geometry" though, these scientific worldviews often clash with perspectives on the world structured by religious or artistic frameworks other characters embody, such as the spirituality of Bernard's wife, June; Jed's religious fanaticism; the aesthetic outlooks of Joe's partner, Clarissa; or the trust in the redeeming power of poetry of Henry's daughter, Daisy. An important aspect of McEwan's works which should be underlined is that, although they stage endless tensions and conflicts between these largely incompatible worldviews, they all create a strong impression that the boundaries between these various perspectives are less stable and clear-cut than one would expect. Jeremy (*BD*'s narrator) describes his parents-in-law and his relationship with them in the following terms: "Rationalist and mystic, commissar and yogi, joiner and abstainer, scientist and intuitionist, Bernard and June are the extremities, the twin poles along whose slippery axis my own unbelief slithers and never comes to rest" (19). Although from various interviews and nonfictional writings,[5] McEwan can certainly be seen as "the New Atheist novelist *par excellence*" (Bradley and Tate 2010: 16; emphasis in original), I strongly disagree though with Bradley and Tate's further claim that "if his fiction did not already exist—Dawkins and company would have had to invent it, so completely does it vindicate their world view" (16). There is clearly a strong tension between the clear-cut, stable (and polemical) ethos of the paratextual McEwan and the ambiguous, unstable, and disquieting ethos emerging from his fiction. The latter can often be seen closer to Jeremy in his unwillingness or incapacity to take a definite stand regarding the epistemological and ethical status of various worldviews.[6]

The instability of the boundaries between different worldviews is already prefigured in "Solid Geometry," where the rationality-spirituality dichotomy is powerfully deconstructed. As many critics have already noticed (e.g., Slay 1996: 26; Head 2007: 37), the narrator's (and his great-grandfather's) scientism repeatedly falls into even stronger forms of mysticism than his wife's, especially when pushed toward extremes. McEwan himself claims in an interview that the "intended irony" structuring this story is based on the fact that the narrator "uses the very system . . . to dispose of her, that Maisie endorses and he has repudiated" (1982 [1981]: 12).

In later novels, similar instabilities are also staged. After his wife's death, Bernard, a person strongly "committed to the elations and limited certainties of science" (*BD*: 19), admits that "grief breeds superstition," and is obsessively looking for "trace[s] of her [-] anything that will keep her alive for [him]" in the faces of young girls in the streets (83); Henry, "the professional reductionist" (*St*: 272), who initially describes his early morning euphoric mood as "a chemical accident . . . prompting dopamine-like receptors to initiate a kindly cascade of intracellular events" (5), and confidently claims that "it interests him less to have the world reinvented" by literature than to "have it explained" through science (66), is later on able to "let [his son's music] engulf him" (171), to "feel . . . lifted up" (67) by its power,[7] and ultimately appears even to accept the fact that one can be "transfixed" (278) by poetry[8]; and even the cynical and deceitful materialist, Michael Beard, who claims that there is nothing in what "arts people . . . talked about . . . that anyone with half a brain could fail to understand" (*Sl*: 278) and is highly skeptical of the fact that "art in its highest forms [could] lift climate change as a subject, gild it, palpate it, reveal all the horror and lost beauty and awesome threat, and inspire people to take thought, take action, or demand it of others" (107–08),[9] nevertheless admits that "the poetic, the scientific, the erotic" are strongly intertwined: "similar daydreams—manic moments, brief neural bursts, compacted but cloudy episodes that braided the actual with the unreal, and threaded gaudy beads of the impossible, the outrageous and contradictory along thought-lines of indeterminate logic—had long ago brought him to formulate his Conflation" (160).

However, the permeability of boundaries between science, art, and spirituality is perhaps never so strongly and beautifully foregrounded than in the character Thelma from *The Child in Time*.[10] Belonging "to an honorable tradition of women theoretical physicists," Thelma holds "great and passionate hopes" that "quantum mechanics would feminize physics, all science, make it softer, less arrogantly detached, more receptive to participating in the world it wanted to describe," and that "informed wonder would have to become integral to the intellectual equipment of scientists" (*CT*: 43). A bit later, getting angry that Stephen, a writer, cannot follow her arguments, she explodes into a powerful, *poetic* defense of science that is worth quoting at length:

> A scientific revolution, no, an intellectual revolution, an emotional, sensual explosion, a fabulous story just beginning to unfold for us, and you and your kind won't give it a serious minute of your time. People used to think the world was held up by elephants. That's nothing! Reality, whatever that word means, turns out to be a thousand times stranger. Who do you want? Luther? Copernicus? Darwin? Marx? Freud? None of them has reinvented the world and our place in it as radically and bizarrely as the physicists of this century have. The measurers of the universe can no longer detach themselves. They have to measure themselves too. Matter, time, space, forces—all beautiful and intricate illusions in which we must now collude. What a stupendous shake-up, Stephen. Shakespeare would have grasped wave functions, Donne would have understood complementarity and relative time. They would have been excited. What richness! They would have plundered this new science for their imagery. And they would have educated their audiences too. But you "arts" people, you're not only ignorant of these magnificent things, you're rather proud of knowing nothing. (44–45)

The use of such a poetic, metaphoric language in describing science points toward another crucial aspect of McEwan's approach to the relationship between scientific and artistic worldviews. The permeability of boundaries between these different perspectives and the discourses in which they are expressed is not only obvious in the *content* of his works, but also reflected in their *form*. As I will discuss in more detail later, McEwan often (ironically/paradoxically) frames scientific discourses and perspectives through a rich literary language, filled both with numerous stylistic devices *and* strong ambiguities, a feature described by scholars like Empson (1930) as the trademark of poetry.

Although deeper reflections on the complex relationship between worldviews and the permeability of their boundaries could be extremely fruitful in shedding more light not only on McEwan's works, but also on the nature of science, religion, and art, as well as in clarifying the meaning and range of application of the concept of "worldview," my aim in this chapter is somewhat different. *Enduring Love*, my case study, is a novel where the *differences* between scientific, religious, and artistic worldviews rather than their similarities are foregrounded. As I will argue later, precisely the *incompatibilities* and sometimes unsurpassable *boundaries* between the worldviews of this novel's characters play a crucial role in structuring both their paralytic ways of sense-making and the instances of invasion emerging during their interactions.

EL is a first-person narrative focused primarily on the plights of the protagonist and narrator Joe Rose, whose initially stable and happy, even if somehow monotonous, life is powerfully destabilized and threatened by various forces in the wake of his involvement in a climactic event, depicted in the first chapter of the novel. During a picnic at the countryside with his partner Clarissa, Joe gets involved in a rescue mission that ends in a tragic failure: an old man flying a balloon together with his nephew lose control of their machine, and Joe, together with four other men, desperately struggle, and ultimately fail, to hold the balloon down, one member of their "team,"[11] John Logan, dying as a consequence of being the only one still holding on the ropes when a strong gust of wind violently pushes the balloon away.

The rest of the novel painstakingly traces the consequences this failure in joint action and cooperation has on the life of the protagonist. Not only are he and Clarissa endlessly analyzing the event, engaging, as I will argue later, in complex forms of narrative sense-making and joint reminiscing which are ultimately doomed to fail, while trying to understand whose fault it was that Logan died, but also Joe's life becomes strangely intertwined with that of Jed Parry, another member of their "team," a religious fanatic who becomes pathologically obsessed with Joe, seeing the balloon incident as a piece of a divine puzzle meaning to bring him and Joe together. The intrusive force Jed becomes in Joe's previously tranquil life puts under threat both the latter's relationship with Clarissa and his mental stability and health. Increasingly paranoid, the protagonist becomes a more and more unreliable narrator as the plot develops, putting under strain not only his position within the web of relationships structuring the novel, but also the reader's hermeneutic position.

By discussing the intricate ways in which several contexts of joint attention and action are invaded and de-structured by an unnecessary surplus of forms of intersubjectivity, I hope to further enrich and complexify the picture of invasion I started to sketch in the previous chapter. Another crucial claim I will make in this chapter and with which I will actually begin my analysis is that Joe and Jed (and to a certain extent, even Clarissa) suffer also from paralysis: their ways of dealing with alterity are obsessively and monomaniacally filtered through abstract, complex discourses, such as science for Joe, religion for Jed, and art/aesthetics for Clarissa (cf. e.g., Childs 2007a; Möller 2011). Joe's obsession with science (and with its troublesome relation to narrative sense-making) makes almost impossible a clear understanding of other people's intentions, desires, or beliefs, just as Jed's religious fanaticism makes him similarly "blind" to the surrounding (social) reality. Even Clarissa's repeated advocacy of the importance of affect in social relations seems to be tainted by a certain shade of abstractness and distance from immediate experience, due to her framing of such issues in terms taken from literature, aesthetics, and literary criticism.

However, as it will become clear later, McEwan's complex use of stylistic and narrative devices (e.g., the fact that the scientist Joe tells his story in a strongly poetic language) problematizes a clear "diagnosis" of these characters. Considering them as *always* and *continuously* blocked within their worldviews would be a reductive move, and would fail to do justice to McEwan's aesthetic discourse. Moreover, the fact that these characters do not always make sense of alterity in deficient ways points toward a crucial aspect of paralysis: its *intermittent* character / *sporadic* occurrence. Thus, it would be more appropriate to describe paralysis as a phenomenon occurring in scattered and irregular/unpredictable instances rather than compare it to a *chronic* disease.

Moreover, I will argue that their (different types of) paralyses could be important causes of the invasions de-structuring the various contexts of joint attention and action in which they are involved. Hence, further evidence of the *double complementarity* between paralysis and invasion will emerge: my reading of *EL* will strengthen my previous claim that the concepts of "paralysis" and "invasion" should be understood as complementary both as *theoretical/philosophical concepts* (since paralysis refers to a lack of ways of relating to others and invasion to a surplus) and as *concrete phenomena* (paralysis can play a causal role in the emergence of invasion during concrete interactions).

3.2 In a Mess of Their Own Unmaking: *Enduring Love*'s Paralytics

3.2.1 Jed – Inviolable in His Solipsism

I will begin my analysis of the three main characters with Jed, since I believe that focusing first on the character who seems to be closest to what we commonly understand as madness, and then expanding my discussion to the other two, (apparently) less pathological cases, more light can be shed on fundamental aspects of paralysis, a way of social sense-making which appears to move within a range of intermediate positions between pathology and health.

As Joe himself reflects (on the nature of love) in the middle of the story, after he (much too) confidently diagnoses Jed with erotomania, or de

Clérambault's syndrome,[12] the relationship between sickness and health is far from being completely clear-cut, the two appearing to be *interdependent*, as Michel Foucault, for example, in his *Madness and Civilization*, insightfully and forcefully argued (1989 [1961]).[13] "It was a simple idea really," Joe claims,

> but a man who had a theory about pathological love and who had given his name to it, like a bridegroom at the altar, must surely reveal, even if unwittingly, the nature of love itself. For there to be a pathology there had to be a lurking concept of health. De Clérambault's syndrome was a dark, distorted mirror that reflected and parodied a brighter world of lovers whose reckless abandon to their cause was sane. (*EL*: 128)

This way of conceptualizing love is also reflected in the title of the novel. "Enduring love" can be interpreted in two ways. If "enduring" is read as an adjective, that is, as "long-lasting" or "permanent," we come closer to the concept of "healthy" love, one that resists the vicissitudes of time and circumstances (as in the case of Joe and Clarissa's relationship lasting regardless of the external forces that breach upon it). If, on the other hand, we read the word as a verb, that is, "to support" or "to suffer" adverse forces and influences, we approach its pathological side (as in the case of Joe's "fate" of suffering the love Jed forces upon him).

In a similar vein with Joe's understanding of love in terms of its various shades lying in-between madness and sanity, with pathological cases helping in elucidating the nature and structure of the more widespread, "normal" ones, I will argue that paralysis can be more accurately conceptualized by initially focusing on instances where it seems to come closer to pathological forms: in this case, on Jed Parry's religious fanaticism.

As I already mentioned, Jed, a twenty-eight-year-old unemployed man, living on an inheritance, is one of the five persons who try unsuccessfully to hold the balloon down, in the incident from the opening of the novel. His obsessive reliance on religious frameworks in structuring his worldviews and his interactions with others is foregrounded from his first meeting with Joe, close to the corpse of Joe Logan, whose "skeletal structure had collapsed internally to produce a head on a thickened stick" in the wake of his fall (23). In response to Joe's quite reasonable statement that "there's nothing we can do but wait" (24), Jed replies, "with a seriousness which warned against mockery [while] lowering himself . . . on his knees" that they could "pray together." Since the rationalist Joe understandably refuses to join Jed in his ritual, the latter becomes increasingly insistent. "Look, we don't know each other and there's no reason why you should trust me," he starts preaching to Joe. "Except that God has brought us together in this tragedy and we have to, you know, make whatever sense of it we can. . . . You shouldn't, you know, think of this as some kind of duty. It's like, your own needs are being answered?[14] It's got nothing to do with me, really, I'm just the messenger. It's a gift" (25).

Among all the other characters from McEwan's works, probably the one resembling Jed the most in terms of his worldviews is Adam Henry from *The Children Act* (2015). A close-to-eighteen-year-old Jehova's witness, Adam is hospitalized with a severe, almost terminal case of leukemia, which can only be treated through medication and blood transfusions. Both Adam and his parents, though, refuse to accept these transfusions on religious grounds. In tune with his father's claims that "mixing your blood with the blood of an animal or another human being is pollution, contamination" (*CA*: 76), Adam, "speaking in breathy snatches . . . quoted Leviticus and Acts [and] talked about blood as the essence, about the literal word of God, about pollution" (113). Fiona Maye, the judge dealing with the dispute between the doctors and Henry's family, arguing that Adam's "childhood has been an uninterrupted monochrome exposure to a forceful view of the world," that is, the religious, and that his "life is more precious than his dignity" (123), decides to override his decision and force him to accept the blood transfusions which could save his life. After initially "raging and ranting" (137), Adam begins to reconsider his viewpoints, particularly after his health begins to improve and writes to Fiona that he feels she has brought him "close to something else, something really beautiful and deep" (139), and later, stalking her in Newcastle (a behavior reminiscent of Jed Parry's too), confesses that his "parents' religion was a poison" and Fiona was "the antidote" (163). However, his self-proclaimed maturity and newly acquired secular worldviews seem to be starkly at odds with his behavior. His close to pathological obsession with Fiona, his "savior" who made everything "collapse . . . into the truth" (164) and who could "give [him] reading lists [about] everything [she] thinks [he] should know about" (167), does not seem to be very far from his earlier religious obsessions. In fact, the reader gets the uncanny impression that nothing much has changed besides the fact that the God of Jehovah's witnesses was replaced by a secular Goddess.

In *EL*, although Joe firmly rejects Jed's plea and is "deliver[ed] from the radiating power of Jed Parry's love and pity" (27) by two policemen who arrive at the scene of the accident, this deliverance is only temporary. Later that night, after returning home, he receives a phone call from Jed, who tells him: "I just wanted you to know, I understand what you're feeling. I feel it too. I love you" (37). This phone call is followed by many others, as well as by a large number of letters from Jed, trying to persuade Joe that the balloon accident was an event arranged by God to bring the two of them together "for a purpose" (65).

During their second face-to-face encounter, in front of Joe's apartment, where Jed spends most of his time, the first clear hints of the extent of Jed's delusional beliefs become apparent. "You love me. You love me," Jed obsessively repeats, "and there's nothing I can do but return your love . . . I don't know why you've chosen me. All I know is that I love you too now, and that there's a reason for it, a purpose" (63). Joe's persistent and repeated denial of the veracity of Jed's statements[15] has absolutely no effect in changing the latter's convictions. On the contrary, he becomes even more stubborn in his belief that Joe is simply teasing him due to obscure reasons: "Don't deny what we have. And please don't play this game with me. I know you'll find it a difficult idea, and you'll resist it, but we've come together for a purpose" (65).[16] When Joe, exasperated, asks him what this purpose he keeps mentioning might be, Jed's reply, spoken in a tone "as though explaining the obvious to a simpleton," bears even stronger religious overtones than his earlier behavior at the scene of the accident:

> To bring you to God, through love. You'll fight this like mad because you're a long way from your own feelings? But I know that the Christ is within you. At some level you know it too. That's why you fight it so hard with your education and reason and logic and this detached way you have of talking, as if you're not part of anything at all?[17] You can't pretend you don't know what I'm talking about, perhaps because you want to hurt me and dominate me, but the fact is I come bearing gifts. The purpose is to bring you to the Christ that is in you and that *is* you. That's what the gift of love is all about. (66; emphasis in original)

At first sight, Jed's understanding of love seems to come very close to the Christian notion of *agape* (a Greek term commonly translated as "divine love"), connoting a selfless, altruistic (and sometimes even sacrificial) type of love which would bring one closer both to God and to other people. This understanding of the term has its origins in the *New Testament* where St. John proclaims that "God is love" (John 4:16) and further extends this claim to an incentive to unconditionally love one's neighbor (4:20). As Sheveland puts it, agape "is thus both a divine prerogative, revealed preeminently in the Cross and Resurrection, and the task of Christian disciples who, like Christ, love sacrificially, lose themselves in loving others, and, paradoxically but unmistakably, discover themselves in the process" (2008: 161).[18] In a similar vein, Jed writes in one of his letters, "I know that you'll *come* to God, just as I know that it's my purpose to bring you there, *through love.* Or, to put it another way, I'm going to mend your rift with God *through the healing power of love*" (97; my emphases). Furthermore, the parallel between Jed's love and the Christian *agape* is foregrounded also during the abovementioned meeting in front of Joe's apartment, through the offense Jed takes when Joe asks him if, through using the word love, he actually means sex. "You know very well we can't talk about it like this," Jed replies (67).[19]

Of course, this parallel is challenged repeatedly throughout the novel. To start with the sexual element: Joe's diagnosis of Jed with erotomania, an aspect expanded upon in the first appendix at the end of the novel, written in the form of a scientific article, entitled "A Homo-Erotic Obsession with Religious Overtones: A Clinical Variant of de Clérambault's Syndrome," and allegedly published in the *British Review of Psychiatry*,[20] where Jed's condition is described as an "erotic delusion" (233) puts certain pressures on an interpretation of Jed's love as purely asexual. Furthermore, certain passages from his letters seem unmistakably loaded with sexual undertones: "Love has given me new eyes, I see with such clarity, in such detail," Jed writes. "Everything I see I want to touch and stroke. . . . What a fabulous way to hear of love, through rain and leaves and skin, the pattern woven through the skein of God's sensuous creation unfolding in a scorching sense of touch" (96).[21] Moreover, the ways in which Jed's love quickly escalates into violence[22] can be read as another sign of its fundamental difference from *agape*.[23]

However, although the article mentions Jed's "fear of sexual intimacy" and his "self-protectively vague notions of what [he] actually want[s] from the love-object" (240), McEwan's use of this narrative device (that is, the incorporation of a scientific article in the appendix of the novel) has an ambiguous role: even though, on the one hand, it could be read as re-enforcing Joe's diagnosis of Jed, it can also be, on the other hand, understood as foregrounding the shortcomings of an obsessive application of scientific categories for making sense of alterity (that is, as an implicit critique of *Joe's* paralysis), and thus show that such "methods" are deficient ways of social sense-making, prioritizing one form of intersubjectivity at the expense of others, as already became clear in my discussion of how "applying" categories such as "brain-damaged" and "frigid" in *OCB* destabilize contexts of primary intersubjectivity. I will return to these issues in the next section, where I will discuss Joe's paralysis.

Interestingly, though, in one of the articles McEwan quotes in the bibliography of the appendix (a real article this time, published in 1978), Doust and Christie claim, after reviewing eight cases of erotomania, that "a close relationship may be posited between some pathological aspects of love and tenets of the church for religious believers" (cited in *EL*: 240). Wenn and Camia's explanation of these findings suggests that the sexual inhibitions placed on people belonging to various religious organizations could be a cause of the development of the disorder. They nevertheless admit that Jed "belonged to no particular denomination or sect, and the object of his delusion was an atheist" (241).

This ambiguity at the core of Jed's relation with religion is also noticed and reflected upon by Joe later in the novel, before his first (unsuccessful) visit to the police to complain about Jed's harassment: "There were very few biblical references in Parry's correspondence," Joe ponders, while trying to select passages from Jed's letters that might help him prove to the police that he might truly be in a dangerous situation and thus need their help.[24]

> His religion was dreamily vague on the specifics of doctrine, and he gave no impression of being attached to any particular church. His belief was a self-made affair, generally aligned to the culture of personal growth and fulfillment. There was a lot of talk of destiny, of his "path" and how he would not be deterred from following it, and of fate—his and mine entwined. Often, God was a term interchangeable with self. God's love for mankind shaded into Parry's love for me. God was undeniably "within" rather than in his heaven, and believing in him was therefore a licence to respond to the calls of feeling or intuition. It was the perfect loose structure for a disturbed mind. There were no constraints of theological nicety or religious observance, no social sanction or congregational calling to account, none of the moral framework that made religions viable, however failed their cosmologies. Parry listened only to the inner voice of his private God. (152–53)

Crucial aspects of a form of paralysis I have not yet discussed can be identified from a close reading of this passage in dialogue with philosophical accounts of intersubjectivity. Whereas the characters from *H* and *OCB* were almost exclusively employing explicit 2PP and 3PP for making sense of others (i.e., self-other meta-perspectives developing during tertiary intersubjectivity), at the expense of the implicit 2PP characterizing primary and secondary intersubjectivity (i.e., the pre-reflective self-other awareness, based on embodied interaction), here, Jed appears to want to abolish completely *the necessary distance* between selfhood and alterity characterizing implicit 2PP.

As Dan Zahavi argues, following Edmund Husserl's account of empathy,[25] "The fact that my experiential acquaintance with the mind of the other differs from my first-person acquaintance with my own mind (and from the other's experiential acquaintance with his or her own mind) is not an imperfection or shortcoming. On the contrary, it is a difference that is constitutional. It is precisely because of this difference, that we can claim that the minds we experience are *other* minds. As Husserl points out, had I had the same access to the consciousness of the other as I have to my own, the other would cease being an other and would instead become a part of me" (Zahavi 2014: 130–31; emphasis in original).

Jed's behavior points precisely toward such a desire to abolish this constitutional difference identified by Husserl. The fact that, in his view, "God was a term *interchangeable* with self," together with his powerful wish to *entwine* his fate with Joe's show the deeply problematic nature of Jed's ways of relating to others.[26] Blocked within his obsessive religious worldviews, he endlessly struggles to surpass instead of accept the irreducible difference/distance between selfhood and alterity characterizing social interaction.

Another interesting aspect foregrounded in this paragraph is the complex interplay between community and individuality in the constitution of subjectivity (and implicitly, in the constitution of *inter*subjectivity). As we have seen before, Jed's religious obsessions have their origin in socially and culturally mediated understandings of religion and in shared religious discourses.[27] Nevertheless, his particular ways of experiencing these communal norms is highly idiosyncratic: "no social sanction or congregational calling to account [and] no moral framework that made religions viable" can truly influence his personal, private manner of interiorizing religion and religious discourses. It seems that no identification with a *concrete* social group with a clear ethical stance can be identified in Jed's case.

His situation is thus quite different from that of the characters from *H* and *OCB*. Despite being, due to their life histories, "emotional oddities" (in Head's terms), both Edward and Florence still seem to be strongly anchored within the hypocritical Victorianism discussed by Marcus. The experiences of *H*'s narrator too appear to be powerfully structured by the (admittedly more broad and general) in-group/out-group dynamics between those who have experienced sex and those who have not. On the other hand, Jed is, as Joe puts it, "inviolable in his solipsism" (144).

Solipsism is indeed a good concept to describe not only Jed's relation to religion, but also his paralysis in general. As I will argue later, it is not only Jed who listens just "to the inner voice of his private God." Joe and Clarissa can just as easily be described in these terms, regardless of the fact that their "private God" does not belong to religion, but rather to science and, respectively, art. In his introduction to Paul Edwards's article "Solipsism, Narrative and Love in *Enduring Love*" (2007), Peter Childs defines solipsism as "an individual's tendency toward self-involvement, which, at an extreme, can result in mental and physical withdrawal from society and feelings of paranoia and persecution" (Childs 2007b: 78). This seems precisely to be Jed's case: after a university degree and an unsuccessful job, he is unemployed and living alone in the house he inherited from his mother. There, as Wenn and Camia claim in the appendix, "both his isolation and his religious beliefs intensified" (*EL*: 237).[28] The nature and extent of Jed's solipsism become quite clear to Joe while he is obsessively re-reading Jed's letters:

> The pattern of his love was not shaped by external influences. . . . His was a world determined from the inside, driven by private necessity, and this way it could remain intact. Nothing could prove him wrong, nothing was needed to prove him right. . . . He crouched in a cell of his own devising, teasing out meanings, imbuing nonexistent exchanges with their drama of hope or disappointment, always scrutinizing the physical world, its random placements and chaotic noise and colours, for the correlatives of his current emotional state—and always finding satisfaction. He illuminated the world with his feelings, and the world confirmed him at every turn his feelings took. (143)

Indeed, Jed is almost continuously involved in what Umberto Eco would call a process of "overinterpretation" (1992), or what Paul Ricoeur labels a "hermeneutics of suspicion" (1970 [1965]). No worldly phenomenon is taken by Jed at face value. In a similar vein with Oedipa Mass's paranoid experience,[29] all the elements from his environment appear to be strongly saturated with meaning, that is, they become symbols standing for something else. For Jed, Joe's moving the curtain to look outside the window, for example, becomes an esoteric sign meant to be interpreted. Similarly, after Joe accidentally brushes some leaves with his hand in front of his apartment, Jed writes to him that he "feel[s] happiness running through [him] like an electric current" (93) since he just realized that Joe "touched [the leaves] in a certain way, in a pattern that spelled a simple message" (96). Narratologist James Phelan, in a rhetorical reading of the novel, ironically and (self-)critically compares Jed with a (certain type of) literary critic, since he "refuses to acknowledge the existence of evidence recalcitrant to his interpretive hypothesis [and] finds confirmation of his hypothesis in what everyone else would regard as irrelevant or, even nonsignifying data" (2009: 315). Similarly, Lynn Wells describes Jed as "a deficient reader, since he perceives in the world, and particularly in Joe, only what his madness leads him to see" (2010: 80).

A useful theory which could shed more light on Jed's psychology and behavior, as well as on aspects of what I understand by paralysis, could be found in psychologist Jean Piaget's work on the structure of the process of adaptation underlying psychological development.[30] For Piaget, adaptation consists of two complementary processes, "assimilation," and "accommodation," through which the relationship between the organism and the environment is constantly negotiated. Whereas during assimilation, the organism outwardly projects already internalized cognitive structures in order to "interpret" the environment, during accommodation, structures of the environment are internalized and (can) change the organism's cognitive schemes. Psychological development is thus described as a series of alternations between assimilations and accommodations. Such alternations appear to be utterly absent from Jed's experience. As obvious from Joe's descriptions cited earlier, Jed's cognitive schemes cannot be changed by external, environmental factors. He appears to be blocked in a never-ending process of assimilation, without any possibility of accommodating to reality. Henry Perowne in *Saturday* offers a beautiful description of problems similar to Jed's:

> The primitive thinking of the supernaturally inclined amounts to what his colleagues call a problem, or an idea, of reference. An excess of the subjective, the ordering of the world in line with your needs, an inability to contemplate your own unimportance. In Henry's view, such reasoning belongs on a spectrum at whose far end, rearing like an abandoned temple, lies psychosis. (17)

Jed's assimilative frenzy, his entrapment into an inner, deeply private version of religious belief, and his monomaniac and obsessive worldview, impermeable by external influences, is also foregrounded in his strong incapacity to connect bodily and affectively with the others. I have already mentioned his apparent lack of interest in sex. Besides this, he is not even able (or willing) to maintain eye contact with another person. According to Hobson and Hobson (2011), eye contact avoidance is an important symptom of autism. As Fuchs argues (2015: 198), many autistic persons suffering from disturbances in primary intersubjectivity attempt to compensate their inability to connect in an embodied/affective manner with others through an employment of tertiary forms of intersubjectivity. Thus, Jed's obsessive reliance on religious frameworks could also be understood as such a compensatory strategy.

During their meeting in front of Joe's apartment, Jed "sighed and looked down the street . . . and then his gaze tracked a passing car. He looked up at the piles of towering cumulus, and he examined the nails of his right hand, but he could not look at [Joe]" (*EL*: 62). In the middle of the conversation discussed earlier, Joe notices the strangeness of Jed's behavior, and he describes it as follows: "I was beginning to see a pattern of a conversational tic he suffered when he spoke. He caught your eye, then turned his head to speak as though addressing a presence at his side, or an invisible creature perched on his shoulder" (65).[31] Much later, during the climax of the novel, when Jed takes

Clarissa hostage, Joe's arrival has similar effects on Jed's manner of social interaction: "He glanced away to his right, to the invisible presence on his shoulder, before meeting my eye" (209).

During the same scene, when Clarissa tries to persuade him that he utterly misunderstood Joe's behavior,[32] Jed "tosse[s] his head from side to side. It was an involuntary spasm, an intensification of his nervous sideways glance" (211). At this point, Jed seems to be almost forced to accommodate to reality due to Clarissa's passionate and persuasive arguments. The clash between the strength of his paralysis and the world's power of breaking in through his defenses has visible effects on his physiology: "The tremor in his hands was so bad he clasped them. Sweat was beading on his forehead" (210). Closely watching his behavior, with the detachment of a true scientist, Joe has an important insight about "the core of his condition," as well as, I would add, about the nature of paralysis: "he had to block out the facts that didn't fit" (211). Ironically though, it is not only Jed that continuously blocks the facts that do not fit: both Joe and Clarissa are recurrently doing the same thing.

3.2.2 Joe: A Giant Polyp of Uninspired Logic

At the beginning of the novel, Joe Rose is not a "pure" scientist anymore. His career in physics halted halfway, and at the time the novel's plot develops he is merely a scientific journalist, explaining to the general public various scientific theories. However, not only is he continuously regretting his failure as a scientist, but also his worldview is (still) obsessively structured by scientific frameworks: Joe is continuously making sense of the world and of other people in scientific terms. In this regard, to put it in Piagetian terms, he is almost as much an "assimilator" as Jed, regardless of the fact that their worldviews are so different.

A first example of Joe's paralysis is his desperate attempt to make sense of Jed's behavior by *diagnosing* him, that is, by finding a scientific (in this case, psychiatric) explanation of what he considers to be *symptoms* of an underlying disease. After his moment of insight when he remembers he previously read a study about de Clérambault's syndrome, Joe calls himself, in an understatement, "almost happy," but the reader can easily infer from his tone that he is more than elated: "De Clérambault's syndrome. The name was like a fanfare, a clear trumpet sound recalling me to my own obsessions. There was research to follow through now and I knew exactly where to start. A syndrome was a framework of prediction and it offered a kind of comfort" (124). Taming the chaos that erupted in his life in the wake of the balloon accident is something Joe strongly needs, and he considers scientific thinking as the most appropriate method for achieving such goals.

A similar type of paralysis also structures some of Henry Perowne's social interactions in Saturday. "Regularly penetrating the skull with some modest success" (86), the neurosurgeon Perowne often uses his medical expertise also outside the operating room. When threatened by three hoodlums on the streets of London on his way to his squash game, for example, Henry immediately takes an observational, distant, explicit 3PP toward their leader, Baxter: "The gripped hand extending towards Perowne is large, given the man's height, and papery pale, with black hair coiled on the back, and extending to the distal interphalangeal joints. The persistent tremor also draws Perowne's professional attention. . . . Baxter is one of those smokers whose pores exude a perfume, an oily essence of his habit. Garlic affects certain people the same way. Possibly the kidneys are implicated" (87). During his tense discussion with Baxter, Perowne does not stop observing the former's physiognomy: Perowne's "attention, his professional regard, settles once again on Baxter's right hand. It isn't simply a tremor, it's a fidgety restlessness implicating practically every muscle . . . As Baxter stares at the marchers, he makes tiny movements with his head, little nods and shakes. Watching him unobserved for a few seconds, Perowne suddenly understands—Baxter is unable to initiate or make saccades . . . To scan the crowd, he is having to move his head" (90–91). Even when Baxter erupts in "a shout of rage . . . there still remains in a portion of [Perowne's] thoughts a droning, pedestrian diagnostician who notes poor self-control, emotional lability, explosive temper, suggestive of reduced levels of GABA among the appropriate binding sites on striatal neurons" (91).

All of these observations make Perowne realize that Baxter suffers from Huntington's disease, a genetic, neurodegenerative (and still untreatable) affliction, a proof, in Perowne's view, of "how the brilliant machinery of being [can be] undone by the tiniest of faulty cogs, the insidious whisper of a ruin, a single bad idea lodged in every cell, on every chromosome four" (94). Perowne's diagnosis, together with the false promise he makes to Baxter that he will help him cure his illness, saves him (for the moment at least) from a physical altercation. Nevertheless, his paralytic way of sense-making and the "shameless blackmail" (95) following the diagnosis will trigger unwanted consequences in Perowne's tranquil existence.[33]

The deficiencies inherent in such a way of relating to others are foregrounded when Joe first meets Jed after the latter's "epiphany." Although he is happy that he managed to diagnose his stalker, to turn him into a scientific case study, Joe is far from willing to study directly his "specimen," that is, to engage in any embodied, face-to-face interaction with him, structured by an implicit 2PP: "I walked towards him quickly, hoping to brush right by him and get indoors" (128). Luckily, he manages to escape quite fast and enter his apartment, after Jed gives him an envelope with a letter he wrote about Joe's scientific articles. Relieved, in the safety of his home, Joe admits: "It was like a painkiller, the distance and height I opened between us in fifteen seconds. Studying Parry in reference to a syndrome I could tolerate, even relish, but meeting him yet again in the street . . . had frightened me" (130). In a similar manner with Jed's problems of embodied interaction I discussed above, Joe's paralysis also appears to ruin the latter's capacity, as well as willingness, for immediate human contact.

Jed's religious fanaticism tends to be explained by Joe in similarly abstract ways, drawing this time upon evolutionary theory, rather than psychiatry. "Might there be a genetic basis to religious belief, or was it merely refreshing to think so?" Joe ponders while making some tea. Several evolutionary explanations are (quite sarcastically, if not even maliciously) invoked to explain a behavior which, for a strongly atheist scientist like himself, would not make sense otherwise:

> Suppose religion gave status, especially to its priest caste—plenty of social advantage in that. What if it bestowed strength in adversity, the power of consolation, the chance of surviving the disaster that might crush a godless man? Perhaps it gave believers passionate conviction, the brute strength of single-mindedness.

> Probably it worked on groups as well as on individuals, bringing cohesion and identity, and a sense that you and your fellows were right, even—or especially—when you were wrong. With God on our side. Uplifted by a crazed unity, armed with horrible certainty, you descend on the neighbouring tribe, beat and rape it senseless and come away burning with righteousness and drunk with the very victory your gods have promised. Repeat fifty thousand times over the millennia, and the complex set of genes controlling for groundless conviction could get a strong distribution. (159)[34]

What is ironic in this paragraph is that the terms "passionate conviction," "single-mindedness," "horrible certainty," or "groundless conviction" Joe so spitefully uses in his diatribe against religious worldviews could very easily be employed to describe his paralysis structured by a scientific worldview too. This is precisely what Clarissa points too when she calls his interest in neo-Darwinism, evolutionary psychology, and genetics "the new fundamentalism. . . . Twenty years ago you and your friends were all socialists and you blamed the environment for everyone's hard luck. Now you've got us trapped in our genes, and there's a reason for everything," Clarissa tells him (70).

Another clear example of Joe's paralysis would be his interpretation of the balloon accident, which is also saturated with concepts and theories taken from evolutionary biology and psychology.[35] The failure of his "team's"[36] attempt to hold down the balloon, and the consequent death of John Logan, was caused by one of the five members letting go of the ropes, an action which forced the others (besides Logan) to let go too, in order to save their lives. Obsessively reflecting upon the accident, Joe draws the following conclusion, in an attempt both to explain what happened and to excuse himself:

> I didn't know, nor have I ever discovered, who let go first. I'm not prepared to accept it was me. But everyone claims not to have been first. What is certain is that if we had not broken ranks, our collective weight would have brought the balloon to earth a quarter of the way down the slope a few seconds later as the gust subsided. But as I've said, there was no team, there was no plan, no agreement to be broken. No failure. So can we accept that it was right, *every man for himself*? (14; my emphasis)

Perhaps such an explanation could satisfy a "common" person, unschooled in the intricacies of evolutionary biology, or even an economist, who understands rationality in terms of egoism (i.e., "every man for himself").[37] But the scientist Joe cannot leave it at that, cannot have "that comfort, for there [is] a deeper covenant, ancient and automatic, written in our nature."[38] The "ancient covenant" Joe refers to is our altruistic instinct, our evolutionary predisposition for cooperation, recently identified and discussed at large in evolutionary biology. Against the Hobbesian perspectives prevalent in earlier varieties of social science and economic theory, current evolutionary approaches to social cognition acknowledge the importance of altruism structuring human nature.[39] But as Joe admits, framing his arguments through ideas taken from Robert Wright's evolutionary approach to morality (1994), we are far from being *solely* altruistic creatures. Human nature is constantly riddled by the tensions and conflicts between our selfish and altruistic instincts. It is precisely in these terms Joe continues his (self-justificatory) explanation of the accident:

> Co-operation—the basis of our earliest hunting successes, the force behind our evolving capacity for language, the glue of our social cohesion. Our misery in the aftermath was proof that we knew we had failed ourselves. But letting go was in our nature too. Selfishness is also written on our hearts. This is our mammalian conflict—what to give to the others, and what to keep for yourself. Treading that line, keeping the others in check, and being kept in check by them, is what we call

morality. Hanging a few feet above the Chilterns escarpment, our crew enacted morality's ancient, irresolvable dilemma: us, or me. Someone said *me,* and then there was nothing to be gained by saying *us.* (14–15; emphases in original)

Evolutionary biology and psychology are, nevertheless, not the only abstract discourses that frame Joe's understanding of the accident. Perhaps even more surprisingly, mathematics, physics (especially mechanics), and chemistry also play a fundamental role. As Sean Matthews acknowledges, *EL* "is particularly marked by the prominence in the narrative of geometric motifs and images which generate patterns in and from the material of the story" (2007: 99). Here is how Joe describes the moment when he and the other four men started running toward the balloon:

The convergence of six figures in a flat green space has a comforting geometry from the buzzard's perspective, the knowable, limited plane of the snooker table. The initial conditions, the force and the direction of the force, define all consequent pathways, all the angles of collision and return, and the glow of the overhead light bathes the field, the baize and all its moving bodies, in reassuring clarity. I think that while we were still converging, we were in a state of mathematical grace. (*EL*: 2–3)

It is interesting to notice not only how Joe is describing the scene by using mathematical ("convergence," "geometry," "plane," "angles")[40] and physical ("initial conditions," "force," "direction of force," "collision") terms, but also how much comfort perceiving and subsequently describing this scene in such an utterly abstract way offers him. Moreover, when describing the object toward which they were "converging," it is not sufficient for him to call it "an enormous balloon filled with helium," and leave it at that. On the contrary, he seems to consider extremely important to provide a definition of helium, loaded with chemical terms: "that elemental gas forged from hydrogen in the nuclear furnace of the stars, first step along the way in the generation of multiplicity and variety of matter in the universe, including our selves and all our thoughts" (3). As with his elation caused by scientifically diagnosing his stalker, Joe's framing of the balloon accident in the disembodied "language" of mathematics, physics, and chemistry seems to him the perfect way of bringing order out of chaos.[41] Finally, he also takes an observer perspective on this scene (in which he participated himself) and tries to make sense of it through an extensive employment of a combination of explicit 1PP, 2PP, and 3PP, a sense-making strategy which, as I argued before, can be considered a trademark of (a certain type of) paralysis.

Leaving aside the balloon accident for now, two more striking examples of Joe's paralysis, structured by his obsessive reliance on scientific frameworks, are foregrounded in the novel, this time interfering with and destabilizing what should ideally be a powerful and "pure" combination of primary and secondary forms of intersubjectivity, that is, his relationship with Clarissa.[42] Waiting for her at Heathrow Airport, "after a separation of six weeks, the longest Clarissa and [him] had spent apart in [the] seven years [they have been in a relationship]" (3), Joe, with a "detachment" (5) which seems quite strange considering the circumstances, starts musing about Darwin:

> If one ever wanted proof of Darwin's contention that the many expressions of emotion in humans are universal, genetically inscribed, then a few minutes by the arrivals gate in Heathrow's Terminal Four should suffice. I saw the same joy, the same uncontrollable smile, in the faces of a Nigerian earth mama, a thin-lipped Scottish granny and a pale, correct Japanese businessman as they wheeled their trolleys in and recognized a figure in the expectant crowd. (4)[43]

Initially, his assimilation of the scene by perceiving it from an abstract, evolutionary perspective (as well from a distant, observational 3PP) once more brings Joe comfort. Although he admits that "observing human variety can give pleasure," he is happy to claim that "so too can human sameness." After thirty-five minutes though, and "more than fifty theatrical happy endings," the problems inherent in his paralytic perception start to become increasingly apparent even to himself. Slowly, each meeting he witnesses seems to be "slightly less well acted than the one before," and soon, he begins to "feel emotionally exhausted and [to] suspect . . . that even the children were being insincere" (4). Similarly with Jed's case, a hermeneutics of suspicion (even self-suspicion[44]), begins to color Joe's perspective. However, differently from Jed, Clarissa's arrival pushes him back within primary intersubjectivity: "Immediately my detachment vanished, and I called out her name, in tune with all the rest" (5). As I will show later though, his recurrent paralysis, combined with external circumstances, will make such a connection increasingly difficult to obtain and maintain.

Another instance where his relationship with Clarissa is strained by his paralysis structured by evolutionary thinking is their discussion regarding the nature and functions of smiling in infants, on which Joe is doing research for one of his papers. During "one of [their] late-night kitchen table sessions" (71), he tries to convince Clarissa, backing up his arguments by citing some of biologist E. O. Wilson's "cool phrases" that the infant smile is a "social signal . . . that triggers a more abundant share of parental love and affection [and, in] the terminology of the zoologist ... [it] is a social releaser, an inborn and relatively invariant signal that mediates a basic social relationship."

When Clarissa accuses him of a "rationalism gone berserk," in the wake of which "everything [is] being stripped down [and] some larger meaning [is] lost,"[45] Joe becomes increasingly angry. "If we value a baby's smile," he tells her condescendingly, "why not contemplate its source? Are we to say that all infants enjoy a secret joke? Or that God reaches down and tickles them? Or, least implausibly, because they learn smiling from their mothers? But then, deaf-blind babies smile too. That smile must be hard-wired, and for good evolutionary reasons" (70).

Joe admits, a bit later, that Clarissa's attacks might have deeper roots than a simple philosophical disagreement. "What we were talking about this time," he claims, "was the absence of babies from our lives" (71). The capacity to decode this double layeredness occasionally characterizing human communication (that is, the ability to infer what is implied but not stated from what has been explicitly stated) is a skill developing during tertiary intersubjectivity. However, its successful employment during concrete social interactions crucially depends (in non-pathological cases) on the use of strategies pertaining to primary and secondary intersubjectivity too. Precisely his incapacity to connect with others in such ways makes Joe repeatedly fail to react appropriately to the emotional problems Clarissa's infertility gives rise to, regardless of the fact that he manages to understand the situation perfectly well in theoretical terms.

The absence of children, caused by Clarissa's infertility, could indeed be a significant problem in their relationship, extending well beyond their theoretical disagreements. However, as Greenberg notes, Joe's interpretation of the destructive force such absence has for their relationship might just as well be framed by Joe in evolutionary terms (even if not explicitly). After all, Robert Wright, one of the evolutionary psychologists mentioned in the acknowledgments of the novel, defines love in the following terms: "The genetic payoff of having two parents devoted to a child's welfare is a reason men and women can fall into swoons over one another, including swoons of great duration" (Wright 1994: 59; cited in Greenberg 2007: 99). For the rationalist Joe, paralyzed within an evolutionary worldview, the absence of children could easily be the proximate cause of a love not to endure.[46]

Regardless of his obsession with evolutionary explanations of human cognitive processes and behavior, though, later in the novel, Joe has an insight that such explanations could perhaps be insufficient to make sense of such complex creatures as ourselves. On his way back to London, after buying a gun to defend himself from Jed, and immediately after finding out that Clarissa is held hostage, Joe has to stop at the edge of a forest to defecate. During this most embodied process, paralleled with his (similarly embodied) careful scrutiny of "a handful of soil" (206) he collects in the palm of his hand,[47] he is haunted by doubts regarding the evolutionary/biological explanations that comforted him until then.

"What I thought might calm me was the reminder that, for all our concerns, we were still part of this natural dependency," he reflects. Immediately though, his optimism drops: "But even as I squatted to enrich the forest floor, I could not believe in the primary significance of these grand cycles." After listing various (mostly damaging) cultural artifacts whose manufacture and use differentiates us from other animals ("the poison-exuding vehicle," "my gun," "the enormous city"), he pessimistically concludes: "What, in this description, was necessary to the carbon cycle, or the fixing of nitrogen? We were no longer in the great chain. It was our own complexity that expelled us from the Garden.[48] We were in a mess of our own unmaking" (207). What is again striking about this character is that, even while acknowledging the limits of biological explanation when it comes to such complex, cultural creatures, he still remains blocked within (perhaps even more) abstract thought processes.

This feature recurs in yet another instance. As Joe's fears of Jed increase, and as Clarissa's suspicions regarding both the former's sincerity/reliability[49] and his mental health become more pronounced, Joe himself starts to doubt whether the rationality he previously praised himself for is warranted. After the shooting at the restaurant, for example, Joe realizes, while being interrogated by the police, that many things he thought he reliably remembered happened in fact differently from what his memory testified.[50] His admission of his own unreliability in fact occurs in many instances throughout the entire novel.[51] He is even ready sometimes to admit that he might be more than simply occasionally self-deceived and could perhaps be verging toward madness, as Clarissa implies.

The morning after the first phone call from Jed, for example, when Clarissa prepares to leave for work, Joe thinks: "Standing there on the polished dance floor parquet I felt like a mental patient at the end of visiting hours. *Don't leave me here with my mind*, I thought. *Get them to let me out*" (58; emphasis in original).[52] Also, during his first meeting with Jed, he feels "as if [he] had fallen through a crack in [his] own existence, down into another life, another set of sexual preferences, another past history and future" (67). And in the police station, he ponders: "But exactly what interests were served by my own account of the restaurant lunch" (181)?

However, although he repeatedly doubts his sanity and reliability (both as a witness, as in the restaurant scene, and as a thinker, in his diagnosis of Jed or his application of scientific insights in explaining (social) reality),

Joe finally ends up assimilating these doubts too through the scientific frameworks structuring his worldviews. Evolutionary psychology serves once more as an explanation and justification of his behavior. When he is starting to suspect that Clarissa is cheating on him, and wants to search her study for any "incriminatory" letters, he tries to persuade himself that he is only going there to look for a stapler. He is notably quick though to explain his self-delusional attitudes in evolutionary terms:

> Self-persuasion was a concept much loved by evolutionary psychologists . . . if you lived in a group . . . persuading others of your own needs and interests would be fundamental to your well-being. . . . Clearly you would be at your most convincing if you persuaded yourself first and did not even have to pretend to believe what you were saying. The kind of self-deluding individuals who tended to do this flourished, as did their genes. (104)[53]

Later on, in the police station, after realizing how flawed his perception and memory of the events in the restaurant were, agreeing that "we lived in a mist of half-shared, unreliable perception, and our sense data came warped by a prism[54] of desire and belief, which tilted our memories too" (180), he offers again an evolutionary explanation of his shortcomings:

> We're descended from the indignant, passionate tellers of half truths who, in order to convince others, simultaneously convinced themselves. Over generations success had winnowed us out, and with success came our defect, carved deep in the genes like ruts in a cart track—when it didn't suit us we couldn't agree with what was in front of us. Believing is seeing. (181)[55]

Joe's admission that his beliefs might (de)structure his perception once more points to how often this character becomes aware of his paralysis. Paradoxically enough, his scientific worldview (which structures his paralysis) is also the tool through which he becomes conscious of the deficient ways in which he can relate to others. Through science (in this case, evolutionary theory), Joe manages to acquire an explicit 1PP and 2PP, necessary for the development of his awareness regarding the disrupted ways in which he is making sense of alterity. Regardless of his self-consciousness though, he is not very often able to break free from his paralysis and open himself to the diversity of ways in which he could connect with others.

Yet, even if Joe, an obsessive monomaniac, appears to be almost as paralyzed as Jed, using mostly science to assimilate reality, and thus failing to accommodate to the intricacies of social interaction, the reader is still left at the end of the novel with the impression that Joe is, in fact, more right in his interpretations than both Jed and Clarissa.[56] The events prove that Jed was, indeed, dangerous and that Joe's increasing fears for his and Clarissa's safety were justified.

In her letter at the end of the novel, Clarissa herself admits she was "completely wrong" for "doubting [his] sanity, for not having faith in [his] powers of rationality and deduction and [his] dedicated research into his condition." However, as she further claims, "[his] being right is not a simple matter" (216). Her explanation of this statement comes as a description of not only the nature of Joe's paralysis but also its inherent dangers:

> You went it alone, Joe. Right from the start, before you knew anything about Parry, you became so intense and strange and worked up about it. . . . You became more and more agitated and obsessed. You didn't want to talk to me about anything else. Our sex life dwindled to almost nothing. . . . As the Parry thing grew I watched you go deeper into yourself and further and further away from me. You were manic, and driven, and very lonely. You were on a case, a mission. Perhaps it became a substitute for the science you wanted to be doing. You did the research, you made the logical inferences and you got a lot of things right, but in the process you forgot to take me along with you, you forgot how to confide. (216–17)

At the end of the letter, she tells him that, due to all these reasons, she prefers to stay apart for a while. But is it only Joe's and Jed's fault for the disintegration of their relationship? Is Clarissa the only innocent, perfectly sane character in this trio? By having a closer look at this literature professor specializing in the romantic poets, I will provide some answers to these questions in the last part of this section.

3.2.3 Clarissa: In the Company of John Keats

Joe's partner, Clarissa, is a literature professor and critic, specializing in the romantic poets, particularly John Keats.[57] The criticism on *EL* is quite divided when it comes to interpreting this character. Some critics, like Carbonell, for example, consider *her* to be "the rational one, a nod by McEwan (a novelist) to the power of literature" (2010: 8) and claims that she "functions as the voice of human 'wisdom' that comes to us from the humanities," able to understand that the social world "cannot be reduced to its atomistic parts" (9). Her "wisdom about how humans operate in the narrative-rich social world" (10) makes her aware of the shortcomings of Joe's paralysis. As we saw in the previous section, she harshly criticizes both Joe's scientific understanding of human relationships and his increasing obsession with Jed. As Childs also argues, Clarissa "feels that art, beauty, and happiness, not facts, are at the centre of people's relationships and that these are the important things that underpin life and love" (Childs 2007b: 16).[58]

On the other hand, Alan Palmer voices a harsh criticism of Clarissa's behavior toward Joe, that is, her increasing distrust of his reliability and sanity. "Is Clarissa's why-didn't-you-just-invite-this-homicidal-maniac-in-for-a-cup-of-tea? strategy," Palmer asks, "*meant* to sound as utterly stupid, inadequate, and pathetic as it does to me" (2009: 303; emphasis in original)?[59] He is unable to understand how is it possible that "a highly intelligent, sensitive, self-aware and conscientious person who loves her partner, tries hard to behave well, and has a considerable degree of insight into herself, other people and the mechanics of relationships generally" could be "so utterly distrustful of the man that she loves that she instantly jumps to the conclusion that he is making things up" (303–04).[60] Utterly dumbfounded by her behavior, Palmer can only reach the conclusion that McEwan is "an incompetent author" (306).

In my opinion, a better explanation of Clarissa's behavior could be found somewhere in the middle of these critical extremes. As Childs himself points, the six weeks separation between her and Joe prior to the balloon accident is caused by "her devotion to another man: Keats" (Childs 2007b: 17). After their reunion at Heathrow, Joe admits that for "much of the time [they] walked westward [they] were talking about Clarissa's research" (*EL*: 6), which is focused on tracking a lost letter Keats wrote to Fanny Brawne, a girl he was in love with. Even if Joe is doubtful that Keats ever wrote such a letter, Clarissa is perfectly sure that he did. Her reasoning seems to be based on a concept of romantic love she learns from Keats himself (and other romantic poets). "He knew he'd never see Fanny again," she tells Joe. "He wrote to Brawne and said that to see her name written would be more than he could bear. He was strong enough those days in December, and he loved her so hard. It's easy to imagine him writing a letter he never intended to send" (7).

Finding this letter becomes a true obsession for Clarissa. Not even the disintegration of their relationship can stop her from continuing her desperate scholarly quest. Toward the end of the novel, during their first meeting after their separation, Clarissa is more than eager to tell Joe in great detail about the newest developments in her research:

> There was a new lead in the search for Keats' last letters. She had been in touch with a Japanese scholar who claimed he had read unpublished correspondence twelve years ago in the British Library written by a

distant relation of Keats' friend Severn. There was a reference to a letter addressed to Fanny but never meant to be posted, a "cry of undying love not touched by despair." Clarissa *had spent every spare hour* trying without success to track down the Severn connection. The Library's transfer to King's Cross was complicating the search, and now she was considering *flying to Tokyo to read the scholar's notes*. (221; my emphases)

As Paul Edwards comments on this scene and on Clarissa's "obsessive quest for the perfect Keatsian letter," a "reader from outside the academic world may well surmise that such a research trip is customary in that privileged world (elsewhere a fax or airmailed photocopy would suffice), but it is not." This aspect forces him to admit that "something is not quite right with Clarissa" (2007: 87).

In my view, what "is not quite right" with Clarissa could also be described as a (mild) form of paralysis. Whereas Jed's paralysis is structured by his religious worldviews and Joe's by his scientific ones, Clarissa's *literary/aesthetic* worldviews drastically structure her ways of dealing with the (social) world. The fact that her research interests are not limited just to her professional life, but insidiously seep into all her spheres of activity, *including* her relationship with Joe, becomes apparent from his description of the beginning of their relationship:

Lately I'd had the idea that Clarissa's interest in these hypothetical letters had something to do with our own situation, and with her conviction that love that did not find its expression in a letter was not perfect. In the months after we met, and before we bought the apartment, she had written me some beauties, passionately abstract in their exploration of the ways our love was different from and superior to any that had ever existed." (*EL*: 7)

Furthermore, during the balloon accident, whereas Joe sees everything through his scientific lenses, Clarissa is just as quick and determined to project literary structures upon the world. When later on, while analyzing the scene in the safety of their apartment, Joe tells her that Logan "seemed to hang in the air before falling," Clarissa recounts, how in that moment, "a scrap of Milton had flashed before her: *Hurl'd headlong flaming from th'Ethereal Sky*" (29; emphasis in original). As Möller argues, Clarissa "is so rooted in literary tradition that she views the world almost entirely through the lens of literature" (2011: 66).[61]

The "orientational framework derived from literature" (Möller 2011: 66) which permeates Clarissa's experience makes her unable to accommodate to the reality and seriousness of Jed's threats. When Joe tells her about Jed's first phone call, Clarissa starts laughing and replies jokingly, framing everything in the language of melodrama: "A secret gay love affair with a Jesus freak! I cannot wait to tell your science friends" (*EL*: 57).

Things become more serious later, of course, when she begins to suspect Joe. It is not incidentally, I believe, that her distrust starts to crystallize when Joe shows her one of Jed's letters, that is, precisely the types of objects her research obsessions are centered on. "She read the letter through the medium of a frown," Joe recounts, "pausing to look up to me at a certain point and say, "His writing's rather like yours'" (100). The hermeneutics of suspicion developed through her scholarly research on Keats's letters emerges here with a vengeance. Joe also suspects that the style in which the letter was written—"Parry's artful technique . . . such an unfaked narrative of emotion" (101–2)—would suggest to a literary critic like Clarissa that "a past, a pact, a collusion, a secret life of glances and gestures" (100) could possibly exist between Jed and Joe.[62]

Even in her letter, where, as I argued before, she coherently describes Joe's paralysis, traces of her own paralysis can be noticed. Her insistence on Joe's distancing himself from her, on his inability to confide, on his becoming a "stranger to [her]" (218) seem directly taken from Keats's letters. And her melodramatic ending is also unmistakably similar in both content and tone to the discourse of the romantic poets: "We've been so happy together. We've loved each other passionately and loyally. I always thought our love was the kind that was meant to go on and on" (218–19).

3.3 Their Fatal Lack of Cooperation: Corrupted Teamwork in *Enduring Love*

In the previous section, I discussed the various forms of paralysis the three main characters from *EL* suffered from. Now, I will turn back to the phenomenon of invasion and analyze its various manifestations in *EL* and the ways in which it is connected to paralysis.

In this chapter, after providing an overview of cognitive-scientific and philosophical accounts of joint attention and joint action, I will discuss the balloon accident from the beginning of the novel. This incident is an interesting example of an embodied collaborative activity, involving an interplay between joint attention and action, that is, a form of secondary intersubjectivity, gone tragically wrong due to a failure of coordination. Whereas, as we have seen in the previous section, Joe tends to interpret this failure in terms taken from evolutionary biology and psychology, my approach will be different.

Drawing on Hans-Bernhard Schmid's philosophical analyses of plural action, as well as on recent cognitive and phenomenological explorations of the structure of joint attention and action, I will argue that in order for a proper *team* to emerge, the participants in joint activities should share a common experiential background, necessarily including powerful affective components. A purely rational, "cold" and calculated approach to situations, like the one McEwan stages, will most of the time end in failure.

My hypothesis is that a serious imbalance regarding the experiential background of, on the one hand, Joe, Jed, Joseph Lacey, and Toby Greene, and, on the other hand, John Logan (the only person who continues to hold the rope after all the rest defect, and who consequently dies) can be identified. Of all the five members trying to hold the balloon down, only Logan had children, a feature which, in my view, gave him (and only him) the opportunity to strongly identify with the plights of James Gadd (the pilot of the balloon) and his nephew and therefore to engage in a proper form of altruistic behavior. Here, a similar pattern with Edward and Florence's sexual failure in *OCB* emerges: if in *OCB*, sexuality, a primary form of intersubjectivity, was invaded by tertiary forms of intersubjectivity structured by the characters' life histories, in *EL*, embodied collaborative activity, a secondary form of intersubjectivity, is destabilized by a similar form of invasion: due to the participants' incongruent experiences of parenthood, what should ideally be a smooth form of embodied collaboration turns into a tragic failure.

Moreover, it can be further argued that Joe's and Jed's paralyses, characterized by hyper-reflective[63] and highly abstract thought processes, could seriously interfere with the formation and endurance of any team they participate in: the self-centeredness and solipsism characterizing certain forms of paralysis are serious impediments to the openness and sharing that are necessary components of forms of interpersonal engagement needed in teamwork. Although the identity of the person who was the first to let go of the ropes remains a mystery throughout the novel and, therefore, neither Joe nor Jed could be held directly responsible for the disintegration of their "team," further cases of joint attention staged in *EL* provide evidence that paralysis can indeed sometimes breed invasion.

The balloon incident can be considered a focus of attention for Joe and Clarissa, who endlessly discuss and try to make sense of what happened (mostly unsuccessfully).[64] By discussing this further instance of failure in joint attention, it will become clearer how paralysis can sometimes give rise to invasion in contexts of secondary forms of social interaction. Furthermore, my discussion of these cases will also shed light on the connection between narrative sense-making and complex forms of joint attention and will show how divergences in the construction and negotiation of narratives can open such interactions to invasive, destabilizing forces.

Before analyzing the breakdowns in joint attention and action causing the balloon incident from McEwan's novel, I will provide an overview of contemporary cognitive-scientific and philosophical approaches to these two phenomena characterizing secondary intersubjectivity. If primary intersubjectivity can be described in terms of dyadic, embodied, and affective face-to-face interactions between infants and caregivers, the emergence of secondary intersubjectivity is marked by a shift to triadic forms of interaction: infants become able to focus together with their caregivers on aspects of the external environment and jointly act upon them.

3.3.1 Joint Attention and Joint Action

In a series of articles from late 1970s and early 1980s, developmental psychologist Colwyn Trevarthen and colleagues coined the terms primary and secondary intersubjectivity and discussed them in the context of child development (e.g., Trevarthen and Hubley 1978; Trevarthen 1979, 1980). In their view, the main difference between primary and secondary intersubjectivity can be described in terms of a shift from dyadic to triadic forms of interaction. To put it differently, if initially infants engage with others in a face-to-face, embodied, and affective manner, without being yet capable of understanding the others' directedness toward parts of the world which do not include the infants, with the onset of secondary intersubjectivity, which occurs at around nine months of age, according to Tomasello (1999; a phenomenon he calls a "Copernican revolution" in infant cognition), the *context* in which social interactions take place gains salience.

In this section I will discuss the two main capacities underlying forms of secondary intersubjectivity: the capacity for joint attention and that for joint action and the connections between the two.

Joint Attention

As Gallagher and Zahavi claim, "Expressions, intonations, gestures, and movements, along with the bodies that manifest them, do not float freely in the air; we find them in the world, and infants soon start to notice how others interact with the world." In other words, they learn "to tie actions to pragmatic contexts . . . and enter *contexts* of shared attention—shared situations— in which they learn what things mean and what they are for" (2008: 189; emphasis in original).[65] Pointing and gaze following are the crucial capacities that underlie these new ways of engaging with others (cf. e.g., Desrochers, Morissette, and Ricard 1995; Franco 2005, 2013; Meltzoff and Brooks 2013). The emergence of these abilities is a fundamental prerequisite for language acquisition (cf. Tomasello 1999), for the development of more complex and abstract ways of making sense of others (Böckler and Sebanz 2013: 211; cf. also Reddy 2005), and for helping infants understand the world through their interactions with others (Gallagher 2011a).

One important question that has given rise to much debate in psychology and philosophy concerns what kind of cognitive capacities infants need to possess in order to be able to engage in contexts of joint attention. Psychologists like Tomasello (1995; 2008) or Baron-Cohen (1995), and philosophers like Campbell (2005), for example, conceptualize attention in psychological/mentalistic terms,[66] and describe joint attention as a complex coordination of minds—an ongoing inferential process, dependent upon meta-representational capacities,[67] in which the participants are engaged in what Tomasello calls "recursive mind reading" (2008: 189–90, 198).[68]

To put it differently, if x and y are jointly attending to z, then two conditions must be necessarily satisfied: (1) x is continuously monitoring y to see whether y attends to z, and vice versa; and (2) x is trying to understand whether y understands that x is attending z, and vice versa. This mutual knowledge of each other's mental states is not only much too complex to account for infant cognition,[69] but also, as Gallagher (2011a: 295) argues (regarding especially the second condition), can lead to infinite regress (x infers that y infers that x infers that y infers, etc.)

In contrast with these views,[70] in which joint attention is conceptualized as a coordination of mental/psychological states, Gallagher proposes as an alternative an understanding of joint attention as a deeply embodied type of interaction, based on a coordination of *movements* rather than of thoughts (2011a: 294). Drawing upon Merleau-Ponty's analysis of interaction in the context of a football match, Gallagher argues that in basic instances of joint attention, the participants are neither engaged in conceptual thinking nor do they have to know recursively the directionality of one another's attention. In the (paradigmatic) case of football,[71] he claims, the player's intentions and actions are shaped by the physical environment and by the nature of the game he is playing (299). Furthermore, no inferences are needed to understand the other players' intentions and directionality of attention since they are quite transparent and are specified by the context and rules of the game. Thus, he concludes, joint attention "is perception and context and movement all the way down [and our] understanding of particular others is pragmatic in the sense of a knowing-how rather than knowing-what. It's geared to action and interaction with them" (300).

Gallagher's insistence on the embodied character of secondary forms of intersubjectivity and their non-reliance on more complex ways of interpersonal sense-making is highly significant for my argument. What theory theorists or simulation theorists would claim to be the rule in such cases of social interaction, I will rather claim to be the exception. Conceptual thought and recursive mind reading are far from being the prerequisites for a successful coordination of attention. On the contrary, as I will argue in more detail later, they seem many times to lead to *failure*.

Another important claim Gallagher makes concerns the fact that once a more complex form of intersubjectivity emerges, it does not supersede prior forms. The stages of cognitive development, he argues, are not stages that we go through and eventually leave behind (293). What theory of mind accounts of joint attention leave out, thus, are also discussions of the "traces" of primary forms of intersubjectivity that are "conserved" and have a fundamental role in structuring contexts of joint attention. Most important for my arguments is the fact that the affective/emotional components that characterize dyadic interactions pertaining to primary intersubjectivity play a crucial role also in triadic forms of joint attention. As developmental psychologist Vasudevi Reddy argues, emotions are more closely connected to the understanding of attention than previously thought. Even in the first two months of age, emotional reactions to the attention of others are subtle and varied. Thus, such reactions, arising initially and most powerfully in contexts of mutual attention, can be considered crucial indicators of the infants' basic understanding of attentionality and are probably mediating all their further, more sophisticated, understanding of attention (2005: 106).[72]

In order to explain the intrinsic connection between emotion and attention, Reddy claims that, in fact, a different type of joint attention can also be identified in prior dyadic contexts of *primary* intersubjectivity. *Pace* Tomasello and his Copernican revolution, for Reddy, attention is not something that is "discovered" at nine months of age, but a capacity which emerges gradually. In her article "Before the 'Third Element': Understanding Attention to Self" (2005), she argues that the most primordial form of joint attention is not triadic (infant-caregiver-external object), but rather dyadic, that is, the joint attention of the infant and the caregiver directed toward the infant itself. In Reddy's words, the "self is the first target of others' attention that the infant experiences, and it is from this experience of attention that others' attention to other topics can be understood. Infant responses to, and attempts to direct, attention (to the self, to actions by the self, and to distal targets) demonstrate a clear continuity in, as well as development of, the understanding of attention" (106).

Furthermore, in Trevarthen's view, our attitude toward objects always bears an emotional "coloring," which is in many cases influenced by the emotional attitudes toward such objects of our co-participants in contexts of joint attention. For him, emotions define the direct appreciation of self and other in changing states of being and agency, as well as the appraisal of the liking and disliking of objects that are attended to (2011: 74).

Joint Action

However, the capacity of jointly attending to the world together with others is insufficient for describing secondary forms of intersubjectivity: the ability to *act* jointly is another crucial component, strongly interrelated with joint attention.[73] Although mentalistic approaches which describe attention as an inner, psychological state, would often tend to understand joint action as a separate phenomenon, accounts such as Gallagher's would identify intrinsic connections between attention and action,[74] as it becomes clear from another look at his example of a football match.

Controlling the ball on the field and strategizing on how to get to the goal, Gallagher claims, are not processes occurring solely in the player's head; they are rather laid out across the field from the perspective of the player as he is positioned and as he moves across the grid. In other words, according to Gallagher, the "control of the ball is accomplished in the movement that is elicited by the particular context of here-and-now-on-this-field-as-I-am-running-and-kicking and as these lines on the field are looming and receding in response to my movement" (2011a: 299). Moreover, discussing the nature of the concrete interpersonal interactions on the field, he argues that "the other player is not first someone that I observe as such from a third-person stance in which I measure him up as an adversary. Rather, the other is someone I am already interacting with such that he is facilitating or blocking my goal" (300).

If Gallagher stresses the fact that attention itself should be conceptualized in terms of action, Böckler and Sebanz discuss, even if from their more mentalistic perspective, the ways in which joint attentional processes fundamentally structure joint actions, and help them function more smoothly. Joint attention is a crucial ingredient in joint action, they argue, since it helps establishing a common perceptual ground between co-actors (2013: 209). Since participants in joint actions must be able to, on the one hand, take into account physical constraints and flexibly adjust their actions online, and, on the other hand, predict and keep track of one another's actions and goals, capacities for joint attention allow them to make use of the information that the others' gaze directionality offers about their action goals and opens the possibility of matching one another's perception in order to enhance the chance to detect the same affordances[75] in the environment (208).

In a recent overview of approaches to joint action, John Michael (2011) distinguishes between what he calls classical and minimalist accounts. Classical accounts[76] are highly similar to the "theory of mind" approaches to joint attention Gallagher discusses, in the sense that they explain the coordination of individuals' actions by appealing to shared intentions under conditions of common knowledge, which requires that participants represent complex interrelated structures of intentions, beliefs, desires, and other relevant mental states (Michael 2011: 2). As Michael argues, in a similar vein to Gallagher, such an account "is tailored to complex actions involving rational deliberation and planning [and] requires that each party has the ability to metarepresent the other party's intentions and beliefs, as well as sophisticated concepts such as 'belief' and 'intention'" (3). Due to these heavy cognitive demands placed on the participants, Michael concludes that it would fail to explain joint actions of children or nonhuman animals.[77]

Minimalist accounts,[78] on the other hand, aim to reduce the complexity required by the classical ones, by arguing that joint actions do not require the recursive, mutual knowledge of interconnected structures of intentions, but rather capacities for simpler processes of joint attention, where perception enables co-actors to know that they are engaged in the same task and makes them mutually aware of this (Michael 2011: 5). As Michael claims, such minimalist approaches focus on the online coordination of movements and depend neither upon reasoning or long-term planning, nor upon the understanding and representing of mental concepts such as "belief" or "intention" (5). Instead, participants in joint actions should be able to monitor the *sensory* consequences of one's own and the others' actions, to further predict such consequences, and to maintain an overview of the overall progress toward their shared goals (5–6).

Although he praises minimalist accounts, claiming that they are able to provide explanations for a considerably larger variety of examples of joint actions, Michael criticizes them for not addressing the powerful role shared emotions play in facilitating coordination in joint actions.[79] He defines a shared emotion between two co-actors, x and y, as having to fulfill three minimal criteria: (a) that x expresses his affective state,[80] (b) that y perceives this expression (7), and (c) that y's perception of x's expression leads to effects that function as coordinating factors within the interaction between x and y (8).

Further on, by distinguishing different ways in which the third condition can be fulfilled, he builds a typology of various ways of sharing emotions that can function as coordinating factors in joint actions, which he calls emotion detection, emotion contagion, empathy, and rapport. Y's conscious perception of x's emotion (emotional detection) can facilitate the prediction of x's further actions (9), and the monitoring of x's appraisal of the progress toward the accomplishment of the shared goals. Furthermore, it can also enable emotional expression to serve as a signaling factor, stressing, for example, the presence or absence of dangerous objects or events, or x's approval or disapproval of the way in which y carries his duties in the context of the interaction. Finally, Michael argues that emotion detection can help in establishing or reinforcing a minimal form of commitment[81] between x and y: if y perceives a positive affect in x, he can predict that x will probably accomplish his duties instead of defecting (10). In other words, emotion detection could provide a minimal analogue of explicit promises (11).

Another example he gives is that of emotion contagion, that is, when y's perception of x's affective state causes y to enter into a similar affective state. This phenomenon could happen through unconscious mimicry and cannot be thus subsumed under the previous case of emotion *detection*: in order for y to "catch" x's emotion, he need not be necessarily aware of the latter's affective state. Emotion contagion can facilitate coordination in joint actions since it can increase participants' motivation to act together, it can make it easier to predict each other's actions and synchronize their movements (12), and can increase the likelihood of perceiving the same objects/affordances in the environment (13).

Empathy, which Michael defines (9) as an instance of social interaction in which y's perception of x's emotional expression causes y to enter into an emotional state of the same type *and* to become aware of this state (being thus, in Michael's view, a combination of emotion contagion and detection),[82] would facilitate joint action in similar ways to emotion contagion and detection and, additionally, since it involves perspective-taking, would also increase y's capacity of representing x's tasks and monitoring his behavior (14).

Finally, rapport emerges when y perceives x's positive sentiments toward y and responds by expressing positive sentiments toward x, reinforcing and thus enhancing, in a recursive way, both of their reciprocal positive sentiments, and therefore engendering interpersonal closeness (9; 14–15). Rapport, in Michael's opinion, since it increases behavioral mimicry and movement synchrony, helps in action coordination. Moreover, it can also be understood as a minimal analogue of a reciprocal commitment, lying thus at the roots of more complex forms of commitments, as the ones discussed by Gilbert (14).

By taking into account the fundamental role of affect, Michael's paper does indeed cover a significant gap in the philosophy of joint action. However, a shortcoming of his analysis is that it only addresses the effects of online, transient/"short-lived" emotional states, that emerge during the joint action and soon after fade. As it will become clear later, such an account is insufficient for describing failures in joint action such as that from the balloon incident in *EL*. What needs to be added to Michael's discussion is also an account of emotions emerging from a larger background of affective dispositions, structured by the life histories of the participants. Hans-Bernhard Schmid's philosophical analysis of shared feelings in teamwork from his book *Plural Action: Essays in Philosophy and Social Science* (2009) can help clarify these aspects.

Schmid's brilliant systematic and historical discussion of plural action, drawing not only upon classical and minimalist accounts of joint action, but also upon the work of philosophers and social scientists such as Heidegger, Lazarus, Tarde, or Weber, is much too complex to be summarized here. Before discussing his analyses of shared feelings though, a few introductory remarks regarding his understanding of the terms "team" and "teamwork," are needed. Plural actions, in his view, can be ascribed either to collective agents, as in the case of the Parliament promulgating a law, or to influential individuals, as in the case of Caesar defeating the Helvetii, or to the joint activity of teams, as in the case of friends taking a walk together (xiv). He considers the last case as the most basic and fundamental type of plural agent and argues that the first two cases presuppose it (xv). "Teamwork is *presupposed* in the collective agent view," Schmid claims,

> insofar it is only by virtue of teamwork that there are any collective agents at all; for there to be a collective agent, individuals have to *act jointly* in pursuit of the goal to *create* and *maintain* a collective agent. Also, it seems that most cases of the influence type of plural agency can also be modeled on the teamwork view. If it seems correct to ascribe the Helvetii's defeat in the battle of Bibracte to Cesar, it is no less correct to ascribe this action to *the Romans*, or to those Romans active in the course of the events, acting jointly as a team under Cesar's leadership. Thus it seems that the teamwork view is much more than just one view of plural agency among others. It is the bedrock of plural agency, and should therefore be the main focus of any theory of plural action. (22–23; emphases in original)[83]

Later in his book, Schmid claims that one of the most significant shortcomings of previous discussions of the collective intentionality characterizing teamwork is their focus on shared intentions and shared beliefs (which he also names cognitive and conative types of intentionality) at the expense of what he calls shared feelings or collective affective intentionality. This is understandable, in his opinion, since the philosophy of affect also used to ignore for decades the intentional[84] character of feelings.[85] As he puts it, there is a "rift between an affectivity-free theory of intentionality . . . and an intentionality-free view of the affective" (60).

Although emotions have begun to be understood recently as ways in which, on the one hand, our mind is directed at the world and, on the other hand, the world is given to us, in other words, as *intentional* (60),[86] most paradigms in the philosophy of affect focus almost exclusively on feelings, which are conceptualized as the phenomenal aspects of emotions, that is, (the awareness of) states of bodily arousal *lacking* intentionality. "It is the deep-seated preconception that *feelings are not intentional*—a view that feeling theorists and their cognitivist opponents have held alike," Schmid argues, "which prevents us from seeing how emotions 'disclose' the world. By playing the intentionality of emotions off against feelings, the cognitivists drive a wedge between the intentionality of emotions on the one hand, and the phenomenology of the other, relegating to the feelings the role of mere contingent *accompaniments* of emotions" (63; emphasis in original).

However, certain contemporary theorists belonging to what Schmid calls the "phenomenological turn in the philosophy of emotion" (64) struggle to overcome the emotion/feeling dichotomy and consider feelings as core components of emotion, possessing intentionality (63). This is an important development, Schmid claims, since if affective intentionality is a matter of feelings rather than just of the beliefs and desires on which philosophers of affect discussing the intentionality of emotion tend to focus upon, the question of how affective intentionality can be collective cannot simply be answered by pointing toward received accounts of shared beliefs and joint intentions. It rather needs to be complemented with an account of how feelings can be shared (64).

In order to provide such an account, Schmid discusses the intentionality of feelings in terms of their mode, content, and subject. The mode of a feeling, he claims, defines the feeling as the kind of feeling it is, helping in differentiating thus between various types of feelings such as, for instance, fear and anger. Regarding the content, he distinguishes between the target and the focus of a feeling. Whereas the target is the object toward which the feeling is directed, the focus is "the object in the background of the feeling which is related to the target in such a way as to *make intelligible*, or *rationalize*, the *mode* of the feeling" (64; emphases in original).[87]

However, Schmid argues, the most important thing regarding the intentionality of feelings should be described in terms of the subject experiencing them: in order for a target-focus relation to rationalize the mode of a feeling, the subject must have some *concern* that serves to make the relation between focus and target relevant to the subject. Therefore, feelings can be considered as indicators of what matters to us.[88] Our concerns, Schmid stresses, are not simple inclinations, because they involve patterns of emotional dispositions that structure our lives and, ultimately, determine who we are: they structure our selfhood and identity.

Furthermore, he claims that there is a basic way in which our concerns, and thus our identities, are indicated by our feelings: "Feelings are the light in which we see ourselves. To experience a feeling is to conceive of ourselves in terms of the underlying concern. Our identities as a friend, as a professional, as a lover of art are settled by affective attitudes." Following this analysis, Schmid distinguishes between the ontic subject, the person who has the feeling, and thus answers the "who has it" question, and the phenomenal subject, who is determined by the way in which the subject conceives of himself or herself *in* the feeling, and therefore answers the question *as who* the ontic subject has the feeling he or she has (65).

After laying out these distinctions, Schmid proceeds to answer the crucial question of what does it mean for a feeling to be *shared*. Regarding the mode, he claims that experiencing a feeling of the same kind is not a sufficient condition to consider the feeling to be shared. Something crucial must be added—the fact that a person's being in an affective state of a certain mode cannot be independent of the other person's being in the same state. He continues by discussing three ways in which affective states in the same mode can be interconnected: affective contagion;[89] affective attunement, that is, the conscious regulation of feelings between individuals; and affective agreement, that is, the normativization through habituation of affective attunements, or, as he puts it, a generally shared idea about the level of affective attunement expected to be reached in certain situations.

Pace Michael, Schmid claims that affective contagion per se does not mean that there is anything genuinely shared about the affective states in question.[90] And although he sees the existence of affective attunement and agreement as important conditions for a feeling to be shared in *some* cases, he nevertheless stresses the fact that they are *not* necessary and sufficient conditions. For example, if the content of a feeling is not shared, affective attunement cannot turn individual feelings into shared ones, and, thus, the existence of affective attunement cannot be seen as a sufficient condition for the emergence of a collective affective state (66).

But is it the case then that if both the mode and the content (including both focus and target) of a feeling are the same, the feeling is shared? Surprisingly, Schmid answers negatively and discusses a scene from Homer's *Iliad* where grief *is* a shared feeling between Achilles and Priam, although the content of their grief, in terms of both focus and target, is different (whereas Achilles grieves for his father, Priam grieves for Hector).[91] What makes the grief these characters feel *shared* is, for Schmid, the shared concern behind the target-focus relation. "Priam's grief for his son," he writes,

> combines with Achilles' grief for his father's abandonment so as to move Achilles to an act of goodwill towards Priam *because Achilles recognizes his own concern with Pelleas' being deprived of Achilles in Priam's grief for the loss of Hector.* In order to do so, however, Achilles has to move from Pelleas to fathers *in general.* This involves reconceiving himself *as a son* rather than as Achilles, and that means a shift in the phenomenal subject of his affective attitude. (68; emphases in original)

To conclude, Schmid considers the sharing of concerns much more important and fundamental for feelings to be truly shared and, consequently, for teams to function smoothly, than for feelings to have the same mode and content: "Sharing a concern leads [people] to *identify* with each other, or with the group, by conceiving of themselves, as part of the feeling, in terms of a collective identity" (68; emphasis in original). In the following section I will return to McEwan's novel and analyze the breakdown in joint action causing the balloon incident from the beginning of *EL.* As I will argue, this breakdown can be fruitfully described by employing the concepts of paralysis and invasion.

3.3.2 There May Have Been a Vague Commonality of Purpose, but They Were Never a Team: A Breakdown in Joint Action

In this section I will discuss the tragic failure in embodied cooperative activity staged in the first chapter of *EL,* that is, the balloon incident in which Joe's and Jed's lives become entangled and in which John Logan, "husband, father, doctor and mountain rescue worker" loses his life, perhaps due to the fact that "the flame of altruism must have burned a little stronger" in him, as Joe puts it (*EL:* 15). Whereas in the previous section I discussed the ways in which Joe's paralysis is structured by his projection of scientific frameworks upon the world in order to make sense of what happened, here I will take a more panoramic perspective, thus focusing not on Joe's interpretation of the scene,[92] but rather on the intersubjective dynamics that emerge from "the convergence of six figures in a flat green space," (2) "running towards a catastrophe, which itself was a kind of furnace in whose heat identities and fates would buckle into new shapes" (3).

The breakdown in joint action that will soon occur, as well as further failures in joint attention and action between Joe and Clarissa and Joe and Jed, is prefigured in the first paragraph of the novel, where a mixture of primary and secondary intersubjectivity disintegrates due to "a man's shout" (1). "I was kneeling on the grass with a corkscrew," Joe recounts,

> and Clarissa was passing me the bottle—a 1987 Damas Gassac. This was the moment, this was the pinprick on the time map: I was stretching out my hand, and as the cool neck and the black foil touched my palm, *we* heard a man's shout. *We* turned to look across the field and saw the danger. Next thing, *I* was running towards it. The *transformation* was absolute: I don't recall dropping the corkscrew, or getting to my feet, or making a decision, or hearing the caution Clarissa called after me. (1; my emphases)

As we will find out a few pages later, this instance of secondary intersubjectivity between Joe and Clarissa is highly charged emotionally: they are enjoying a romantic picnic together "by a track that ran through beech woods in the Chiltren Hills [and are] still elated by [their] reunion" after being apart for six weeks. Initially, Joe's attention is entirely focused on Clarissa (and there is no reason to doubt that her attention is focused on him as well): "We set down our path arm in arm . . . ; what was familiar about her—the size and feel of her hand, the warmth and tranquility in her voice, the Celt's pale skin and green eyes—was also novel, gleaming in an alien light, reminding me of our very first meetings and the months we spent falling in love."

This intense, embodied, and affective encounter, a paradigmatic case of primary intersubjectivity, turns, due to the beauty of the scenery, into a similarly emotionally charged instance of secondary intersubjectivity—their joint action of walking together through the woods and jointly attending to their surroundings: "We went through College Wood towards Pishill, stopping to admire the new greenery on the beeches. Each leaf seemed to glow with an internal light. We talked about the purity of this colour, the beech leaf in spring, and how looking at it cleared the mind" (5). And even if later on, their attention focuses on more mundane things, such as the wine and food they are about to share, they still remain interlocked in a self-sufficient form of interaction, oblivious to everything besides the small, Edenic context in which their encounter takes place.[93]

Harry Gadd's desperate shout, though, brutally breaches their shared engagement, destroying it completely in a matter of seconds. Although, initially, their attention remains shared ("*we* heard a man's shout," "*we* turned to look"), a quick "transformation" occurs: the "we" suddenly shifts into an "I": "Next thing, *I* was running towards it." The complete breakdown of both the primary and secondary forms of intersubjectivity between the two lovers—the sudden shift from an implicit 2PP to no 2PP at all—is foregrounded by Joe's confession of his complete oblivion of Clarissa and her warnings: "I don't recall . . . hearing the caution Clarissa called after me" (1).

This first paragraph thus stages a very concrete example of the inherent fragility of primary and secondary forms of intersubjectivity: external, contextual forces (the shout) "pierce through" and destroy an up-to-then self-contained and smoothly functioning social encounter. But if the intrusive contextual forces in this example are purely physical/material (the sound of Gadd's voice), in the case of invasion I will discuss next, they are more subtle and complex.[94]

In the second half of the first paragraph, Joe describes the crystallization of another context of secondary intersubjectivity which, at the first sight, seems very similar to Merleau-Ponty's and Gallagher's phenomenological descriptions of football: "There was the shout again, and a child's cry, enfeebled by the wind that roared in the tall trees along the hedgerows. I ran faster. And there, suddenly, from different points around the field, four other men were converging on the scene, running like me" (1).

The similarities with Merleau-Ponty's and Gallagher's accounts emerge not only from Joe's description of their movement while approaching the balloon in terms such as planes, directions of forces, or angles of collision and return (2–3), taken from mathematics and physics,[95] but also from the foregrounding of the embodiment and contextuality of their shared attention (that is, their collective focus on the balloon), and its close connection to movement and action, both before and after reaching the balloon:

> The pilot had the rope in his hands and was lifted two feet clear of the ground. If Logan had not reached him and taken hold of one of the many dangling lines the balloon would have carried the boy away. Instead, both men were now being pulled across the field, and the farm workers and I were running again. I got there before them. When I took a rope the basket was above head height. . . . Jed Parry was on a rope seconds after me, and the two farm workers, Joseph Lacey and Toby Greene, caught hold just after him. (10)

The first aspect of this scene that differentiates it from the football example, though, is the combination of activity *and* passivity that characterizes it. Active verbs highlighting the men's goal-directed movements (running, reaching, taking, holding) are juxtaposed with passive verbs (being lifted, pulled, carried). The joint actions this impromptu, would-be team aims to engage in are continuously thwarted by insensate yet threatening natural forces: "The wind renewed its rage in the treetops before I felt its force on my back. Then it struck the balloon [which] broke free. . . . A mighty fist socked the balloon in two rapid blows, one-two, the second more vicious than the first. . . . It jerked Gadd right out of the basket on to the ground, and it lifted the balloon five feet or so, straight into the air" (9–13). Of course, one could argue that, in the case of football, players can be *acted upon* by the members of the opposite team. But if, in football, the goal-directed movements of the players from *both* teams follow pre-established rules, here, the rules need to be "created" on the spot and continuously change according to the "demands" of the natural environment these actions are embedded in.

Yet, from all this unruly chaos, once all five men take hold of the ropes, a simple general rule nevertheless seems to emerge, as Joe himself acknowledges: "With five of us on the lines the balloon was secured. We *simply* had to keep steady on our feet and pull hand over hand to bring the basket down, and this, despite what the pilot was shouting, was what we began to do" (10; my emphasis). As can be clearly noticed, this rule implies nothing more than an embodied form of coordination ("keep steady on our feet and pull hard"), ideally unencumbered by more abstract (e.g., linguistically mediated) ways of interaction.

However, Joe insists that he "should make something clear. There may have been a commonality of purpose," he claims, "but we were never a team. There was no chance, no time" (10). Such remarks recur throughout the first chapter. Earlier on, he speaks about "their fatal lack of co-operation" (2) and a bit later, he stresses the fact that "there was no team, there was no plan, no agreement to be broken" (14). But why would this be the case? Why is this utter failure of a team to emerge followed by such disastrous consequences? Here is Joe's explanation, once more colored by language taken from evolutionary psychology:

No one was in charge—or everyone was, and we were in a shouting match. The pilot, red-faced, bawling and sweating, we ignored. Incompetence came off him like heat. I know that if I had been uncontested leader the tragedy would not have happened. Later I heard some of the others say the same thing about themselves. But there was not time, no opportunity for force of character to show. Any leader, any firm plan would have been preferable to none. No human society, from the hunter-gatherer to the post-industrial, has come to the attention of anthropologists that did not have its leaders and the led; and no emergency was ever dealt with effectively by democratic process. (11)

It is obvious here that Joe understands teamwork in terms of what Schmid called the "influence model." In Joe's opinion, a team cannot function without a powerful leader to decide the types of collective actions needed to accomplish a shared goal and to provide guidance for their execution. However, as Schmid argues, the influence model is *not* the most primordial way of understanding teamwork, but rather presupposes and emerges from more fundamental kinds of interactions. Therefore, Joe's explanation of their failure in terms of the impossibility of a leader emerging and taking control of the situation appears to be neither necessary nor sufficient. In what follows, I will identify and discuss what I believe to be more fundamental problems in teamwork haunting this interaction than the one Joe describes.

Immediately after all five men take hold of the ropes, and the simple rule that none of them should let go seems to be tacitly established, silence is suddenly broken by a polyphony of voices. "We were all talking at once," Joe recounts. "Two of us, myself and the motorist, wanted to walk the balloon away from the edge. Someone thought the priority was to get the boy out. Someone else was calling for the balloon to be pulled down so that we could anchor it firmly. . . . The pilot had a fourth idea, but no one knew or cared what it was" (10). What should ideally be a nonlinguistic form of embodied coordination, anchored in affective attunement, agreement, and shared concerns, is forcefully invaded and de-structured by forms of intersubjectivity structured by language.

There are similarities here with the linguistic excess destabilizing sexuality in both *H* and *OCB*. What is different though is the fact that, in this chapter, language is not a background force as in the previous cases, slowly yet insidiously working its way into concrete, face-to-face interactions and de-structuring them, but rather explodes suddenly within the collective action of holding the balloon down, making the emergence of a nonlinguistic embodied coordination impossible.

Furthermore, this scene appears to reinforce Schmid's insight (against Michael's arguments) that emotion contagion is insufficient for collective affective intentionality to emerge. Indeed, emotions such as fear, and perhaps even anger, seem to quickly "travel" within this group: the "shouting and swearing" (11) or the "adrenally incensed heartbeat[s]" (14) characterizing these "breathless, excited" (13) men are clear indicators of the highly charged affective contagion the interaction is steeped in. And yet, none of this helps their "team" to endure: "hanging there below the basket, we were a bad society, we were disintegrating," Joe laments (15).

Soon after one of the five men lets go of the ropes, enacting what Joe-the-scientist calls "our mammalian conflict—what to give to others and what to keep for yourself [that is,] morality's ancient, irresolvable dilemma: us, or me" (14–15), everyone besides Logan lets go too, saving their lives, and, at the same time, condemning Logan to a painful death. "I didn't know, nor have I ever discovered, who let go first. I'm not prepared to accept that it was me," Joe apologetically explains. "But everyone claims not to have been first." "What is certain," he continues, "is that if we had not broken ranks, our collective weight would have brought the balloon to earth a quarter of the way down the slope a few seconds later as the gust subsided."

But although who was the first to let go remains an unresolved mystery, what is clear is who *didn't* let go: "John Logan, husband, *father*" (14; my emphasis). Their group brutally splits into two: on the one hand, Logan, on the other hand, all the rest. Joe's reason for defecting and, implicitly, Logan's reason not to defect emerge quite clearly from the former's reflections: "The child was not my child, and I was not going to die for it" (15). However, the child neither was Logan's. Nevertheless, out of all the five men, Logan was the only one having children of his own. Therefore, following Schmid's terminology, I would argue that the main reason for the breakdown in joint action staged in this chapter is the impossibility of emergence of a *shared concern* (based on a common experiential-affective background, or in Schmid's words, a social identity) among the members of the group. To paraphrase Schmid, Logan is the only one able to make the crucial move from the child in the balloon to children *in general*, and from himself as the father of *his* child to fathers in general, and thus to identify and empathize with this particular child's plight. And this, in my view, is the main reason why, as Joe puts it, in Logan "the flame of altruism must have burned a bit longer" (15).

Such an interpretation appears to be confirmed by Clarissa later, when together with Joe she "obsessively re-examines" the events: "He was a good man ... The boy was in the basket, and Logan wouldn't let go. He had children of his own. He was a good man" (*EL*: 31). In the wake of her "pleading" (31) words, Joe himself seems to come close to this insight: "The boy was not his own, but he was a father and he understood" (32).

Thus, my hypothesis is that the invasion causing the breakdown of what should have remained, as Joe himself admits, a *simple* coordination of movements and affects, an instance of plural action pertaining to secondary intersubjectivity, can be described in the following terms: the implicit 2PP needed for the successful carrying out of the action is burdened by the emergence of a surplus of explicit 1PP, that is, by an intense self-scrutiny of all the members of the "team" regarding their status and duties in the context of the interaction they are part of. Since the child in the balloon was not theirs, and since none of them besides Logan had children of their own, why risk their lives? The lack of a shared concern causes an eruption of explicit 1PP, brutally invading and tragically corrupting their attempted teamwork.

However, further instances of paralysis and invasion also characterize Joe's and Clarissa's attempts to make sense of the incident. In this case, McEwan stages the breakdown of a more complex form of joint attention: instead of focusing on an event or object from the present, the two characters turn their attention on a *narrative* dealing with *past* events. In order to understand the development, structure, and functions of such instances of joint attention, I will initially provide an overview of the passage between secondary and tertiary intersubjectivity, by focusing on (1) how embodied and affective forms of joint attention and action play a fundamental role in the emergence of language, (2) how linguistic abilities further structure the development of narrative sense-making, and (3) how narrative competency allows us to attend together to past events in contexts of joint reminiscing.

3.3.3 The Emergence of Language in Contexts of Joint Attention

As Gallagher and Zahavi claim, the acknowledgment of the capacities for understanding others that define primary and secondary intersubjectivity is not yet sufficient to address new developments occurring around the ages of two, three, or four years. The "elephant in the room" around the age of two years is language (2008: 192–93).[96] Although, as I already argued, Tomasello's mentalistic approach to joint attention can be criticized in certain important aspects, his discussion of the emergence and development of language out of previous capacities for joint attention (1999) is, in my opinion, compelling and worthwhile to summarize here.

In his view, infants begin to engage in joint attention the moment they begin to understand the others' behavior as intentional, that is, as having goals and as making active choices from a behavioral repertoire regarding what to pay attention to in order to accomplish these goals (68). Around nine months of age, children start to be able to understand both *on what* the adult's attention is focused and *why* the attention is focused in that direction and they are able to follow the adult's gaze or finger pointing (69). The most important effect of these newly acquired capacities is that they "open the child to the uniquely human forms of cultural inheritance" (78).

As I have already stressed, the environment in which human beings develop cannot be understood as just a physical one. An adequate understanding of the world in which humans are embedded *must* take culture into account. Human infants are not born and do not grow in forests. On the contrary, the environment that they inhabit from the very start is deeply cultural. Our world, as Tomasello writes, is "populated by material and symbolic artifacts and social practices that members of [our] culture, both past and present, have created for the use of others" (91). And in order for children to start to understand the affordances such an environment offers, they need the guidance of adults. In other words, they need to embark upon a long and arduous process of cultural learning (80).

The capacity for joint attention opens for children the possibility to learn how to use various tools and artifacts from their surroundings. Observing the adults manipulate various objects from the environment, and imitating their behavior, children slowly learn for themselves what affordances these objects offer (81–82). Concomitantly, they begin to learn a first, pre-linguistic, form of communication with adults: gestural communication. In an imitative manner, for example, they learn to point at objects in the environment in order to draw the attention of the adults at the aspects of the world the children are attentive to (87–89).

Around the same time, according to Tomasello, another important development occurs. Although in many contexts of joint attention, the child and the adult focus together on outside entities from the world, it sometimes happens that the other person whose attention is monitored by the child focuses his or her attention on the child him/herself. Because of this, children learn to monitor also the adults' (emotional/intentional) attitudes toward them. Consequently, they become able to view themselves from an outside, external perspective, thus, as participants who can assume various roles, which they can interchange with adults, in joint attentional scenes (89–90).[97]

The understanding of gestures as communicative signals in contexts of shared attention, as well as the child's ability to view the joint attentional scene, together with his/her and the adults' roles in it, from an external perspective, are the next crucial steps toward language acquisition. First, understanding *communicative* intentions, a feature that is crucial in linguistic use, requires more than simply understanding *intentions*. As discussed earlier, at a first level, the child learns to understand the adults' intentions toward objects from the environment, that is, the child understands that the adult reaches toward a cup from the table in order to lift it. Only later, though, can the child understand that the adult's intention was not only to lift the cup, but also to direct the child's attention to the action of lifting the cup. In order for such an understanding to be possible, the child has to be able to monitor not only the adult's directedness toward objects in the environment, but also the adult's directedness toward the child him/herself. Only when the child can understand this *double* directedness of the adult's attention (toward the world and toward the child), we can claim that the child is able to understand *communicative* intentions (100–03).

But this is still not enough for the capacity of linguistic acquisition to emerge. A capacity for role-reversal imitation is also a crucial prerequisite.

It is not sufficient that the child understands the adult's communicative intention when the latter is using a linguistic symbol in order to direct the child's attention to a (now named) object from the environment. The child must also learn how to use the symbol toward the adult just as the adult used it toward the child (105). And this is only possible if the child manages to gain an external perspective on the joint attentional scene, and therefore to understand his/her role in this scene as interchangeable with that of the adult. Only at this stage, can a truly linguistic symbol—"a communicative device understood intersubjectively from both sides of the interaction" (106)—emerge.

To sum up, linguistic acquisition requires children to have the following capacities: an understanding of other people as intentional agents; an ability to participate in joint attentional scenes which set the social-cognitive grounds for acts of linguistic communication; an understanding not only of intentions, but of *communicative* intentions, that is, an understanding of the other's intention that the child attends to certain aspects from the environment; and an ability to reverse roles with adults in the learning process, that is, an ability to use toward the adult the (same) linguistic symbols used by the adult toward the child (107).

3.3.4 Narrative Sense-Making

Nevertheless, as Gallagher and Zahavi argue, if language development is something that depends on the capacities underlying primary and secondary intersubjectivity, language also has the fundamental role of carrying these capacities forward and of putting them into service in much more sophisticated social contexts (2008: 193). However, instead of using language as a prop for detached theorizing or internal simulations, as theory of mind scholars of both TT and ST persuasions would argue, more primordial ways in which this new cognitive instrument can be employed in order to make sense of puzzling actions which are not directly comprehensible through their expressive, bodily manifestations, are to either employ conversational skills and ask the others for explanations or to construct narratives to explain their reasons for actions (193; cf. also Bruner 1990; Nelson 2003, 2007; Hutto 2007, 2008; Gallagher and Hutto 2008; Gallagher 2011b).

Gallagher and Hutto, following Lamarque (2004), provide a neutral, minimal definition of narrative as a structure containing at least two interconnected events and having a temporal dimension. They further identify a subset of narratives they call "folk psychological narratives" and which they claim to be about agents who act for reasons. In their opinion, narratives of this kind can play a special role in development by being the objects of joint attention in early learning (2008: 30).

Children's capacity to understand narratives emerges around two years of age (cf. Nelson 2003) and becomes a crucial aid in the development of folk psychology, that is, (simplistically put) an ability to understand actions in terms of the *reasons* behind them (*why* someone acted the way he/she did; cf. Hutto 2007: 45).[98] In his "Narrative Practice Hypothesis," Hutto argues that narrative competency develops due to the fact that caregivers expose children continuously to a variety of stories about agents acting for reasons (2007: 53), where the "principles" of folk psychology

> are revealed to children not as a series of rules but by showing them in action, in their normal context of operation. In this way, narratives not only show which features are constant to folk psychological explanation but also, importantly, what can vary in such accounts—such as the particulars of what a person believes and desires, how these attitudes can change over time and why, and also how character, history, and other commitments might impinge on why a person acts as they do. (56; cf. also Hutto 2008: 23–40; Gallagher and Hutto 2008: 28–32)

The concreteness of these stories that Hutto identifies and discusses, that is, their ability to show reasons in the context of their operation instead of as a series of behavioral rules, is shown by Gallagher and Zahavi also to underlie the "application" of the acquired narrative competency in making sense of others in real life. "I encounter the other person," they claim, "not abstracted from their circumstances, but in the middle of something that has a beginning and is going somewhere. I see them in the framework of a story in which either I have a part to play or I don't. The narrative is not primarily about what is 'going on inside their heads'; it's about what is going on in our shared world and about how they understand and respond to it" (2008: 193). Furthermore, these narratives also shape our evaluative judgments about these people's actions (194).

What Gallagher and Hutto stress, though, following Bruner (1990), is that the employment of folk-psychological narratives in order to explain behavior is the exception rather than the rule in social interaction. Since most everyday social interaction takes place in normal/normalized environments, well-rehearsed patterns of behavior and coordination are sufficient for making sense of others' actions. Folk-psychological narratives come into play when culturally based expectations are violated, Gallagher and Hutto argue, paraphrasing Bruner,[99] that is, in those cases when the others' actions deviate from what is normally expected in such a way that it becomes difficult to understand them (2008: 30).

3.3.5 Joint Reminiscing

After having discussed the emergence of language in ontogeny out of contexts of joint attention, as well as the development of narrative competency, I will now return to joint attention, this time in its more complex, narratively structured forms and, following Hoerl and McCormack (2005), I will discuss joint reminiscing (or memory sharing) in terms of joint attention to the past.

Hoerl and McCormack admit from the very beginning of their article that most of the philosophical and scientific analyses of joint attention focus primarily on the phenomenon of children and adults jointly attending to physical objects in the visual field. And although they claim that there is an obvious parallel between more basic forms of joint attention and joint reminiscing, in the sense that when two persons are engaged in sharing memories of an event they have experienced together, that past event becomes the focus of their joint attention, in a similar way in which an object in their current environment could become the focus of their joint attention through their looking at that object together, they also identify a crucial difference—the fact that joint reminiscing necessarily involves the use of a shared language (2005: 260). In other words, whereas, as Tomasello argued, language emerges out of basic, embodied joint attentional contexts, joint reminiscing *presupposes* the existence of rather highly developed linguistic capacities in order to function.

Hoerl and McCormack, however, make an even more radical claim. In their view, it is not only the case that joint reminiscing presupposes a quite sophisticated command of language, but also that "the very ability to make the past a possible focus of one's attention . . . only emerges in the context of learning how to participate in linguistic interactions that involve the sharing of such attention to the past with others" (261–62). To put it differently, their claim is that memory itself, particularly what they call "episodic memory,"[100] develops out of contexts of joint reminiscing. Thus, social interaction seems to be a fundamental prerequisite for the development of memory in general (cf. also Nelson 2007).

One crucial cognitive capacity that enables us to turn our attention to the past in episodic recall is, according to Hoerl and McCormack, causal understanding. As they put it, in order to substantiate the distinction between the past and the present, children need to understand that how things are in the present depends not only on what happened at one point in the past, but also on what happened subsequently, thus, to grasp "the way in which causality unfolds over time."[101] In their view, the development of children's understanding of causality depends crucially on their social interactions, in particular, on their joint reminiscing of past events in the company of adults. Children, they argue, first grasp how causality functions during conversations in which an adult is trying to exert some rational influence on the child by reminding him/her of particular events from the past. Thus, children acquire causal understanding "in the context of learning how to participate in a particular kind of rational engagement with others that turns on the sharing of episodic memories" (262).[102]

Finally, following Nelson (1996), Hoerl and McCormack identify and discuss another specific set of linguistic skills necessary for learning to engage in joint reminiscing (278) and having a crucial role to play in making genuine episodic memory possible in the first place (280): narrative abilities. The importance they give to narrative competency emerges not only from the (obvious) fact that the abovementioned conversations in contexts of joint reminiscing are structured by narratives. Since narratives embody an understanding of how the overall outcome of a sequence of events depends on the temporal order in which they happened, that is, how later events from the sequence might have changed or even obliterated the effects of earlier events (279), they can be understood as "vehicles for the particular kind of causal understanding" (280) a fully developed mnemonic capacity requires.

Another important aspect they stress is the potential function of narratively structured contexts of joint reminiscing not only in helping children develop their memory through the fine-tuning of their abilities to understand causality, but also in helping them arrive at a shared appreciation of how certain attitudes are, or are no longer, rationally appropriate. In other words, narratives of the past are not just the vehicle of a certain form of causal understanding, but also the vehicle of a certain form of "normative understanding," and they can thus "serve as a means of resolving differences between two people's perspectives," and help them arrive to "a shared personal and emotional evaluation of the past" (282).

In the following section, I will return to McEwan's novel and discuss the breakdowns in narrative sense-making and joint reminiscing characterizing Joe's and Clarissa's attempts to build a coherent story of the tragic incident they witnessed. As it will become clear, their paralytic ways of dealing with reality caused by their monomaniac worldviews play a crucial role in giving rise to invasive processes destabilizing their attempts of narrative sense-making and joint reminiscing.

3.3.6 The Obsessive Reexamination That Followed: Breakdowns in Narrative Sense-Making and Joint Reminiscing

Most of the scholars reflecting on *EL* acknowledge and discuss in great detail the importance of narrative sense-making both at the thematic and formal level.[103] Although their approaches are different, all of them agree that *EL* is a strongly metafictional novel, that is, it is a narrative about (the making of) narratives.[104] As Greenberg notices, the "entire novel is saturated with references to story and narrative" (2007: 110; cf. also Randall 2007: 56), and is thus foregrounding its own narrative structures (Greenberg 2007: 95).

This aspect is evident in the first chapters of the novel, with the recurrent employment of words such as "story," "chapter," "beginning," "events," or "end." "The beginning is simple to mark," reads the first sentence (1). Later, Joe describes Gadd's shout in the following terms: "It was a baritone, on a rising note of fear. It marked the beginning and, of course, an end. At that moment a chapter, no, a whole stage of my life closed" (8). "What idiocy," Joe complains, "to be racing into this story and its labyrinths, sprinting away from our happiness among the fresh spring grasses by the oak" (1). Similar expressions also accompany his reflections upon the balloon incident: "The struggle with the ropes, the breaking of ranks and the bearing away of Logan—these were the obvious, large-scale events that shaped our story" (18).

The immediately following sentences, though, foreground a crucial aspect of the novel, already identified by various critics (e.g., Edwards 2007: 85; Greenberg 2007: 110; Randall 2007: 57–58), that is, its incessant reflection upon the contingency, incompleteness, ambiguity, and, ultimately, artificiality and unreliability of the process of trying to make sense of reality in narrative terms: "But I see now that in the moments immediately after his fall there were subtler elements exerting a powerful sway over the future. The moment Logan hit the ground should have been the end of this story rather than one more beginning I could have chosen. The afternoon could have ended in mere tragedy" (18). And although Joe claims that he "already marked [his] beginning, the explosion of consequences, with the touch of a wine bottle and a shout of distress," he nevertheless admits that "this pinprick is as notional as a point in Euclidean geometry, and though it seems right, I could have proposed the moment Clarissa and I planned to picnic after I had collected her from the airport, or when we decided on our route, or the field in which to have our lunch, and the time we chose to have it" (17). The conclusion seems inescapable: "There are always antecedent causes. A beginning is an artifice, and what recommends one over another is how much sense it makes of what follows" (17–18).

EL's strongly metafictional character is also foregrounded in Joe's explicit discussion of the use of narratives in science and literature in the nineteenth and twentieth centuries. Struggling to write an article about the role of narratives in science (which he describes as "a narrative in itself, a little tired perhaps, but it had served a thousand journalists before me"), Joe argues that "storytelling was deep in the nineteenth-century soul," and since the "dominant artistic form was the novel, great sprawling narratives which not only charted private fates, but made whole societies in mirror image and addressed the public issues of the day" (48), it is no wonder that science itself used narrative devices (cf. also e.g., Beer 1983 who discusses (among other issues) the narrative structure of Darwin's *The Origin of Species*). During the twentieth century, Joe claims, "science became more difficult, and it became professionalized. It moved into the universities, parsonical narratives gave way to hard-edged theories that could survive intact without experimental support and which had their own formal aesthetic. At the same time, in literature and in other arts, a newfangled modernism celebrated formal, structural qualities, inner coherence and self-reference" (48–49).

Although he initially concludes his article full of confidence by claiming that "the meanderings of narrative had given way to an aesthetics of form, as in art, so in science," soon after, doubts regarding the veracity of his theory start to creep in: "Counter arguments welled from between the neat lines of text. What possible evidence could I produce to suggest that the novels of Dickens, Scott, Trollope, Thackeray etc. had ever influenced by a comma the presentation of a scientific idea? Moreover, my examples were fabulously skewed. I had compared life sciences in the nineteenth century . . . to hard sciences in the twentieth. In the annals of Victorian physics and chemistry alone there was no end of brilliant theory that displayed not a shred of narrative inclination. And what in fact were the typical products of the twentieth-century scientific or pseudo-scientific mind? Anthropology, psychoanalysis—fabulation run riot. Using the highest methods of storytelling and all the arts of priesthood, Freud had staked his claim on the veracity, though not the falsifiability of science. And what of those behaviorists and sociologists of the nineteen twenties? It was as though an army of white-coated Balzacs had stormed the university departments and labs. . . . What I had written wasn't true. It wasn't written in pursuit of truth, it wasn't science" (50). Joe's reflections point toward not only the deep interrelation between narrative and science but also the ultimate unreliability of *both* narratives and science in making sense of reality. Furthermore, his obsession with producing a *scientific* account of the role of narratives in science is further proof of his paralysis.[105]

Regardless of the unreliability of narratives, Joe still struggles to justify his choice of a particular beginning for his story. His explanation comes very close to Bruner's analysis of the ways in which narrative sense-making emerges out of our need to deal with the unexpected and the noncanonical: "The cool touch of glass on skin and James Gadd's cry—these synchronous moments fix a transition, a divergence from the expected: from the wine we didn't taste (we drank it that night to numb ourselves) to the summons, from the delightful existence we shared and expected to continue, to the ordeal we were to endure in the time ahead" (18).

As I will further argue, Joe's description of Gadd's shout as a "divergence from the expected" can also be employed to describe the balloon incident as a whole. The exceptionality of this event, and its power to brutally destabilize the characters' previously tranquil existences, forces them to try to make sense of it in narrative terms. Therefore, in what follows I will take a closer look at chapter three of the novel, where, in the night after the incident, Joe and Clarissa "obsessively re-examine" it, in an intense context of joint reminiscing, trying to make sense, and therefore, gain some control, of this event which borders on incomprehensibility.[106] Here is how Joe describes the beginning of this arduous process of shared remembering:

> We hadn't said much in the car. It had seemed enough to be coming through the traffic unharmed. Now it came out in a torrent, a post-mortem, a re-living, a de-briefing, the rehearsal of grief, and the exorcism of terror. There was so much repetition that evening of the incidents, and of our perceptions, and of the very phrases and words we honed to accommodate them that one could only assume that an element of ritual was in play, that these were not only descriptions but incantations also. There was comfort in reiteration. (28)

The event which they obsessively reiterate, "back[ing] away from [it] again and again, circling it, stalking it, until they [have] it cornered and began to tame it with words" is, of course, Logan's death. The incomprehensibility of this horrific event, and of their role in it, makes it, on the one hand, an inescapable attraction and focus in the context of their joint reminiscing, but on the other hand, also something to be feared and avoided. A dialectics of attraction and repulsion characterizes their joint remembering of this episode: "We were back with the fall again, and how long it had taken him to reach the ground, two seconds or three. Immediately we backed off into the peripheries, the police, the ambulance men . . . and the garage break-down truck that had towed away Logan's car."

However, the "peripheries" in the remembrance of which they seek shelter from the horror of the fall deviously, yet unavoidably, lead them back again to the central point of their obsessions. Their reflection on Logan's car, for example, makes them "imagine . . . the delivery of this empty car to the home in Oxford where Mrs. Logan waited with her two children." But, as Joe acknowledges, "this was unbearable too, so [they] returned to [their] own stories" (29).

Their manic "movements" of approaching and retreating from Logan's death, and the consequent resistance of this event to being "tamed into" a coherent narrative, are powerfully expressed by Joe through a metaphorical mapping which juxtaposes their attempts at story-making and storytelling to running around chaotically inside a prison cell: "Along the narrative lines there were knots, tangles of horror that we could not look at first time, but could only touch before retreating, and then return. We were prisoners in a cell, running at the walls, beating them back with our heads" (29–30).

Surprisingly, one digression that makes their "prison [grow] larger" and helps them feel "on safer ground" is Joe's shift of attention to his meeting with Jed Parry and his recounting of this event to Clarissa. "I told the prayer story as comedy," Joe confesses, "and made Clarissa laugh. She locked her fingers into mine and squeezed" (30). Here, we see a primary form of intersubjectivity infiltrating into the painful context of joint reminiscing *caused by* the powerful impact on Clarissa of the genre in which Joe frames his story.[107]

This is not the only moment when forms of primary intersubjectivity arise in this chapter, giving the couple moments of respite during their feverish remembrance. After one of their most powerful disagreements, caused mainly by Joe's paralysis, Clarissa tries to pacify him and bring him back "to the essentials." "We've seen something terrible together," she tells him. "It won't go away, and we have to help each other. And that means we'll have to love each other even harder." Although at the beginning, Joe is "trying to deny [himself] even the touch of her hand, assuming that affection was inappropriate, an indulgence, an irreverence in the face of death" (33), they finally go "hand in hand into the bedroom [where the] world would narrow and deepen, [their] voices would sink into the warmth of [their] bodies [and] everything was touch and breath" (33–34).

And yet, their descent into primary intersubjectivity is continuously invaded by a surplus of forms of intersubjectivity their (joint) memories force upon their interaction. "A high price had been paid for this ecstasy," Joe confesses, "and I had to repel an image of a dark house in Oxford, isolated, as if set in a desert, where from an upstairs window two baffled children watched their mother's somber visitors arrive" (35). A similar type of invasion de-structures also their precarious attempt to connect affectively after Joe's recounting of his meeting with Jed. The comedic overtones structuring his story cannot help him forget its *situatedness*, that is, in the vicinity of Logan's corpse:

I wanted to tell her I loved her, but suddenly between us there sat the form of Logan, upright and still. I had to describe him. It was far worse in recollection than it had been at that time. Shock must have dulled my responses then. I began to tell her how his features appeared to hang in all the wrong places, and I broke off my description to tell her the difference between then and now, and how a certain dream logic had made the unbearable quite ordinary, how I had thought nothing of carrying on a conversation with Parry while Logan sat shattered on the ground. And even as I was saying this it occurred to me that I was still avoiding Logan, that I had shied away from the description I had begun because I still could not absorb the facts, and again, I wanted to tell Clarissa this fact too. (30)

Joe's explicit 1PP, an almost pathological form of hyper-reflection (in this situation), and his similarly explicit 2PP in his previous interaction with Jed continuously interfere with the implicit 2PP between him and Clarissa. Only through Clarissa's prompt intervention can this invasion be parried off and can they return, at least for a while, to a primary form of interaction: "Clarissa pushed back her chair and came round my side of the table. She drew my head against her breasts. I shut up and closed my eyes" (30).

Yet, no matter how much they struggle both to interpret through narrativization what they have lived during that day, and to escape from their memories through engaging in affective forms of interaction, Joe and Clarissa fail to find peace and continue to be haunted throughout the novel by what they have witnessed. All they can manage to do is to atrophy their affective involvement through the obsessive retellings of the same events.

After their failure to build together a coherent story, they invite friends over and tell the story "in the married style, running along with it for a stretch, talking through the partner's interruption sometimes, at others, giving way and handing over." Slowly, Joe claims, "our story was gaining in coherence; it had shape, and now it was spoken from a place of safety. . . . Over the days and weeks, Clarissa and I told our story many times to friends, colleagues and relatives. I found myself using the same phrases, the same adjectives in the same order." His following remark, though, points to the fact that the increasing in coherence of their story is not an effect of their working through the traumatic event they witnessed, but simply a matter of emotional atrophy: "It became possible to recount the events without re-living them in the faintest degree, without even remembering them" (36).

What could be the causes of Joe and Clarissa's failure to make sense together, in the context of narrative joint reminiscing, of what they experienced? In my opinion, one of the most important is their different interpretations of the events, rooted in their divergent worldviews. As Randall argues, "The competing narratives" the characters from *EL* build emphasize "the multiple ways in which individuals, groups and systems make sense of the world through the use of narratives. It can also be seen that each character looks to order and control their lives through the use of a particular narrative viewpoint. There are the 'grand narratives' of science, religion, and art that respectively Joe, Jed, and Clarissa embody" (2007: 57).

Take for example the strongest disagreement that emerges in chapter three during Joe and Clarissa's discussions. At one point, she insists that Logan's death "must mean something." Joe's response foregrounds his paralysis structured by his scientific worldview: "I hesitated. I'd never liked this line of thinking. Logan's death was pointless—that was part of the reason we were in shock. Good people sometimes suffered and died, not because their goodness was being tested, but precisely because there was nothing, no one, to test it. No one but us" (32). Clarissa's reply to this rather cynical worldview, prompted, in my view, by her (mild) paralysis structured by her artistic worldview, leaves no room for dialogue and understanding. "You're such a dope," she tells him. "You're so rational sometimes you're like a child" (33). Here is a clear example of how paralysis breeds invasion. Their narrative sense-making in the context of their joint reminiscing (i.e., a secondary form of intersubjectivity) is de-structured by their two divergent, highly abstract ways of sense-making, grounded in science, in Joe's case, and romantic aesthetic theory, in Clarissa's.[108]

Such a situation is paralleled also in the ways in which Joe and Jed make sense of the incident. As I discussed at length in the previous part of this chapter, whereas Jed, obsessively assimilating the world through his religious perspectives, tends to see the balloon incident as an event staged by God in order to bring him and Joe together, Joe can only see blind chance operating in a Godless world.

To conclude, my discussion of the failure in narrative sense-making and joint reminiscing of the balloon incident of Joe, Jed, and Clarissa (1) illustrates the importance of these forms of secondary intersubjectivity in social interaction, and (2) complements cognitive and philosophical theories by showing how paralytic worldviews can de-structure and destabilize these ways of sense-making. McEwan's novel can certainly serve as an intuition pump that can challenge and refine reductive philosophical and scientific theories, and give directions for future empirical and theoretical research.

3.4 The Dangers of Monomaniac Worldviews

In this chapter I argued that disrupted forms of intersubjectivity such as paralysis and invasion can de-structure and destabilize not only sexuality, but also various other types of human interactions, such as those pertaining to secondary intersubjectivity, that is, contexts of joint attention and action, in both their nonconceptual, embodied, and affective manifestations and their more complex, linguistically/narratively mediated varieties (e.g., narrative sense-making and joint reminiscing).

Furthermore, the careful investigation of *EL*'s three main characters unveiled different types of paralyses than the ones haunting the social interactions of the characters from *H* and *OCB*: the obsessive, monomaniac "inhabitance" of abstract worldviews, structured by scientific, religious, or artistic/literary-critical frameworks, can give rise to highly deficient ways of relating to others, characterized by (1) futile attempts at abolishing the necessary, constitutional distance/difference between selfhood and alterity during an obsessive, solipsistic process of assimilating (social) reality rather than accommodating to it (as in Jed's case), (2) a manic employment of explicit 1PP, 2PP, and 3PP at the expense of the implicit 2PP underlining primary and secondary intersubjectivity (Joe), or (3) an excessive reliance on a hermeneutic of suspicion in experiential contexts where trust had better play a leading role (Clarissa).

Moreover, in contrast with other works of McEwan, where the permeability of boundaries between science, religion, and art is often foregrounded, *EL* stages powerful *clashes* of the worldviews Joe, Jed, and Clarissa embody. As I argued, the irreconcilable differences between these characters' worldviews, together with their paralytic sense-making strategies, can sometimes give rise to invasion during their concrete social interactions: an unnecessary surplus of ways of relating to others is often employed in contexts where more basic forms of intersubjectivity, such as the primary or secondary ones, are clearly more appropriate.

A haunting meditation on how easily faith can turn into obsession and rationality slide into madness and on how methods of analyzing works of literature, if used outside their academic context, can wreak havoc in a relationship, *EL* remains one of the most complex of McEwan's attempts to diagnose the discontents of our contemporary civilization.

4

Coda

4.1 The Hermeneutic and Heuristic Potential of the Concepts of Paralysis and Invasion

In this book I discussed two forms of disrupted intersubjectivity, paralysis and invasion, as staged and reflected upon in three of McEwan's works: the short story "Homemade" and the novels *On Chesil Beach* and *Enduring Love*. An important result of my analyses was the insight that paralysis and invasion should be understood as complementary in both theoretical and experiential terms. Whereas paralysis refers to a lack/deficiency of ways of relating to others, invasion refers to an unnecessary surplus, making thus the two *concepts* theoretically complementary. However, my study of the concrete instances of social interactions represented in McEwan's works also show that the two *phenomena* are usually strongly intertwined during social encounters: paralytic ways of dealing with alterity often breed invasion during concrete intersubjective encounters. In other words, paralysis and invasion should also be understood as experientially complementary phenomena.

As I hope to have clearly shown, the introduction of these two concepts into the vocabulary of literary studies, philosophy, and cognitive science has both a hermeneutic and a heuristic potential. On the one hand, paralysis and invasion can be used as categories for critical reading of literary works, helping to provide new approaches for disentangling the complex webs of social relationships these artifacts stage. On the other hand, by gathering under two "conceptual umbrellas" various intersubjective phenomena lying between health and pathology, which have not yet been discussed in philosophy and cognitive science, my analysis can serve as a starting point for further philosophical and scientific research (both theoretical and empirical) on the nature of intersubjectivity.

I began this book with an overview of a set of contemporary philosophical and cognitive-scientific theories of intersubjectivity (the philosophical and developmental alternatives to/critiques of the theory of mind debates), which I proposed to consider as the interpretive ground against which to project my figure, that is, the cognitive-thematic reading of a selection of McEwan's works. In my opinion, the particular theories I chose can be seen as representing highly important scientific and philosophical developments in the contemporary study and understanding of social phenomena.

For more than thirty years, a large number of researchers from both philosophy of mind and empirical psychology took as axiomatic a strongly reductive view of intersubjectivity, in which social interaction was understood as consisting of complex, inferential processes of various kinds and where the fundamental role of embodiment, environmental embededness, and affectivity had been largely ignored.

The philosophical and developmental alternatives to theory of mind, which emerged gradually in recent decades and are still in the process of theoretical and empirical clarification, aim to redress such reductive approaches. Scholars working within this paradigm argue that complex forms of intersubjectivity (e.g., like those discussed by theorists of mind) emerge from and are structured by more fundamental ways of social sense-making during ontogeny. Thus, they draw a picture of intersubjectivity as developing in various stages: from primary intersubjectivity (the dyadic, embodied, and affective attunement with others) to secondary intersubjectivity (the triadic, embodied, and affective participation with others in contexts of joint attention and action) to narrative sense-making and joint reminiscing, and finally, to tertiary intersubjectivity (the acquisition of a self-other meta-perspective and the emergence of an ethical stance following an expansion and consolidation of self- and other-consciousness).

The philosophers and scientists involved in the development of these theories further argue that newly emergent forms of intersubjectivity build upon previous ones, and that, at the same time, the previous ones remain functional even when more sophisticated forms emerge. Therefore, during adulthood, all forms of intersubjectivity function in tandem, although some are prioritized over others in different instances of social interaction.

My criticism of these theories, or rather of the application of these theories, emerges from the fact that, although they have already proved to be very useful in providing systematic explanations of both successful (e.g., empathy, affect attunement, embodied collaboration) and highly pathological (e.g., autism, schizophrenia) types of social interaction, they have not yet addressed intersubjective processes pertaining to the vast area in between health and pathology. Both experience and theoretical reflection point toward the fact that social interaction can often be characterized in terms of *failures* of understanding, even if such failures rarely reach the critical level of those which autistic or schizophrenic persons experience.

One of the aims of my book was precisely to identify and discuss some of these forms of disrupted intersubjectivity haunting human encounters.

Employing a cognitive-thematic approach to a selection of Ian McEwan's works, I sketched various types of disrupted intersubjectivity and classified them into two categories: paralysis and invasion. By paralysis, I labeled forms of intersubjectivity characterized by a lack or deficiency of ways of relating to others, a blockage within a *single* way of social sense-making at the expense of other possible types of intersubjective connections. The characters from McEwan's works about sexuality, for example, are usually approaching their sexual partners from distant, observational perspectives, or, in Thomas Fuchs's terminology, from a combination of explicit 1PP/2PP and implicit 3PP, which are the trademarks of tertiary intersubjectivity.[1] They are thus sidestepping not only the implicit 1PP and 2PP needed for a smooth intermingling of bodies, movements, and affects, but also any trace of an explicit 3PP (which could help them take the perspectives of the others, imaginatively transpose themselves into the others' perspectives, and thus empathize with the others' plights).

Enduring Love's characters too, obsessively and monomanically "inhabiting" their abstract worldviews (structured by religious, scientific, and artistic/literary-critical frameworks), are incapable of experiencing the variety of ways in which they could relate to others. Their paralyses give rise to highly deficient types of social sense-making, characterized by: futile attempts at abolishing the necessary, constitutional difference between selfhood and alterity during obsessive, solipsistic processes of assimilating (social) reality instead of accommodating to it; manic employments of explicit 1PP, 2PP, and 3PP at the expense of the implicit 2PP underlying primary and secondary intersubjectivity; or an excessive reliance on a hermeneutics of suspicion in experiential contexts where such a way of sense-making is quite unnecessary.

My discussion of McEwan's works also brought to light the intermittent aspect of paralysis. Instead of considering it similar to a chronic psychopathology, paralysis should better be understood as a sporadic occurrence, emerging in scattered, irregular, and largely unpredictable instances. Moreover, although it is obviously a form of disrupted *inter*subjectivity, having to do with ways in which individuals make sense of *other* persons, paralysis nevertheless has a more pronounced subjective/individualistic character than invasion: instead of erupting, like invasion, *only* within concrete social encounters, it rather permeates an individual's perspective upon his/her social world.

However, as I have shown, when paralytic individuals try to engage in forms of primary or secondary intersubjectivity which should remain unencumbered by more complex ways of social sense-making, the lack/deficiency characterizing their social perspectives can often breed an unnecessary surplus of ways of relating to others *during* their concrete interactions, that is, invasion. In the sexual encounters McEwan stages, for example, the participants' incapacity to relate to each other otherwise than in the intricate ways underlining tertiary intersubjectivity strongly de-structures and destabilizes what should remain a simple instance of primary intersubjectivity—a thoughtless form of nonlinguistic embodied and affective coordination of movements, expressions, and affects.

The balloon incident from the beginning of *Enduring Love* too can be discussed in terms of invasion: what should have remained within the bounds of secondary intersubjectivity—that is, a nonlinguistic, embodied, and affective form of cooperation—turns into a tragic failure due to a polyphonic eruption of linguistically mediated forms of interaction, and to the incapacity of the persons involved in the incident to share their concerns, and, thus, to align their implicit 2PP—a necessary requirement for the smooth functioning of a team. The implicit 2PP needed for the successful carrying out of their plural action are burdened by the sudden emergence of a surplus of explicit 1PP, brutally invading and tragically corrupting their attempted teamwork.

Finally, I have argued that forms of social interaction lying between secondary and tertiary intersubjectivity, such as narrative sense-making and joint reminiscing, can also be invaded by an unnecessary surplus of tertiary forms, a process caused by the participants' paralyses structured by abstract, mutually exclusive worldviews; the two "couples" from *Enduring Love* (Joe and Clarissa; Joe and Jed) fail to jointly create a coherent story out of the balloon incident due to their monomaniac, solipsistic "inhabitance" of their religious, scientific, and artistic/literary-critical worldviews.

After providing this brief overview, it is time to acknowledge what still remains to be done in future research. A highly interdisciplinary venture like mine will unavoidably contain gaps which only further systematic reflections can attempt to fill. In my opinion, however, the existence of such gaps should not be seen as a shortcoming of my research. On the contrary, I strongly believe that it should be considered a virtue rather than a sin. By opening crucial questions regarding both the nature/functions of literature and the structures of human relationships in general, my current project also implicitly enacts what I consider to be a proper understanding of the nature of knowledge: its open-ended rather than closed character. If the acquisition of knowledge fails to point toward the *necessity* of acquiring more knowledge, not only the existence of universities be jeopardized, but also life itself will risk losing precisely that which differentiates it from inert matter: its inherently *dynamic* character, its perpetual fight against stasis, and hunger for change.

4.2 Topics for Further Research

4.2.1 Systematic Theoretical and Empirical Studies of Paralysis and Invasion

Although I have provided a sketch of two types of disrupted intersubjectivity lying in the area between health and pathology, much more theoretical (scientific *and* philosophical) as well as empirical research is needed to properly explain the phenomena of paralysis and invasion. In my view, a good starting point could be a systematic investigation of the similarities and differences between these phenomena and full-blown psychopathologies such as autism, schizophrenia, obsessive-compulsive disorders, or mania (and perhaps other afflictions too).

My discussion of McEwan's characters often pointed toward the inherent fragility of the boundaries between health and pathology. Some forms of paralysis I discussed, characterized by an excessive employment of abstract ways of social sense-making at the expense of more concrete ones, are strongly reminiscent of afflictions pertaining to the spectrum of autistic disorders (cf. e.g., Hobson 1993; Sacks 1995). Other types of paralysis, such as those structured by religious or literary-critical frameworks, seem to be capable of occasionally giving rise to experiences and behaviors similar to those of schizophrenics: both the dissolution of boundaries between selfhood and alterity and the excessive and uncontrollable hermeneutics of suspicion, sometimes dangerously bordering toward delusional behavior are well-known symptoms of schizophrenia (cf. e.g., Bleuler 1911; Parnas 2003). Furthermore, the manic obsession of interpreting the world through a *single* frame of reference (be it scientific, religious, or artistic/literary-critical) makes paralysis share some features with both mania and obsessive-compulsive disorder.

However, as I repeatedly stressed, paralysis has an intermittent/sporadic rather than a chronic/continuous character, a feature which differentiates it from the psychopathologies I mentioned. Furthermore, the intensity of the disruption of social relations which paralysis engenders (that is, invasion) is sometimes less pronounced than in the case of autism and schizophrenia, and perhaps even than in the case of the other two illnesses. Nevertheless, both the similarities and the differences I briefly sketched give rise to important questions regarding not only the nature of paralysis, but also that of psychopathologies. How can one classify, for example, types of paralysis (and thus, of invasion)? Should they be classified in terms of their intensity? Of their frequency? Of their consequences (e.g., the types of invasion they give rise too)? And consequently, how should one delimit the borderline separating paralysis from pathology? Moreover, what do the experiential and behavioral similarities between paralysis and certain forms of pathology imply for our understanding of the latter? Can they be seen as exacerbations of paralytic forms of sense-making? An affirmative answer would lead to another question: what are the precise causes prompting the passage from mild cases of disrupted intersubjectivity to full-blown pathologies? Furthermore, since the phenomenon of paralysis in general bears similarities to *various* psychopathologies, clarifying which particular type of paralysis can develop into which particular pathology could open paths not only toward identifying the structure and etiology of different psychological illnesses but perhaps also toward preventing their emergence. Finally, the insights regarding the fundamental experiential connection between paralysis and invasion could open different perspectives on understanding what happens when autistics or schizophrenics interact with others. Could the disrupted forms of intersubjectivity emerging be described in terms of invasion? If so, what types of invasion do interactions structured by different pathologies give rise too?

In order to answer these questions, further interdisciplinary research is needed. A combination of theoretical and methodological frameworks from clinical and developmental psychology, psychiatry, and neurobiology can open paths toward a deeper understanding of paralysis and invasion and of their intricate connections to various psychopathologies. However, due to the clear importance of the *experiential* dimension of these disrupted forms of intersubjectivity, science by itself is insufficient for their proper explanation. Phenomenological investigations of how paralysis and invasion manifest themselves in lived experience are crucial for a comprehensive understanding of these phenomena.[2]

Although phenomenological reflections on intersubjectivity (e.g., Husserl's, Heidegger's, Merleau-Ponty's)[3] have been studied intensively by certain contemporary philosophers of mind and cognitive scientists,[4] and crucial phenomenological insights have already been incorporated within philosophy of mind and cognitive science, no systematic study of failures of understanding has yet been conducted from such a perspective.[5] The classical phenomenologists' reflections on intersubjectivity should be re-read with an eye open for examples of disrupted intersubjectivity.[6] Furthermore, their general theories of intersubjectivity should be re-assessed in order to see whether they would confirm or not my findings regarding the nature and manifestations of paralysis and invasion.[7] Finally, their phenomenological reflections on intersubjectivity should be complemented with the linguistic, philosophical, and cognitive literary analyses of misunderstandings provided by scholars like Austin, Grice, Cavell, Derrida, or Spolsky.

Having sketched these possible directions for further research regarding the theoretical and empirical clarification of the concepts/phenomena of paralysis and invasion, I will now briefly turn to another work of McEwan, *Atonement* (2001). As I will argue, a reflection on this highly challenging novel can point toward other areas for future research.

4.2.2 *Atonement*'s Open Questions

I initially planned to include another chapter in my book, containing an extended critical reading of McEwan's novel *Atonement* in terms of paralysis and invasion. After deeper reflection though, I realized that the complexities of this novel would have expanded my analyses far beyond what I have proposed to do in this project. McEwan's artful and intricate staging of the inherent dangers underlying the processes of reading, writing, and interpreting literary works opens extremely important, yet very complicated questions which cannot be comprehensively answered without further extensive research. In the remainder of this book, I will identify some of the pressing problems *Atonement* poses and will give brief directions regarding the possible paths toward their solution.

Briony Tallis, the main character of *Atonement*, suffers from a type of paralysis similar in many respects to Clarissa's from *EL*. Briony's paralysis, though, is not only much more intense than Clarissa's, and with definitely more tragic consequences (the deaths of her sister Cecilia and her sister's lover Robbie), but also more ambiguous and harder to define and describe.

In the first part of the novel, she is introduced by the (apparently) heterodiegetic third-person narrator as a thirteen-year-old developing writer (of both stories and theater plays) and voracious reader of a great number of romances and melodramas. The common feature characterizing both her readings and writings is their simplicity and naivety: all seem to be structured by clear-cut binary oppositions—the "cumbrous struggle between good and bad, heroes and villains" (*At*: 40).

Her strong immersion within these fictive story worlds powerfully structures her worldviews, which she "inhabits" with the same monomaniac obsessiveness with which Jed, for instance, "inhabits" his religious worldviews. As her mother reflects, Briony, "struck . . . dumb . . . by the demons of self-consciousness and talent . . . was always off and away in her mind, grappling with some unspoken, self-imposed problem, as though the weary, self-evident world could be re-invented by a child" (68).

Since she is continuously assimilating (social) reality instead of accommodating to it, similarly to other paralytics in McEwan's works, it is no wonder that Briony repeatedly misinterprets the others' actions. Like most of

McEwan's novels, *Atonement* is structured around a crucial event, a crisis that breaks unexpectedly into the lives of its characters and wreaks havoc in their prior more or less tranquil existence. This event is Briony's misidentification of Robbie as the assailant of her cousin, Lola, at the end of the first part of the novel. Her action has tragic consequences: Robbie is sent to prison and later to war where, as we learn from the novel's Coda, he dies without having the chance to see Cecilia again.

Although "what she knew was not literally, or not only, based on the visible" since it "was too dark for that," when Briony "said, over and over again, I saw him, she meant it, and was perfectly honest, as well as passionate." Her conviction is based, in fact, on two previous misunderstandings: "Her eyes confirmed the sum of all she knew and had recently experienced . . . . The truth instructed her eyes" (169).[8] Led by "her controlling demon" (5), that is, "her instinct for order" (41), symmetry, and consistency, it is only natural for Briony to misinterpret reality in the light of prior misinterpretations.

Close to the beginning of the novel, Robbie and Cecilia experience an awkward moment, filled with sexual tension, near the Triton fountain in the Tallises' estate. Going to the fountain to put water in a vase, Cecilia meets Robbie who, "with an urgent masculine authority," insists on helping her, managing only to break the vase in his struggle to take it from her hands, "two triangular pieces [dropping] into the water and [tumbling] to the bottom in a synchronous, see-sawing motion" (29). Enraged, Cecilia takes off her clothes and plunges into the water to recover the pieces: "Her movements were savage, and she would not meet his eye." After recovering the pieces, the "frail white nymph" dresses and departs quickly, while he "stood there dumbly as she walked away from him, barefoot across the lawn, and . . . watched her darkened hair swing heavily across her shoulders, drenching her blouse" (30).

The same scene, "that could easily have accommodated, in the distance at least, a medieval castle" (38) is observed by Briony from "one of the nursery's wide-opened windows" (37). At the beginning everything seems clear to her:

> A proposal of marriage. Briony would not have been surprised. She herself has written a tale in which a humble woodcutter saved a princess from drowning and ended by marrying her. What was presented here fitted well. Robbie Turner, only son of a humble cleaning lady and of no known father . . . had the boldness of ambition to ask for Cecilia's hand. It made perfect sense. Such leaps across boundaries were the stuff of daily romance. (38)

However, when Cecilia undresses, Briony's sense of understanding starts to falter. "The sequence was illogical," in her view—"the drowning scene, followed by a rescue, should have preceded the marriage proposal." She is left in darkness by "the strangeness of the here and now, of what passed between people, the ordinary people that she knew, and what power one could have over the other, and how easy it was to get everything wrong, completely wrong" (39). The sexual tensions between Robbie and Cecilia, so obvious to the reader as well as to the old Briony recounting the scene, remain completely unobserved by the young aspiring writer, who, rather than using elements from the real world to give substance to her fictional creations, interprets and even more frequently misinterprets the world by assimilating it through previously internalized literary structures. Deeply immersed in literature from an early age, Briony is constantly "failing to make a distinction between the fictive and the real" (Finney 2004: 70).

Such failures of understanding are pushed to extremes later on, when Briony stumbles upon Robbie and Cecilia having sex in the library and interprets the scene as an act of aggression, "a realization of her worst fears" (123). Here is how Briony perceives Robbie and Cecilia's passionate, and ultimately, tender first (and probably last, if we choose to believe Briony's claim from the Coda that both of them died during the war without having the chance to meet again) sexual encounter which I already discussed in the introduction of my chapter on sexuality:

> Briony stared past Robbie's shoulder into the terrified eyes of her sister. He had turned to look back at the intruder, but he did not let Cecilia go. He had pushed his body against her, pushing her dress right up above her knee and had trapped her where the shelves met at right angles. His left hand was behind her neck, gripping her hair, and with his right he held her forearm which was raised in protest, or self-defense. (123)

Her misunderstanding is fueled by an earlier event. After their encounter at the fountain, Robbie writes a letter of apology to Cecilia in which he also makes a first attempt at expressing his feelings toward her. Undecided about what precisely to write in the letter, he writes draft after draft, one of them being a vulgar, explicit rendering of his sexual desires. Unluckily, this draft is the one that actually reaches Cecilia, *through* Briony, who reads it "shamelessly in the center of the entrance hall" (114) before delivering it to her sister.

The effects of reading this letter on Briony's understanding of Robbie are devastating: "With the letter something elemental, brutal, perhaps even criminal had been introduced, some principle of darkness and . . . she did not doubt that her sister was in some way threatened and needed her help" (113–14). Inspired once more by her literary background, Briony sees Robbie as an "incarnation of evil" (115), threatening "the order of their household"

(114). In the wake of this series of misunderstandings, Briony falsely accuses Robbie of assaulting Lola, trapping herself "into the labyrinth of her own construction" (170).

Two observations can be extracted from this discussion of Briony's misunderstandings. On the one hand, we encounter here forms of intersubjectivity, based on narrative practices, gone deeply wrong. Quite unexpectedly, taking into account the philosophical and scientific theories concerning narrative sense-making discussed earlier in this book, Briony's excessive exposure and use of storytelling has clearly damaging effects on her understanding of alterity. Secondly, we also notice that Briony's stance toward the others is a disengaged and distant one. She is always an *observer* of situations in which social interactions take place, never a *participant*: a combination of explicit 1PP/2PP and implicit 1PP structures her relation to others. Furthermore, she obsessively wants to *know* the others, therefore her standpoint is almost purely epistemological with, as we saw, dire ethical consequences.

Such a strong paralysis, structured by literary frameworks, unavoidably gives rise to invasion in the (rare) moments when Briony actually *interacts* with others. As we learn in the second part of the novel, filtered through Robbie's perspective, when Briony was ten years old, a "drama" occurred "by the river" (233) close to the Tallis estate, during "a swimming lesson he had promised her" (229). Immediately after hearing Robbie's affirmative answer to her question regarding whether he would save her if she fell in the river, Briony does not hesitate to test his assertion and jumps into the water. After being saved by Robbie, she confesses to him that she loves him and that she acted as she did to see whether he loves her too.[9]

But is the connection between Briony and Robbie here an embodied and affective one, resembling interactions pertaining to primary intersubjectivity? Her declaration of love is quickly, and probably correctly, judged by Robbie as "lines, surely, from one of her books, one she had read recently, or one she had written" (232). And her supposed romantic attachment to him is described in the following terms: "For three years she must have nurtured a feeling for him, kept it hidden, nourished it with fantasy or embellished it in her stories. She was the sort of girl who lived in her thoughts" (233). Moreover, her actions too, that is, the ways in which she tests his love, are obviously also taken from literary romances and melodramas. Thus, an unnecessary and damaging surplus of ways of social sense-making, structured by the literary frameworks underlying her worldviews, clearly invades her embodied and affective engagement to Robbie.

In contrast to the characters from *H*, *OCB*, or *EL* though, the older Briony is occasionally able to engage in what seems to be more successful social interactions, unencumbered by invasive processes. In one of the key scenes of the novel, she experiences a powerful moment of intimacy and openness to alterity characteristic of primary forms of intersubjectivity. While working as a nurse in London during the war, she is summoned by Sister Drummond, the head nurse, to attend to a wounded French soldier, Luc: "You see that soldier sitting up, at the end of the row? Acute surgical, but there's no need to wear a mask. Find a chair, go and sit with him. Hold his hand and talk to him." At the beginning, Briony is offended, believing (mistakenly, as usual) that Sister Drummond thinks she is tired and needs some rest. She nevertheless obeys and begins a conversation with the delirious soldier, who is confusing her with a girl from his past whom he loved, while Briony holds his "cold and greasy to the touch" hand and looks at his "delicate face, with dark eyebrows and dark green eyes" (305).

Initially, Briony thinks that "it wasn't right to lead him on" (307) and tries to explain to him that he is confusing her and that he is not in Paris, as he mistakenly believes, but in London. However, at his request to loosen his head bandages, she suddenly realizes the gravity of his condition: "The side of Luc's head was missing. . . . Below the jagged line of bone was a spongy crimson mess of brain, several inches across, reaching from the crown almost to the tip of his ear" (308). This horrendous "epiphany of the brain" convinces her that, in this case, truth is less important than a deeper and more direct human connection, "a subtle kind of intimacy" (O'Hara 2010: 83–84), desperately needed by Luc in his last moments of life. As O'Hara argues, Briony is finally able to "willfully imagine herself into the foreign and uncertain terrain of an Other's narrative world" (83). With his "pale, oily face gleam[ing] and bobb[ing] in front of her eyes" (*At*: 307) she "plays along, allowing her imagination to be transfigured, rather than disfiguring the Other for the sake of self-centered certainty" (O'Hara 2010: 97).

The young Briony seems to be unable though to enter such moments of intimacy. Contexts of secondary intersubjectivity in which Briony is involved are also occasionally destabilized and de-structured by ways of sense-making pertaining to tertiary intersubjectivity. At the very beginning of the novel, Briony forces her mother, Emily, to read her melodramatic theater play, *The Trials of Arabella* "in [Emily's] bedroom, at her dressing table, with the author's arm around her shoulder the whole while." Whereas Emily is able to connect bodily and affectively with her daughter,[10] Briony is continuously bombarded with self-other conscious emotions pertaining to tertiary intersubjectivity: she "studied her mother's face for every trace of shifting emotion, and Emily Tallis obliged with looks of alarm, snickers of glee and, at the end, grateful smiles and wise, affirming nods" (4).

This is obviously far from being a simple, straightforward context of joint attention. The shared focus on the theater play is highly charged with more complex ways of sense-making, which could definitely be described in terms taken from theory of mind: Briony is continuously monitoring Emily's attention, struggling to infer what her mother thinks about her artwork, and thus, what she thinks about its author too. In a similar vein, while reading "her stories aloud in the library," Briony performs "so boldly, making big gestures with her free arm, arching her eyebrows when she did the voices, and looking up from the page for seconds at a time as she read in order to gaze into one face after the other, unapologetically demanding her family's total attention as she cast her narrative spell" (6–7). Thus, Briony's self-centeredness and solipsism characterizing her paralysis do not allow her to connect in more direct ways to others.

Several years later, though, nurse Briony *is* able to engage in contexts of joint action unburdened by any surplus of ways of social sense-making. Returning from a walk with one of her fellow nurses, Briony is immediately ordered by a doctor to help him carry a stretcher with a wounded soldier on it. During their trip from the hospital's entrance to the emergency room, no direct contact between her and the doctor takes place, aside (of course) from the fact that they are each holding their end of the stretcher: "[the doctor] was oblivious to Briony's presence [;] his back was to her as he slammed the lift gates apart, and told her to take her end" (291). Nevertheless, they are partners in a joint pragmatic project—they must carry the stretcher together as quickly as possible to the emergency room in order to save the soldier's life.

Just as in the case of Gurwitsch's cobblers I discussed earlier, there is no need for Briony to infer the doctor's mental states nor vice versa. Their cooperation in a pragmatic context is sufficient to give rise between them to a powerful connection which can be understood in terms of secondary intersubjectivity. Until late in the night, Briony is continuously involved in such forms of social interaction: "there was always another job, always a sister demanding help or a soldier calling from his bed" (302). To paraphrase Heidegger in his analyses of "being-with" (*Mitsein*), Briony is interacting with her colleagues "by way of the world." It is through co-involvement in pragmatic contexts that she encounters alterity in these cases. And in contrast with her previous misunderstandings, here she manages to successfully collaborate with her fellow nurses and doctors. In the "floating timelessness of those first twenty-four hours" (315), Briony learns that the other is not always someone to be *known*; sometimes the other is simply someone to *be with*. And such lessons help her achieve what was impossible for her to experience before: "a touch of rapport in adversity" (302).

The interplay between young Briony's recurrent misunderstandings and older Briony's more elaborate capacities for successful social interaction is not the only issue this novel deals with. *Atonement* is also a powerful and complex meditation on the (obsessive) consumption and, especially, production of literature. Briony's paralysis structured by literary frameworks is highly similar to those of Miguel De Cervantes's Don Quixote, Gustave Flaubert's Madame Bovary, or Jane Austen's Catherine Morland (from her novel *Northanger Abbey*). An interesting direction for future research would be an in-depth comparison between (the representation of) their paralyses. Such an attempt would not only shed more light on the general nature of paralysis but, since these characters belong to different historical, cultural, and literary periods and traditions, would also provide a starting point for understanding how (1) paralysis manifests itself in various historical and cultural contexts, and (2) what strategies of representation various literary conventions offer for staging such cases of disrupted intersubjectivity.

However, instead of providing a straightforward critique of paralytic ways of social sense-making structured by literary frameworks (and of the instances of invasion they engender), McEwan stages a much more elaborate reflection on the dangers underlying the processes of reading and writing, employing narrative strategies which, as I will argue, strongly destabilize the relationship between the reader and the text and, thus, seriously hinder the process of interpretation, *regardless* of what ground the reader chooses.

The process of writing is described from the first pages of the novel as characterized by an intricate interplay between secrecy and self-exposure. The first story Briony writes, "a foolish affair, imitative of half a dozen folk tales and lacking, she realized later, that vital knowingness about the ways of the world which compels a reader's respect," nevertheless teaches her "that imagination itself was a source of secrets: once she had begun a story, no one could be told. Pretending in words was too tentative, too vulnerable, too embarrassing to let anyone know" (6). From the first pages of McEwan's novel, the creative act, at its onset, seems to be fundamentally characterized by an element of secrecy, a boundary between the self and others.

A few sentences later, the narrator provides an explanation of these peculiar effects: "Self-exposure was inevitable the moment she described a character's weakness; the reader was bound to speculate that she was describing herself. What other authority could she have?" (6). Suddenly, yet indirectly, the *connective* powers of storytelling can also be felt. Briony is scared that writing could bring herself into the light, could throw herself under the eyes of another, and she fears this because she is "discovering, as had many writers before her, that not all recognition is helpful" (7).

Nevertheless, Briony also loves her readers' attention. Self-exposure through literature does not always trouble her. She often seems to deeply enjoy it. A dialectic between fear of self-exposure and desire for it is thus established from the beginning of the novel and is strongly connected to the process of writing. Indeed, the reader of *Atonement* realizes at the end of the novel that the third-person narrator of the first three parts was Briony herself, writing in order to confess her sins and atone for them. Yet, even if she clearly desires to expose her deepest flaws in front of the reader and ask for forgiveness, she nevertheless chooses to hide her authorship beyond an anonymous, impersonal, and apparently omniscient narrator.[11]

The series of misunderstandings thematically underlying the novel is thus also closely mirrored by its form. The way in which McEwan stages the relationship between reader and writer (in itself a very complex form of intersubjectivity)[12] at the level of the novel's narrative structure has a deep affinity with the characters' almost ubiquitous failures of understanding.[13] The fact that the reader learns only at the end of the novel that Briony herself was its narrator breaks his/her initial trust in the narrator and in the veracity of the narrated events.[14] The suspension of disbelief suddenly turns into a hermeneutics of suspicion, utterly confusing the reader's understanding of the narrator's (and consequently, the author's) intentions, beliefs, and desires. Through such strategies attempting to deceive the reader, McEwan forces him/her to identify to a certain extent with the young Briony witnessing the scene at the fountain: her "confusion and misunderstanding" (40) regarding the dynamics between Robbie and Cecilia also characterize the reader's standpoint toward the novel as a whole, and implicitly his/her relationship with the narrator and the author.

This complex narrative structure gives rise to a wide range of questions only future research can deal with. One of the most striking features of Briony's atonement for the sins caused by her paralysis is the fact that she attempts to achieve it through literature, that is, the very medium which initially caused her paralysis. In this respect, Briony somehow resembles Joe from *EL*, who, as I argued, becomes conscious of his paralysis structured by scientific frameworks *through* his scientific reflections. The difference is that Briony is not only becoming conscious of her paralysis by writing about it; she also tries to atone for its tragic consequences through this method.

The first question which emerges, of course, is whether such an attempt is successful or not. Briony's views on this issue are ambivalent: "How can a novelist achieve atonement," she asks herself, "when, with her absolute power of deciding outcomes, she is also God? There is nothing outside her. In her imagination she has set the limits and the terms. No atonement for God, or novelists, even if they are atheists. It was always an impossible task, and that was precisely the point. The attempt was all" (371).

Her romantic views on the nature and powers of novelists, together with her claim that "there was nothing outside her" seem to point toward the fact that she has not yet overcome her paralysis. However, as O'Hara convincingly argues in his discussion of the differences between Briony's "mature narrative identity" and her "immature solipsism," (2010: 93), the fact that she manages to transpose herself imaginatively into Robbie's position and render so powerfully his war experiences *from his perspective* can be seen as a proof that "she comes, as the author of the novel, to respect the *otherness* of others, to repeal the primacy of her subjectivity and to imagine empathetically other, uncertain possibilities of experience" (94; emphasis in original). In Fuchs's terminology, Briony appears to have acquired the capacity to transform her implicit 3PP (a distant observation of others) into an explicit 3PP (an imaginary transposition into the others' perspectives), helping her empathize with others, and, thus, indirectly, open herself toward ways of sense-making pertaining to primary and secondary intersubjectivity.[15]

Such an interpretation points toward interesting questions about the general nature of paralysis within tertiary intersubjectivity: Would it be possible, for instance, to (indirectly) cure such an affliction through capacities pertaining to tertiary intersubjectivity too (that is, the ability of employing explicit 3PP)? Consequently, could training in literature (reading and/or writing), which, according to O'Hara,[16] develops such capacities, help overcome paralytic ways of social sense-making? If so, could it also cure paralyses structured by science or religion? More systematic (theoretical and empirical) research needs to be done to begin answering these puzzling questions.

There are two other directions for future research *Atonement* points to. On the one hand, the hermeneutic problems this novel creates due to its strongly metafictional character open up more general questions regarding cognitive-thematic approaches to literature such as mine, which aim to extract knowledge about cognition from literature. As scholars as varied as John Dewey, Marshal McLuhan, Jacques Derrida, Rita Felski, or Derek Attridge have argued at great length,[17] ignoring the form in which any kind of knowledge is transmitted is, for various reasons, quite risky, particularly when such knowledge is transmitted in artistic forms,[18] and can even turn out to be deeply unethical. Doing justice to a literary work involves, as Attridge argues, taking seriously into account its specificity and uniqueness, that is, its *form* (2015: 111–32).[19]

Although in my analysis of McEwan's works I have occasionally discussed the ways in which the generic, stylistic, and narrative peculiarities of my case studies influenced their representation of paralysis and invasion, much more research needs to be done in order to clarify how the literary medium (de)structures the message we are trying to extract from it. Since works of literature are *not* anthropological databases, pointed attention to the *specificity* of the literary works under discussion is crucial for a deeper understanding of not only what kind of knowledge we can "extract" from them, but also how such knowledge should be "extracted."

Questions of how different genres, literary periods, and stylistic and narrative strategies enable and/or constrain our attempts to acquire knowledge about extraliterary issues from our case studies are essential for the cognitive-thematic approach to become more than just another variety of analogical approaches. In order to clarify the status of literary interpretation within cognitive literary studies, in-depth reflections on the different epistemological affordances particular literary works offer are indispensable.

Finally, another important direction for future research that the curious case of *Atonement* opens up concerns the problem of ethics. In an interview with Brian Appleyard in the *Sunday Times* (2007), McEwan describes his aesthetic project in the following terms: "For me the moral core of the novel is inhabiting other minds. That seems to be what novels do very well and also what morality is about: understanding that people are as real to themselves as you are to yourself, doing unto others as you would have done to yourself." This aesthetic program is mirrored by Briony's in *Atonement*. In her view, as a writer, "She need only show separate minds, as alive as her own, struggling with the idea that other minds were equally alive. . . . And only in a story could you enter these different minds and show how they had an equal value" (*At*: 40).

In his brilliant and erudite article,[20] O'Hara insightfully argues that *Atonement* should be read precisely as an enactment of such claims, both thematically and formally. McEwan's novel, in his view, successfully stages "the *ethical* complex that lies between author and reader, text and world" (74; emphasis in original). Furthermore, he shows how McEwan's novel "explores the same self-Other dynamics that underpin the work of Lévinas, Merleau-Ponty, and Zygmunt Bauman while *metafictionally* making claims about narrative not unlike those found in the hermeneutic philosophies of Richard Kearney and Paul Ricoeur" (74–75; emphasis in original).

O'Hara's insights about *Atonement* are crucial not only for a better understanding of McEwan's novel, but also in pointing toward directions for further research that a systematic and comprehensive analysis of paralysis and invasion should follow. Although I have implicitly referred to the ethical consequences of paralysis and invasion during my discussion of their representation in McEwan's works, more investigations regarding the ethical status of these disrupted forms of intersubjectivity are required. An in-depth study of the various ethical theories of intersubjectivity elaborated by philosophers such as Lévinas, Bauman, Ricoeur, or Kearney[21] is needed for shedding more light on both the general theoretical structure of paralysis and invasion and on their intricate relationship with the larger social/historical/cultural contexts in which they operate. Furthermore, an integration of these philosophers' insights within the philosophical/developmental alternatives to theory of mind could help fill a significant gap in the latter's explanation of *mature* intersubjectivity, that is, their current ignorance of the ethical issues structuring *all* forms of intersubjectivity during adulthood.

To answer all these questions, much more time and reflection is needed. But endless time and infinite powers of reflection will still be insufficient if I pursue this path alone. One crucial lesson I have learned and I hope I have successfully transmitted through this study is that intersubjectivity is indispensable in human affairs of whatever type. Not only sex, but also academic research needs dialogue in order to continue and bear fruit. In Roger Waters's terms, together we stand, divided we fall. My hope at the end of this project is that my obsessive, meta-paralytic thoughts invading the years in which this book was written, my endless struggles to understand misunderstanding, will not fail to open a space for dialogue and understanding.

Notes

Chapter 1

1   Attridge mentions as predecessors to his approach Derrida, Blanchot, and Adorno (7). However, Susan Sontag's manifesto "Against Interpretation" (1966), calling for an "erotics" instead of a hermeneutics of art, seems to be another important precursor of such a way of thinking, even if it is less systematic in its arguments than Attridge's book.

2   Derrida himself would argue, according to Liesbeth Korthals Altes, that one of the specificities of the literary medium is that it "in fact parasitizes upon all kinds of discourses. It incorporates these, taking over their reference function and truth pretensions, while suspending them, resisting the illusion of immediate reference and of truth" (Korthals Altes 2009: 410).

3   For insightful philosophical discussions of how artistic experience relates to other types of experiences, see Dewey (1934); see also Paul Ricoeur for phenomenological, hermeneutic, and narrative analyses of the power of literature to "transfigure" our ordinary experience (1983, 1984, 1985). More recently, much work in the cognitive literary studies has been dedicated to showing how reading helps in the acquisition and development of various cognitive, social, and moral capacities (e.g., Hakemulder 2000; Herman 2003; Mar et al. 2006; Zunshine 2006; Schreier 2009; Vermeule 2010; Kidd and Castano 2013), studies pertaining to what Caracciolo (2016) calls "functional" approaches to literature.

4   Important recent collections of articles pertaining to this field are Richardson and Spolsky (2004), Leverage et al. (2010), Aldama (2010), Herman (2011a), Jaén and Jacques (2012), Bruhn and Wehrs (2013), Bernaerts et al. (2013), Zunshine (2015), Burke and Troscianko (2016).

5   In the *Stanford Encyclopedia of Philosophy*, for example, Paul Thagard defines cognitive science as "the interdisciplinary study of mind and intelligence, embracing philosophy, psychology, artificial intelligence, neuroscience, linguistics, and anthropology" (2014). For a succinct, yet relevant account of the historical development of the cognitive sciences, see Thompson (2007: 3–15). For more comprehensive historical accounts, see Boden (2006) and Dupuy (2009).

6   For example, Iser (1974, 1978), Eco (1979), Jauss (1982). See also Tompkins (1980) and Suleiman and Crosman (1980) for selections of relevant works in this field.

7   Recent processual approaches include Schneider (2001), Bortolussi and Dixon (2002), Kuiken, Miall and Sikora (2004), Miall (2006), Kuzmičová (2012), and Sanford and Emmott (2012). Whereas the works of Bortolussi,

Dixon, and Miall are strongly empirical, relying on experimental testing of actual readers, the others are slightly more speculative, striving nevertheless to propose hypotheses that could be subsequently tested experimentally (cf. Caracciolo 2016: 194).

8   See footnote 3 for a list of functional approaches.

9   Cognitive literary scholars such as Jackson (2000, 2002), Abbott (2001), Hart (2001), Adler and Gross (2002), and Spolsky (2003) argue that one of the main problems facing cognitive literary studies (and cognitive humanities in general) is the *uni*directionality of knowledge transfer, that is, *from* cognitive science *to* the humanities, and very rarely the other way around.

10 Importantly, Caracciolo argues that the nature of the ground cannot serve as a justification for the quality of the interpretation. He defines a *good* literary interpretation as being "novel and stimulating, speaking to the interests of a given interpretive community . . . as yielding insight into the text it sets out to interpret [and as] being well argued and sufficiently grounded in textual evidence" (2016: 188), *regardless* of its ground. Hence, readings using cognitive science as a ground are not necessarily better than readings using other grounds. This is very important because many cognitive literary scholars continue to claim that their interpretations are better (i.e., more valid, truthful) *because* of their use of *science* as ground (such as the "Literary Darwinists"; see, for example, Carroll (1995, 2004, 2008); Storey (1996; Boyd 1998).

11 See, for example, Palmer (2004, 2010) and Herman (2011a).

12 See, for example, Abbott (2008), Alber (2009), Alber et al. (2010), and Alber and Heinze (2011).

13 Abbott makes the same point, by bringing in an example from McEwan's work. "Do authors fails to the extent that they contravene the hard evidence of kinship studies?" he puzzles (2001: 205). But if this were so, "what does this say about narratives like Ian McEwan's richly erotic portrayal of incest in *The Cement Garden*? Why does this novel, with its climactic scene of intercourse between a brother and sister, move so many so powerfully? Have its enthusiastic readers and the author gone wrong because they are ignorant of the fact that children raised together don't want to sleep together? Or is there something more complex going on in the sexual dynamics of this novel? . . . And if the latter is the case, can we still account for this complexity in evolutionary . . . terms?" (205–06).

14 To exemplify these metacognitive questions, Caracciolo writes: "During its long history, literature has always tended to ask—or, more precisely, has been interpreted as asking—questions such as: What is the self? Can it exist autonomously from intersubjective interaction? What is consciousness? How reliable is our knowledge of the world, and what role do emotions play in shaping it? These concerns seem to stubbornly resist definitive answers, thus forming some sort of 'deep' background to readers' engagement with literary texts" (2016: 199).

15 A term coined by Daniel Dennett, who uses it in order to describe (the nature of) philosophical thought experiments (1991). For a more elaborate discussion of intuition pumps as tools for thinking, see Dennett (2013).

16 What is called in the scientific literature, rather unfortunately, "the theory theory of mind (TT)." See Baron-Cohen (1995), Wellman et al. (2001), and Carruthers (2005).

17 "The simulation theory of mind (ST)." For example, Gallese (2001, 2005), Goldman (2005), and Gordon (2005). For a critical overview of both TT and ST, see Gallagher and Zahavi (2008: 171–87).

18 In many philosophical and scientific debates, this experience of inwardness is claimed to be a universal aspect of human subjectivity. However, as Taylor shows (1989: 111–99), this phenomenon is better understood in historical terms, as a feature of *modern* subjectivity.

19 A beautiful extended literalized metaphor of such an inferential, mediated way of dealing with alterity can be found in chapter six from *Atonement* (63–71), focalized through Emily, Briony's mother. Suffering from debilitating migraines, Emily takes refuge in her "cool and darkened bedroom" (63) and "breathing quietly in the darkness, [she] gauge[s] the state of the household by straining to listen" (65), sending "her raw attention into every recess of the house" (69). In the absence of direct (visual) perception, Emily develops "a sixth sense, a tentacular awareness that reached out from the dimness and moved through the house, unseen and all-knowing" (66). Auditory signals must be continuously deciphered in order to infer the others' beliefs, desires, and intentions.

20 I am referring here to Heraclitus's famous claim that Φύσις κρύπτεσθαι φιλεῖ (translated as "nature loves to hide" or "nature loves to conceal itself"; Fragmentum B 123, in Diels 1903). For an interesting discussion of Heraclitus's conception of nature, see Hadot (2006 [2004]: 39–91).

21 For an overview of current debates regarding the nature and functions of folk psychology, see Hutto and Ratcliffe (2007).

22 A typical false-belief experiment was performed by Baron-Cohen, Leslie, and Frith in order to test their hypothesis that autistic children lack a theory of mind (1985). Children (healthy, autistic, and with Down's syndrome) were presented with two dolls, Sally and Ann. The story the experimenters told them ran as follows: Sally has a basket and Ann a box. Sally also has a marble which she puts in her basket and then goes out for a walk. While she is away, Ann steals her marble and puts it in her box. The question the children had to answer was: Where will Sally think the marble is when she returns? Most of the autistic children answered that Sally will believe that the marble is in Ann's box. Therefore, they could not understand that other persons can have different beliefs than them.

23 Initially formulated, among others, by J.S. Mill (1867: 237–38).

24 Clusters of so-called mirror neurons (discovered by a group of scientists led by Giacommo Rizzolatti at the University of Parma in the 1990s), that

is, neurons from the pre-motor cortex and Broca's area which are activated both when we engage in specific motor actions and when we see other people performing the same actions. As Gallagher and Zahavi explain this phenomenon, "One's motor system reverberates or resonates in one's encounters with others" (2008: 177). For a comprehensive overview of these discoveries and their implications, see Rizzolatti and Sinigaglia (2008).

25 If perception is understood as a temporal, enactive phenomenon, that is, as also *including* motor processes. See Merleau-Ponty (1962 [1945]), Noë (2004), Thompson (2007: 243–67).

26 See, for example, Gallagher (2001, 2004, 2008), Gallagher and Zahavi (2008: 187–95), Ratcliffe (2007), and Zahavi (2008).

27 This inborn capacity for imitation was acknowledged by Aristotle in his *Poetics*: "Imitating is co-natural with human beings from childhood, and in this they differ from the other animals because they are the most imitative and produce their first acts of understanding by means of imitation" (10). The abovementioned discovery of resonance systems in the brain seems to provide neuroscientific support for such claims.

28 For an account of the emergence of language from contexts of joint attention, see Tomasello (1999: 56–134).

29 See also De Jaegher and Di Paolo (2007) for an analysis of what they call "participatory sense-making."

30 As an example, Gallagher and Zahavi (2008: 191) discuss Gurwitsch's description of two workers cobbling a street (1979: 104, 108, 112), where one worker lays the stones while the other cobbles them into place. As they argue, the workers understand each other in virtue of the roles they play in this common situation, rather than through grasping hidden mental states.

31 See Tomasello (1999) for an account of the development of our understanding of the other as animate being (one to twelve months of age), intentional agent (one to four years of age), and finally mental agent (four to five years of age; cf. Gallagher and Zahavi 2008: 192–93).

32 As it can be clearly seen from this discussion, narrative practices do not only help us refine our understanding of other persons' behavior, but also teach us what types of actions are right or wrong and why, entering thus in the domain of ethics and morality.

33 That is, the capacity to create rudimentary sentences containing a subject and a predicate.

34 For an in-depth discussion of the development of the verbal and narrative self and their relationship to changes in children's understanding of temporality, see also Nelson (2005).

35 "Here," Fuchs claims, "lies the (limited) justification of simulation theory" (2012: 657).

36 To exemplify this, Fuchs cites Oliver Sacks's description of Temple Grandin, an autistic woman: "She has . . . to 'compute' others' intentions and states of mind, to try to make algorithmic, explicit, what for the rest of us is second

nature. . . . She is now aware of the existence of these social signals. She can infer them, she says, but she herself cannot perceive them, cannot participate in this magical communication directly, or conceive the many-level kaleidoscopic states of mind behind it. Knowing this intellectually, she does her best to compensate, bringing immense intellectual effort and computational power to bear on matters that others understand with unthinking ease" (Sacks 1995: 270–72; cited in Fuchs 2015: 198).

Chapter 2

1 For example, Byrnes (2009) and Summers-Bremner (2014).
2 Or, as Jack Slay puts it, "the initiations into the alien world of the adult" (1996: 12).
3 *The Comfort of Strangers* still remains the novel where McEwan deals in greatest detail with these problems. A fable about sexuality and gender set in the eerie labyrinths of (an unnamed but clearly recognizable) Venice, *The Comfort of Strangers* reflects deeply upon the connections between sadism, masochism, and pleasure and powerfully and vividly shows that eroticism is far from being totally amenable to rationality and that human desire might be fundamentally underwritten by a master/slave dialectic, in which roles are not fixed but contested, and individuals can endlessly move between the position of sadist and masochist, subject and object, dominator and dominated (cf. Childs 2006: 58; for a summary and selections of relevant critical approaches to this novel, see Childs (2006: 46–58).
4 See, for example, Butler (1990, 2004).
5 For example, "Homemade," "Disguises," "In Between the Sheets," *The Cement Garden, On Chesil Beach.*
6 For example, "Butterflies," "In Between the Sheets."
7 For example, "Dead as They Come," *The Child in Time.*
8 For example, "Reflections of a Kept Ape," *Black Dogs* (1992). This story and novel stand in an almost complementary relation regarding McEwan's treatment of inter-species sexuality. Whereas in the story, a Kafkaesque monologue of an ape kept as a sexual slave by a female writer, the unquenchable human sexuality violently infiltrates into the animal kingdom too; in the novel, dogs are trained by the Gestapo during the Second World War to rape women, pointing not only toward the inherent cruelty and lack of morality characterizing animal life but also toward the equally strong ethical dilemmas haunting the *human* animal, particularly in conditions of crisis such as war.
9 And perhaps even *The Innocent* in certain scenes (such as those marking the beginning of the relationship between Leonard and Maria). Nevertheless, by subsequently zooming in on Leonard's sadistic inclinations and on the disgust such inclinations engender in Maria's perspective upon her lover

and their relationship, the novel problematizes clear normative judgments of the characters' sexuality. I will reflect in more detail later on how McEwan's works tend to deconstruct normative binary divisions such as those between health and pathology, normality and deviance, or success and failure.

10 In *Atonement*, Robbie and Cecilia are in their early adulthood, are still virgins prior to their sexual encounter in the library, and share a long-term friendship (though ambiguous and fraught with misunderstandings as well as sexual undercurrents) where romance and sexuality do not yet play a crucial role; in *The Child in Time*, on the other hand, Stephen and Julia are a middle-aged married couple whose marriage falls apart after their young daughter is kidnapped.

11 Lawrence, however, is not the only literary predecessor McEwan engages with in his complex staging of sexual relationships. Besides the obvious figures of Marquis de Sade and of Sacher-Masoch behind his renditions of sadomasochist behaviors, both direct and indirect references to writers dealing extensively with sexuality (particularly *male* sexuality) such as Henry Miller, Norman Mailer, Vladimir Nabokov, or Thomas Mann abound in his stories and novels. See Childs (2006: 8–58) for further references and discussions of the intertextual frameworks structuring McEwan's approach to sexuality.

12 See also his theoretical works *Psychoanalysis and the Unconscious* and *Fantasia of the Unconscious*, both published in 1923, for similar descriptions of sexuality.

13 For a discussion of Lawrence's novel *Women in Love* in terms of Foucault's theories, see Doherty (1996).

14 Scholars like Gibbs, for instance, trace the dualism haunting Western thought back to Plato, and single out other important thinkers from the history of philosophy with similar viewpoints: "Separation of the mind and body and the hierarchical ordering of mind over body haunt the history of Western philosophical accounts of knowledge from Plato, Aristotle, and Augustine through to Descartes and Kant" (2005: 3).

15 Husserl, Heidegger, Merleau-Ponty, and Sartre are not the only phenomenologists discussing the body. Practically the entire phenomenological tradition seems to have recognized and discussed embodiment as our most fundamental way of being-in-the-world. For more examples, see Gallagher and Zahavi (2008: 134–35).

16 The analyses of how cognition is shaped and structured by dynamic interactions between body, brain, and physical and social environments are currently called 4E (embodied, embedded, enactive, and extended) approaches. See Newen, De Bruin, and Gallagher (2018) for a recent overview of this interdisciplinary field.

17 This idea is inspired, as Gallagher and Zahavi admit, by Gibson's theory of affordances (1986). Put simply, Gibson claims that objects from the

environment afford different action capacities for different kinds of being. For example, if we take as example a wooden chair, we find that it offers strikingly different affordances to a human being (e.g., sitting) than to a woodpecker (e.g., pecking).

18 A comprehensive collection of articles addressing imitation from cognitive and social scientific perspectives is Hurley and Chater (2005) (two volumes).

19 For an enactivist critique of the innateness of imitation, see Lodder, Rotteveel, and van Elk (2015).

20 A group of scientists led by Giacommo Rizzolatti was trying to identify the regions of the brain responsible for arm movement in Macaque monkeys at the University of Parma. After they managed to map these regions in a monkey's brain, the researchers took a break but forgot to take down the electrodes connecting the monkey to the computer. At one point, they noticed that the areas responsible for arm movement became active again, even if the monkey was standing still. After the initial puzzlement and the subsequent brainstorming, the researchers understood that the activation of the regions in question was caused not by motor processes but by perceptual processes. When the monkey *saw* the researcher move his arm, the same areas from the brain were activated as if the former would actually be *performing* the same action.

21 For a recent overview, see Rizzolatti and Sinigaglia (2008).

22 After all, mirror neurons were first discovered in *monkeys*.

23 Which Rochat calls "the two-month revolution," when "infants begin to manifest socially elicited smiling" which he describes as "an unmistakable expression of positive affect in the presence of another individual," and considers it to be a highly different phenomenon from the automatic, reflex-like smiles exhibited by infants before (Rochat 2009: 68).

24 Reddy (2013: 32–33) also considers these capacities as laying the ground for the development of joint action, a fundamental process pertaining to secondary intersubjectivity which I will discuss in more detail in the next chapter.

25 In a similar vein, Reddy characterizes imitation as "bi-directional" (2008: 60).

26 That is, the theory focusing on the bodily component of emotions, originally postulated by William James (1884), in which emotions are defined as the feelings of bodily changes vs. the more recent cognitive approaches to emotion (e.g., Solomon 1976; Lyons 1980; Nussbaum 2001) which claim that emotions are acts of evaluation and appraisal of a given situation (cf. Fuchs and Koch 2014: 1). Fuchs and Koch argue that both theories are reductive and advocate an understanding of emotions that combines the two positions (2–5).

27 See Sander and Scherer (2009) for a comprehensive companion to emotion and the affective sciences. For an enactive approach to emotion, see Colombetti (2014).

28 A term taken from the work of the psychologist and psychoanalyst Daniel Stern (1985). Stern describes interaffectivity, which he also calls affect attunement, as "a match between the feeling state as experienced within and as seen 'on' or 'in' another" (1985: 132). In his opinion, affect attunement is not a form of communication but of communion—participation, sharing without altering, maintaining the thread of feeling connectedness. Furthermore, he argues that affect attunement contributes to attachment and a sense of security and also helps in the development of psychic intimacy (cf. Stern 1985: 138–61; see Beebe et al. 2003: 824–27) for a summary of Stern's arguments and experiments).

29 They are careful nevertheless to argue that such claims *should not* be understood as similar to the ones in which simulation theorists of mind describe social interaction: "We certainly do not simulate the other's angry gaze or voice, even less his anger, but rather feel tense, threatened or even invaded by his expressive bodily behavior. Bodily sensations, tensions, action tendencies, etc. that arise in the interaction do not serve as a separate simulation of the other person, but are fed into the mutual perception" (Fuchs and Koch 2014: 6).

30 For a recent in-depth discussion of attachment based on findings in developmental psychology, see Owen (2017).

31 For example, Ridley (1993), Buss (1994), Miller (2000).

32 Note my previous caveat remains in this case too: although my focus will be on the representation of sexuality in these two works, the works themselves are *not only* about sexuality.

33 As he admits in the same interview, he wrote this story as a parody of the tendency toward "sexual aggrandisement" characterizing Henry Miller's and Norman Mailer's male characters (McEwan and Hamilton 1978: 18).

34 Contemporary cognitive scientists appear to take for granted the fact that real-life events have a narrative structure, or at least, that narrative structures are employed in order to make sense of such events (particularly if they appear to deviate from what is expected). Although such an undertaking would take me too far from my arguments in this chapter, the narrator's agnosticism regarding claims taken for granted in cognitive science could certainly be used as a starting point for challenging and attempting to re(de)fine specific scientific theories.

35 Sternberg (2003a, b) describes at length what he calls the three universals of narrative, that is, suspense, curiosity and surprise.

36 For the relationship between space and time in mythical thought, see Cassirer (1955 [1925]: 83–144) and Eliade (1957: 20–116); for a cognitive account of the general human propensity of conceptualizing time through spatial metaphors, see Lakoff and Johnson (1999: 137–69); for a discussion of the mythical and ritual aspects of the passage into adulthood see Van Gennep (2004 [1960]: 65–145); and for a cognitive-developmental approach to the ways in which puberty is structured by mythic and romantic frames, see Egan (1997: Chs 2, 3).

37 According to Zahavi and Rochat, by the middle of their third year, children learn to correctly identify their gender; by age four to five, they become aware of their ethnic and racial identity (2015: 548).

38 Of course, another question which emerges here is *why* the older, knowledgeable narrator would feel the need to confess such a shameful thing. As we will see later though, this tendency toward exhibitionism is highly developed in his younger self too. The fact that the retrospective narrator still has it makes the reader wonder whether (*pace* Head and Broughton) one could still consider him as having developed much since puberty.

39 While playing "Mommies and Daddies" with his sister in order to ultimately deceive her into having sex with him, the narrator reflects: "I was plunged into the microcosm of the dreary, everyday, ponderous banalities, the horrifying, niggling details of the life of our parents and their friends, the life Connie so dearly wanted to ape" (*H*: 38). This scene, together with his earlier sarcastic comments regarding his parents' and relatives' futile struggles to earn money (31–32) probably make Broughton claim that our "hero" is celebrating his separateness from society. However, as his attitudes toward his virginity I discussed earlier testify, his position toward society appears to be more ambivalent than Broughton argues.

40 "Used in French as an insulting epithet, as well as a pejorative term for the vulva and the vagina" (Broughton 1991: 141).

41 Shoshana Felman, in 1977, tracked how a series of academic critics were trapped in certain ways of interpretation already thematized and problematized in the novel they were trying to interpret: Henry James's *The Turn of the Screw* (1898).

42 Head's examples are his mythic description of Lulu, as well as the sensation of his first orgasm (caused by masturbation): "I was lifted by the scruff of the neck, my arms, my legs, my insides, haled, twisted, racked, and producing for all this two dollops of sperm" (*H*: 26).

43 Here, the narrator employs what Fuchs calls an implicit 3PP, that is, an observer perspective, a one-way, remote *observation* of others, highly different from an *interaction* with others.

44 One of the most troublesome features of this encounter is, of course, its incestuous character. However, a systematic discussion of the theme of incest in McEwan's works (which he expands in more detail in his first novel, *The Cement Garden*) lies beyond the scope of this study.

45 I am calling this interaction paradoxical since it can be described in terms of a surplus (invasion) caused by a lack (paralysis).

46 It is beyond the scope of this chapter to comprehensively discuss the ways in which sexuality is structured by various timescales (e.g., the "spacious" present, the personal-historical, the public-historical, the evolutionary-biological, and the cosmic-geological) as well as how the failure haunting the protagonists loses its importance when seen from a cosmic-geological perspective. However, it is important to mention briefly how the complex framings of *OCB* problematize value judgments such as those provided

by *H*'s more straightforward framing and, thus, clearer evaluative stance, that is, from the (limited) perspective of its retrospective narrator. In *OCB*, recurrent references to the physical/geographical setting of the novel, in which the cosmic-geological time-scale embedding the characters' encounter is often foregrounded (e.g., "Chesil Beach with its infinite . . . shingle between the sea and the lagoon" [4–5], where "thousands of years of pounding storms had sifted and graded the sight of pebbles along the eighteen miles of beach" [19], "the sound of waves collapsing onto the shore at regular intervals" [131], "the solid darkness of the hills" [150], "the immense straight road of shingle gleaming in the pallid light" [166]) open perspectives where moral/ethical judgments regarding the characters' behavior become irrelevant. Their sexual encounter, seen from their limited perspective as a tragic failure, loses its importance when seen from this larger, cosmic-geological perspective. As Edward and Florence too meditate toward the end of the novel, "the relentless laws and processes of the physical world, of moon and tides . . . were not remotely altered by [their] situation" (131) and, thus, "what they had there, on the shores of the English Channel, was only a minor theme in a larger pattern" (146).

47 Head discusses the ways in which McEwan's work deconstructs the classical distinction between a novel and a novella (2013). In his view, novellas are usually "determined overtly by structure and device" (116) and "depend upon a single symbolic setting or motif" (118), features which "restrict the experimental treatment of larger issues and themes" (116). Although he claims that *OCB is* in fact structured around a symbolic setting, that is, the beach, read as an allegory of the borderline between two historical contexts, Victorianism and contemporaneity (cf. Childs 2009; Wells 2010; however, see my significantly different reading of the geographical setting in the footnote above), he nevertheless argues that the psychological depth of the characters, which makes them *more* than just representative of their historical-cultural context, is something usually novels rather than novellas deal with (118–21).

48 Head describes him as "a sexually knowing narrator manipulating his innocent creations" and further claims that "the gap between [the characters'] understanding and experience, and the knowledge of the narrator—and also the author, as the governing intelligence—is discomfiting" (2013: 122). See also Caracciolo's insightful and in-depth discussion of how McEwan's use of such a narrator has a paradoxical effect on the readers, prompting them *both* to identify and empathize with the characters' plights *and* to maintain, at the same time, an ironic distance (2014b: 144–54). As he puts it, the "feat McEwan accomplishes is that his characters remain poised between the status of puppets in a semi-comic experiment that he carries out jointly with the reader, and their being creatures whose all-too-human interpersonal fiasco stirs the reader's sympathies and emotions" (145).

49 Here is the poem: "Sexual intercourse began/ In nineteen sixty-three/ which was rather late for me)—/ Between the end of the 'Chatterley'

ban/ And the Beatles' first LP.// Up to then there'd only been/ A sort of bargaining,/ A wrangle for the ring,/ A shame that started at sixteen/ And spread to everything.// Then all at once the quarrel sank:/ Everyone felt the same,/ And every life became/ A brilliant breaking of the bank,/ A quite unlosable game.// So life was never better than/ In nineteen sixty-three/ (Though just too late for me)—/ Between the end of the 'Chatterley' ban/ And the Beatles' first LP."

50 A clear example would be the conflict between feminists and Hugh Hefner's *Playboy* culture (cf. Garton 2004: 223–24).

51 A period loosely associated with the reign of Queen Victoria over the British Empire (1837–1901), yet for some scholars (particularly those advocating the revolutionary aspects of the developments from the late twentieth century), extending up to the 1960s. This points toward an important aspect which should be taken into account in the context of these debates about sexual revolutions: they are relevant *only* for a limited geo-historical context, that is, the Western (or perhaps, even only the British) one, spanning the (late) nineteenth and twentieth centuries.

52 For example, Marcus (1966), Pearsall (1969), and Trudgill (1976).

53 Foucault's analyses of sexuality and of its relation with knowledge and power are much too complex to be comprehensively summarized here. For a good introduction to the first volume of *History of Sexuality*, see Kelly (2013).

54 For example, the hysterical woman, the masturbating child, the Malthusian couple, or the pervert adult (Foucault 1978 [1976]: 103–14).

55 For example, Childs (2009), Wells (2010), and Head (2013).

56 For a different and rich perspective on turning points, see Christopher Norris's verse-essay "Ectopiques," published online in the *In/Stead* journal (http ://www.insteadjournal.com/article/ectopiques/).

57 For a historical overview of the development and proliferation of such medical/normative discourses about sexuality in the twentieth century, see Garton (2004: 189–209). Furthermore, these passages, as many others in *OCB*, are characterized by double-voicedness (see Bakhtin (1981) for complex analyses of literature in terms of double-voicedness, heteroglossia, and polyphony). The strategies of *OCB*'s knowledgeable, ironic, and manipulative narrator, discussed by Head and Caracciolo, make the reader oscillate between an empathic identification with and an ironic distance from Florence: the anguish she feels while reading these manuals is only *partly* transmitted to the reader, who cannot escape noticing, at the same, the quasi-humorous tone of the narrator's rendering of the passages Florence reads.

58 As the narrator ironically claims, "During [Edward's] three years as a student, the nights at the club represented the peak of his cultural experience" (38)—a strong parallel with *H*'s narrator's sexual "education" prior to his first sexual encounter.

59 Mostly tragic for the characters, of course, yet, due to the narrative framing, quite comic for the reader.

60 The staging of this interplay between the particular and the general with the purpose to let the two illuminate each other is similar with McEwan's strategy in *H* of building a parallel between the narrator's paralysis and Raymond's more general disconnection from experience.

61 For more detailed (cognitive scientific) accounts of categorization see also Jackendoff (1987: Ch. 8) and Lakoff (1987).

62 Here, the crucial role of narratives in shaping identity and in structuring social interactions contemporary philosophers and cognitive scientists acknowledge and analyze is also foregrounded. What *OCB* adds to the philosophical and scientific debates is the crucial insight that even clearly *false/deceitful* narrative accounts can powerfully structure (inter) subjectivity.

63 For a discussion of the theme of secrecy and its connection with identity in *OCB* see Byrnes (2009). Cf. also Childs (2009), who discusses the "conspiracy of silence and denial" surrounding Edward's family (33). I will address secrecy and the ways in which it structures (inter)subjectivity in greater depth when I will discuss *Atonement*. For the moment, another brief return to *Sabbath's Theater* can provide sufficient food for thought on these issues. When Roseanna, his alcoholic second wife tells him that, in her opinion, "You're as sick as your secrets," Sabbath immediately corrects her, since it "was not the first time that he was hearing this pointless, shallow, idiotic maxim:" "Wrong . . . You're as adventurous as your secrets, as abhorrent as your secrets, as alluring as your secrets, as courageous as your secrets, as vacuous as your secrets, as lost as your secrets; you are as human as [your secrets]." Manufacturing secrets, Sabbath concludes, "is mankind's leading industry" (Roth 2007 [1995]: 88).

64 The deep influences social interactions have on the development of selfhood foregrounded in this passage are reminiscent of, for example, Vygotsky's, Nelson's, Fuchs's, or Schore's theoretical reflections on the fundamental role of intersubjectivity in the constitution of subjectivity (Vygotsky 1986; Nelson 2007; Fuchs (2012); Schore 2019).

65 As I will discuss in the next chapter, similar types of paralysis are also staged in the novels *Enduring Love* and *Saturday*.

66 Speaking in an interview about Florence's probable childhood abuse, McEwan claims: "In earlier drafts it was much clearer and in subsequent drafts I made it less obvious. In the final draft it's there as a shadowy fact for readers to make of it what they will. I didn't want to be too deterministic about this. Many readers may miss it altogether, which is fine" (cited in Byrnes 2009: 26–27).

67 For the importance of embodied and affective interactions between caregivers and children for the latter's future psychological and social development, see Stern (1985), Nelson (2007), and Schore (2019).

68 I will discuss in more detail in the next chapter how monomaniac "blockages" within various worldviews (scientific, religious, artistic, philosophical) can give rise to paralysis and invasion.

69 As I already mentioned above, Caracciolo provides an insightful interpretation of how McEwan's narrative strategies in these passages give rise
paradoxically to both ironic distance and empathetic identification with the
characters' plight in the readers (2014b: 144–54).
70 "Who, for decorum's sake, has even slowed his heart, or muted a blush?"
(*OCB*: 86).
71 Edward's expectations for their wedding night are highly reminiscent
of Lawrence's idealization of sexuality: "here was a boundless sensual
freedom," Edward meditates,

> theirs for the taking, even blessed by the vicar—*with my body I thee
> worship*—a dirty, joyous bare-limbed freedom, which rose in his
> imagination like a vast airy cathedral, ruined perhaps, roofless, fan-
> vaulted to the skies, where they would weightlessly drift upwards in
> a powerful embrace and have each other, drown each other in waves
> of breathless, mindless ecstasy. It was so simple! Why weren't they
> up there now, instead of sitting here, bottled up with all the things
> they did not know how to say or dared not do? (Ibid.: 96)

Besides the hopes for a "worshiping of the body" leading to a "mindless
ecstasy," also the references to the "airy cathedral" remind the reader of
Lawrence's novel *The Rainbow*, where, if not the birth, at least the intensification of the sexual desire between Ursula and Skrebensky takes place in a
cathedral.
72 In an interview McEwan claims that the disastrous sexual encounter was
"no one's fault. Edward and Florence are of their time, and they are not
armed of getting themselves out of this mess" (D'Ancona 2007; cited in
Byrnes 2009: 14).
73 Mathews mentions two works by Strachey, *Eminent Victorians* (1918) and
Queen Victoria (1921), which he describes as "polished reflections on the
generational shift from the Victorian to the modern period" (2012: 84). He
also draws a parallel between *OCB*'s Florence and Florence Nightingale,
one of Strachey's "eminent Victorians": when he first saw Florence, Edward
"thought for a moment she was a nurse—in an abstract, conventional way
he found nurses erotic, because—so he liked to fantasize—they already
knew everything about his body and its needs" (*OCB*: 47–48; cited in
Mathews 2012: 85).
74 Broader reflections, however, regarding the peculiar position within the
animal kingdom of the *clothed* animal, continuously ashamed of and
trying to cover its nakedness, point toward the perils of the characters'
unavoidable identification with a much larger social group, that comprises
the entire human species. After Edward's premature ejaculation and
Florence's departure to the beach, he obsessively thinks about what
happened ("thought it through all over again"), only to conclude that it "is
not easy to pursue such hard truths in bare feet and underpants" and to

immediately draw "his trousers on and grope . . . for his socks and shoes"
(*OCB*: 135). When he reaches Florence on the beach, she is "bothered . . .
that he thought he had to bring a jacket with him." "At least he had not
put on his tie!" she bitterly reflects. "God, how irritable she suddenly felt,
when minutes ago she was so ashamed of herself" (143). Sabbath's quasi-
philosophical ruminations on the theme of clothing, tinged with his usual
sarcasm and bitterness, can, once more, be read as interesting counterparts
of these scenes from *OCB*: "Clothes are a masquerade anyway. When you
go outside and see everyone in clothes, then you know for sure that nobody
has a clue as to why he was born and that, aware of it or not, people are
perpetually performing in a dream. It's putting corpses into clothes that
really betrays what great thinkers we are" (Roth 2007 [1995]: 413).

75   The essentialist approaches from the contemporary cognitive sciences
     where sexuality is conceptualized in biological, universalist terms and
     where the phenomenology of the sexual act is largely ignored (and in the
     rare cases when it is not ignored is mainly seen as pertaining to primary
     intersubjectivity).

76   Both phenomenological accounts of sexuality in terms of primary forms of
     intersubjectivity such as Merleau-Ponty's and social constructivist views of
     sexuality as a social-historical construct such as Foucault's.

77   Mainly D. H. Lawrence's idealization of sexuality as a nonlinguistic, non-
     conceptual, embodied, and affective form of interaction.

Chapter 3

1   The concept of "worldview" has a long and complex philosophical
    history. Originally introduced by Kant in *The Critique of Judgment*
    (*Weltanschauung*) in 1790, this concept has been further elaborated
    in various directions by a great number of philosophers (e.g., Hegel,
    Kierkegaard, Dilthey, Nietzsche, Husserl, Jaspers, Heidegger, Wittgenstein,
    Foucault), psychologists (Freud, Jung), social scientists (Mannheim, Berger,
    Luckmann, Marx, Engels), and theologians (Orr, Kuyper, Dooyeweerd,
    Schaeffer). It is beyond the scope of this study to address the various debates
    surrounding this concept, as well as its relation to other similar concepts
    such as William James's "sub-universes"(1890), Alfred Schütz's "finite
    provinces of meaning" (1945), or Owen Flanagan's "spaces of meaning"
    (2007). For a detailed history of this concept, as well as further references,
    see Naugle (2002). For an insightful discussion of how worldviews are
    created through metaphorical, ideological, and linguistic frameworks,
    see Underhill (2011). In the context of this book, the concept "worldview"
    should be understood as designating the frameworks of understanding
    structuring our perception of and interaction with the world and would
    thus bear similarities with Underhill's concept of "world-perceiving"

(2011: 7). Of course, this preliminary definition of the concept, as well as that of the (slightly) more specific concept of *"monomaniac* worldview" will be fleshed out in more detail during my analysis of McEwan's novel.

2 Head claims that the "story's chief interest is that it is an early treatment of the opposition between the mystical or intuitive and the rational, an idea that assumes great importance in McEwan's later work" (2007: 37).

3 McEwan himself, in his introduction to *The Imitation Game*, claims that the narrator and his wife, Maisie, are "the exaggerated representations" of "the highly rational and destructive" and "the loving but self-deluded" (1982 [1981]: 12). For a brief, yet powerful discussion of the connections between this dichotomy and gender dynamics, see Ryan (1994: 11–12).

4 As well as in the theater play *The Imitation Game* (1980) and the oratorio *Or Shall We Die?* (1983).

5 See McEwan's website for a comprehensive list of interviews and articles dealing with these issues: http://www.ianmcewan.com/science.html

6 See, for example Wally (2012), for a discussion of *Saturday* as a *deconstruction* of the "New Atheist novel."

7 Although Henry enjoys listening to classical music while performing neurosurgery, claiming it to have much more "purity" than fiction, which he describes as the "too humanly flawed, too sprawling and hit-and-miss to inspire uncomplicated wonder at the magnificence of human ingenuity, of the impossible dazzlingly achieved" (*St*: 68), he nevertheless admits that his relation to music cannot enter such depths as his son's: "There's nothing in his own life that contains this inventiveness, this style of being free. The music speaks to unexpressed longing or frustration, a sense that he's denied himself an open road, the life of the heart celebrated in the songs. There has to be more to life than merely saving lives. . . . Theo's playing carries this burden of regret into his father's heart. It is, after all, the blues" (28).

8 See Childs (2006) for overviews of the critical reception of *BD* (90–103) and *St* (144–51).

9 For an in-depth discussion of the narrative strategies McEwan uses to represent the environmental crisis in *Solar*, see Ionescu (2017).

10 For an overview of *CT*'s critical reception, see Childs (2006: 59–75).

11 I am putting the term "team" between inverted commas since I will later on argue, drawing upon philosophical and scientific research on joint action, that it would ultimately be mistaken to describe this group of people as a team (in the sense of the word given by Hans-Bernhard Schmid in his work on plural action from 2009).

12 This condition is named after the French psychiatrist Gaëtan Gatian de Clérambault (1872–1934), one of Lacan's most influential teachers, who discussed erotomania, that is, an affliction characterized by delusional beliefs someone holds that another person, usually of higher social status, is in love with him or her (cf. de Clérambault 1942 [1921]).

13   For an interpretation of *EL* in Foucaultian terms, see Matthews (2007: 95–96).

14   As Joe describes it, in his usual quasi-scientific vocabulary, "Parry had his generation's habit of making a statement on the rising inflection of a question—in humble imitation of Americans, or Australians, or, as I heard one linguist explain, too mired in relative judgments, too hesitant and apologetic to say how things were in the world" (*EL*: 24). Through the incorporation of this and other idiosyncratic traits within the construction of his character (largely unnecessary for the development of the plot), McEwan adds more nuance to what otherwise would be just an allegorical representation of a religious worldview (in Forster's terminology (1927), Jed becomes a "round" character; for a brilliant discussion of such methods of characterization, see Kermode 1979: 75–100).

15   "I've met you once before and I can tell you now that I have no feelings for you either way" (*EL*: 63). "Believe me, I have no feelings to control" (64). "I don't know who you are. I don't understand what you want, and I don't care" (65).

16   Similarly, in one of his letters, Jed accuses Joe again that he is just playing with him by denying the love between them, and once more frames his "argument" in religious terms: "It's a game you're playing with me, part seduction, part ordeal. You are trying to probe the limits of my faith" (*EL*: 97).

17   As I will argue in the next section, Joe's "detachment," steeped in reason and logic, giving Jed the impression that Joe "is no part of anything at all" can be seen as quite a good description of the latter's paralysis (or, perhaps, of the consequences of his paralysis).

18   For a more detailed analysis of this concept, see Nygren (1953: 61–159).

19   For a detailed discussion of the differences between *agape* and *eros*, see Nygren (1953).

20   The scientific manner in which the article is written tricked some reviewers into believing that it is genuine. In fact, it is written by McEwan (the surnames of the alleged authors, Wenn and Camia, are an anagram of Ian McEwan). As he claims in an interview, "I devised what they call in Hollywood a back story for Wenn and Camia: that they are a couple of homosexuals, who are only interested in homoerotic behavior. If you look at their other published paper, it is called 'Homosexual Erotomania,' and was published in *Acta Psychiatrica Scandinavia*, which is a real journal and the most obscure that I could find. I submitted the fictional paper for publication but now I feel terribly guilty because the journal I sent it to has written back saying that it is considering it for publication" (cited in Childs 2007b: 35).

21   See Davies (2007) and Ryan (2007) for in-depth analyses of the sexual ambiguities staged in the novel.

22   Toward the end of the novel, Jed hires hit men for killing Joe and personally threatens Clarissa after breaking into their apartment.

23 There are hints in some of Jed's letters though that his understanding of divine love does not necessarily exclude violence: "God's love . . . may take the form of wrath. It can show itself to us as calamity. . . . His love isn't always gentle. How can it be when it has to last, when you can never shake it off? It's a warmth, it's a heat and it can burn you, Joe, it can consume you" (*EL*: 152). In such passages, Jed's God seems to come closer to the one from the Old, rather than the New Testament.

24 Although in the next section I will describe Joe as obsessively/ monomanically employing scientific frameworks for making sense of (social) reality, his behavior in this scene already problematizes such an interpretation. His critical reading of Jed's letters, characterized by an intense hermeneutic stance of reading "between the lines" and "against the grain" seems quite different from his usual way of analyzing the world and other people through scientific lenses. Here, Joe appears closer to a literary critic rather than a scientist. By foregrounding the fact that Joe is able sometimes to break out of his rigid, scientific stance, McEwan once more points toward the intermittent nature of paralysis.

25 An embodied and affective way of "understanding" the other, steeped in an implicit 1PP and 2PP (cf. Zahavi 2014: 95–196).

26 However, the reader should always keep in mind that almost everything we know about Jed is filtered through Joe's perspective. Thus, taking into account also the fact that Joe himself has serious deficiencies in relating to others (which I will discuss in the next section), his judgments of Jed should never be taken for granted. Yet, regardless of their accuracy, they nevertheless provide interesting descriptions of a peculiar form of paralysis.

27 Cf. my previous discussion of the similarities between Jed's understanding of love and the Christian notion of *agape*.

28 For a psychoanalytic interpretation of Jed's solipsism, see Sistani, Hashim, and Hamdan (2014) who attempt to show "how deprivation from the establishment of a satisfying contact with [the] primary love object (mother) can wreak havoc in the character's psyche and cause his ego to move toward establishing relations with his internal objects instead of natural, real objects in his external world" (142). Yet, as psychiatrists like Thomas Fuchs argue, pathologies of intersubjectivity can also intensify due to lack of social contact (2015).

29 In Thomas Pynchon's novel *The Crying of Lot 49* (1965).

30 For example, Piaget (1928 [1926], 1952 [1936]). See Flavell (1963) for an excellent overview of Piaget's psychological research.

31 The possibility that Jed might hallucinate brings his condition closer to schizophrenia rather than to autism.

32 "I'm sure Joe didn't mean you any harm," she pleads to Jed. "He was actually very frightened of you, you know, standing outside the house, and all the letters. He didn't know anything about you" (*EL*: 211).

33 For a powerful discussion of the ethical consequences of Perowne's deficient ways of relating to Baxter, see Gauthier (2013).

34 For similar evolutionary explanations of religion, see, for example, Andresen (2001), Boyer (2001), and Atran (2004).

35 Joseph Greenberg (2007) discusses at length the ways in which McEwan integrates evolutionary biology in the novel. McEwan's interest in this scientific field is transparent not only from a variety of interviews, but also from the acknowledgments at the end of *EL*, where he stresses his indebtedness to various evolutionary biologists/psychologists, such as E. O. Wilson, Steven Pinker, and Robert Wright.

36 Joe himself acknowledges that "there might have been a commonality of purpose, but we were never a team" (*EL*: 10).

37 Hans-Bernhard Schmid, though, provides a powerful critique of such an understanding of rationality which is prevalent in contemporary economic theory (2009: 87–154).

38 Historically, evolutionary biology/psychology emerged as a powerful critique of what Barkow, Cosmides, and Tooby (1992) call the "Standard Model in Social Science," that is, a variety of strong *cultural* constructivism, claiming that the human mind is a *tabula rasa*, waiting for culture to fill it in. In contrast with this, evolutionary biologists and psychologists argue for the *innateness* of various psychological traits which, in their opinion, would constitute human *nature*. Here are McEwan's views on this issue: "There is a subject matter which would have been completely ruled out of court 15 years ago as a matter of scientific inquiry, and now it's central. It's called human nature. That interface between biology and social sciences, between biology and psychology, is increasingly clear. And . . . anthropology . . . is now exploring not how exotically different we are from each other, but how exotically similar we are. Which seems to me a really fascinating problem" (interview with Dwight Garner, cited in Childs 2007b: 113).

39 See, for example, Wright (1994), De Waal (2009), and Tomasello (2009).

40 For an extended list of mathematical motifs in *EL*, see Matthews (2007: 100).

41 Alan Palmer (2009) provides an insightful discussion of Joe's desire for control (cf. also Matthews 2007: 99).

42 Here, I offer a first glimpse on how paralysis breeds invasion in *EL*. I will leave for later though a more detailed discussion of these issues.

43 A succinct yet pointed contemporary discussion of the universality of the (expression of) emotions can be found in Ekman (1999). Spolsky, however, persuasively argues that "although understanding what others think, feel, believe, and intend may be crucial to our well-being, perhaps to our safety on a moment to moment basis, even the best mind reading can never provide fully reliable information. Other minds are simply not transparent, and we normally get better at hiding as we get older, learning, for example, to control facial muscles to disguise our feelings almost at will" (2015a: 62–63).

44 "I was just wondering how convincing I myself could be now in greeting Clarissa" (*EL*: 4–5).

45 "The truth of the smile," in Clarissa's opinion, "was in the eye and heart of the parent, and in the unfolding love which only had meaning through time" (*EL*: 70).

46 We find from the first appendix, however, that Joe and Clarissa "were reconciled and later successfully adopted a child" (*EL*: 242). Such an outcome can be read as a critique of a Darwinian view of love as based in biological parenthood, such as Wright's (and, implicitly, Joe's).

47 Which immediately give rise to biological reflections we are already used to hear from him: "Some people find their long perspectives in the stars and galaxies; I prefer the earthbound scale of the biological. . . . The blind compulsion of these organisms to consume and excrete made possible the richness of the soil, and therefore the plants, the trees, and the creatures that live among them, whose number once included ourselves" (*EL*: 206–07).

48 Just like his recurrent framing of scientific discourses in literary terms, his use of this religious metaphor here points toward the permeability of boundaries between scientific and religious worldviews, as well as to the fact that Joe's paralysis should be better understood as an intermittent occurrence rather than a chronic condition.

49 Many critics discussed Joe as an unreliable narrator (Matthews 2007 offers the most comprehensive analysis of the various types of unreliability this narrator could be accused of).

50 "What a sorry picture memory offers," he reflects in highly poetic terms, "barely a shadow, barely in the realm of sight, the echo of a whisper" (*EL*: 182). Such a way of expressing scientific facts, that is, through a complex metaphor, structured by a powerful synesthetic mixture of vision and sound, foregrounds once more the permeability of the boundaries between science and art, and the intermittent nature of Joe's paralysis.

51 Matthews calls such admissions acts of "candid" unreliability (see Matthews 2007: 96–98 for a list of examples).

52 An interesting example of how one can occasionally become *conscious* of one's own paralysis.

53 Spolsky discusses these findings from evolutionary biology in terms of a "divergence between truth and fit" (2015a: 19): "Evidence that truth and fitness are not always productively aligned may be glimpsed in the discussion about the origins of altruism, where it has been hypothesized that the ability to fool oneself about one's motives may well be adaptive. Hypocrisy and even self-delusion, on these arguments, are part of the necessary equipment for living in social groups" (2015a: 18–19). The hypothesis that most successful behavior results from self-delusion was first proposed by Alexander (1975, 1979) and Trivers (1976, 1985). See Nesse and Lloyd (1992: 603ff.) for an overview.

54 Notice also the mathematical term he uses.

55 See Childs (2007a) for an in-depth discussion of the "believing is seeing" metaphor in the context of McEwan's novel, and Spolsky (1994) for a bril-

liant discussion of the opposite metaphor ("seeing is believing") as structuring Apostle Thomas's experiences in the Bible.

56 McEwan admits in an interview with James Naughtie that this was precisely his intention in the novel: "I wanted a man at the center of this who was a clear thinker, who appears to be right but then perhaps is wrong, but in fact is right. . . .I wanted, in other words, to write a book somewhat in praise of rationality which I think gets a very poor showing in western literature" (cited in Childs 2007b: 5). McEwan's claims give rise to very important questions regarding the relationship between certain forms of paralysis and rationality, an aspect that is beyond the scope of this study.

57 Whom Joe criticizes harshly; in his opinion, Keats was "a genius, no doubt, but an obscurantist too who had thought science was robbing the world of wonder, when the opposite was the case" (*EL*: 71). Joe's belief that science can engender wonder while, at the same time, demythologizing the world, comes close not only to Thelma's poetic defense of science I cited in the introduction to this chapter, but also to Henry Perowne's endowment of Charles Darwin's concluding sentence of his *Origins of Species* (1859), that is, "there is grandeur in this view of life." "Those five hundred pages deserved only one conclusion," Henry claims, "endless and beautiful forms of life, such as you see in a common hedgerow, including exalted beings like ourselves, arose from physical laws, from war of nature, famine and death. This is the grandeur. And a bracing kind of consolation in the brief privilege of consciousness" (*St*: 56).

58 Interestingly enough, some contemporary scientists, such as Ellen Disannayake (2000), also come close to such views.

59 "I found myself getting angry at Clarissa," Palmer confesses (306).

60 In a milder tone, Paul Edwards also claims that "Clarissa's suspicions are quite misplaced" (2007: 84).

61 As I will argue later, Briony Tallis in *Atonement* embodies a similar, yet much more pathological form of paralysis caused by an excessive reliance on artistic/literary frameworks.

62 Again, one should not ignore the destabilizing effect on the hermeneutic process arising from the fact that these judgments are filtered through Joe's limited/deficient perspective.

63 For a philosophical and cognitive discussion of the psychopathologies of hyper-reflexivity, see Fuchs (2010).

64 This incident can also be considered a focus of attention for another "couple," Jed and Joe, whose disagreements (to put it mildly) emerge, as previously discussed, from their highly divergent interpretations of this incident.

65 The last two decades witnessed a wide range of discussions of joint/shared attention from interdisciplinary perspectives (combining philosophy of mind, social neuroscience, developmental psychology, and evolution theory). The most important collections of articles dealing with these issues are Moore and Dunham (1995), Eilan et al. (2005), Seemann (2011a), Metcalfe and Terrace (2013). These phenomena, however, have been

discussed in earlier continental philosophy too. Merleau-Ponty, for example, famously argued that "in so far as I have sensory functions . . . I am already in communication with others. . . . No sooner has my gaze fallen upon a living body in process of acting than the objects surrounding it immediately take on a fresh layer of significance; they are no longer simply what I myself could make out of them, they are what this other pattern of behavior is about to make of them" (1962: 353). See also Gallagher and Jacobson (2012) for a discussion of Heidegger's philosophy as an analysis of secondary forms of intersubjectivity and Szanto and Moran (2015) for a collection of phenomenological approaches to joint attention and action.

66 That is, as a mental state, involving conceptual understanding, rather than as an embodied openness toward the world (as phenomenologists, for example, would see it).

67 Gallagher describes meta-representation as the ability to represent or understand the fact that both my attention and the attention of the other are directed outward toward the same object (2011a: 294).

68 Böckler and Sebanz also follow a similar path when they describe joint attention as having two components: the perceptual component of processing and gaze following, and the conceptual component of knowing about the other's attention (2013: 206–7).

69 Roessler claims that the "problem is that while there is compelling intuition to the effect that 1-year-olds have some grasp of others' attention, there is also prima facie grounds for doubting that they have the conceptual abilities for interpretation (such as the ability to give causal explanations)" (2005: 236; cited in Gallagher 2011a: 296).

70 Which Gallagher calls "theory of mind versions of joint attention" and ties to theory theorists and simulation theorists of social cognition (Gallagher 2011a: 296).

71 Another paradigmatic example of an embodied collaborative activity in need of no mind-reading abilities is Gurwitsch's analysis of two workers cobbling a street (1979). As Gallagher and Zahavi argue, in such a case each worker "is related to the other in his activity and comportment. When one worker understands the other, the understanding in question does not involve grasping some hidden mental occurrences. There is no problem of other minds. There is no problem of how one isolated ego gets access to another isolated ego. Rather, both workers understand each other in virtue of the roles they play in the common situation" (2008: 191).

72 However, Reddy (2005, 2008, 2011, 2013) is not the only scholar discussing the importance of affect in joint attention. In the first important collection of articles about joint attention (Moore and Dunham 1995), Adamson and McArthur discuss the role of emotion in structuring contexts of joint attention, by addressing how emotional messages about objects may vary as a function of infants' gender (1995: 205, 212–14), as well as how affective deficits characterizing autistic children can impede their capacities to engage in joint attention (214–17; cf. also Sigman and Kasari 1995;

Gomez 2005; Hobson 2005; Hobson and Hobson 2011). For other analyses of the fundamental role of emotion in secondary forms of intersubjectivity, see Adamson and Russell (1999), Seemann (2011), and Trevarthen (2011).

73 For the relationship between joint attention and joint action, see the articles collected in Metcalfe and Terrace (2013), especially the one by Böckler and Sebanz.

74 In fact, the recent, enactive paradigm in cognitive science tends to describe perceptual processes in general as fundamentally connected to action tendencies (cf. e.g., Noë 2004; see, also, Thompson 2007: 243–66, and Gallagher and Zahavi 2008: 89–106 for overviews).

75 This concept is taken from Gibson's ecological psychology (1986). See Costantini and Sinigaglia (2011) for a neuroscientific discussion of joint attention in terms of affordances.

76 For example, Gilbert (1990), Bratman (2007), Tuomela (2007).

77 He admits, however, that classical accounts could be useful in explaining more sophisticated instances of joint action (2011: 3, 16).

78 For example, Tollefsen (2005), Pacherie and Dokic (2006), Sebanz, Knoblich, and Prinz (2005), and Vesper et al. (2010).

79 A similar critique can be found in Schmid (2009: 59–86).

80 He is careful to emphasize though that the expression of emotions *need not* be necessarily verbal (Michael 2011: 7).

81 A concept analyzed in depth in classical accounts such as Gilbert's. However, Michael claims, the complex ways in which Gilbert defines commitment (in terms of "obligations" and "entitlements") would not make it a viable explanatory term for, e.g., interactions in infancy (Michael 2011: 4, 10).

82 This definition of empathy would be considered too simple by several phenomenologists. Although I cannot expand more upon this here, see Zahavi's comprehensive and systematic recent analyses of empathy (2014: 95–196).

83 For a more detailed analysis of the relationship between the collective agent model, the influence model, and the teamwork model of plural action, as well as in-depth arguments regarding why the first two presuppose the third, see Schmid (2009: 3–28). For an account of "team thinking" and the ways it structures coordination, see Schmid (2009: 111–18). A comprehensive collection of articles on teamwork, bringing together developmental, evolutionary, and social scientific perspectives is Gold (2005).

84 Here, he refers to the phenomenological understanding of intentionality as directedness/aboutness.

85 "In this view," Schmid claims, "a theory of the affective should be concerned with a taxonomy of feeling experiences, and with the analysis of the causal role of states of arousal, rather than with such ventures as intentional analysis" (2009: 60).

86 As Schmid stresses, though, the intentionality philosophers of emotion talk about is more mentalistic than the phenomenological understanding

of intentionality as an embodied directedness/openness toward the world, that is, it implies cognitive and conative aspects, such as beliefs and action dispositions (2009: 60).

87 He gives the following example: when encountering a threatening dog coming toward oneself while jogging in a park, the target of the fear is the dog, and the focus of the fear of the dog is oneself. If, on the other hand, the dog is approaching a group of children, the target will still be the dog, yet the focus will be the children (Schmid 2009: 64–65).

88 If, for instance, the subject in the previous example does not care about his or the children's safety, the fact that the dog attacks him or the children will not rationalize the feeling of fear (Schmid 2009: 65).

89 Which I already discussed earlier in connection to Michael's arguments.

90 Although he does not explain explicitly why this is the case, I believe that his argument would revolve around the fact that, in cases such as the spreading of a feeling of fear within a group, such a feeling would lack content.

91 For a more elaborate discussion of this scene from Homer, see Schmid (2009: 67–68).

92 Although this scene is also rendered through and mediated by Joe's perspective.

93 See Ryan (2007) for a discussion of the Biblical references in the first chapter (the parallels between the Chiltern Hills and the Garden of Eden as well as those between John Logan's fall and the Biblical "fall" from Genesis).

94 Although I discussed the breakdown in Joe and Clarissa's interaction in terms of "intrusive" forces "breaching" their encounter, it is important to realize that this is *not* a case of invasion: no surplus of forms of intersubjectivity causes this breakdown; on the contrary, Gadd's shout has the effect of suddenly dissolving all traces of intersubjectivity between the two characters.

95 A symptom of his paralysis, as I previously argued.

96 Gallagher and Zahavi would see the emergence of language and the development of narrative sense-making as processes lying way beyond secondary intersubjectivity. However, I would consider them, together with Fuchs, as intermediary cases, strongly rooted in secondary intersubjectivity, and marking the transition to more complex forms of sense-making pertaining to tertiary intersubjectivity.

97 As I argued before, following Reddy, attention to the self seems to be developmentally more primordial than attention to objects and events. However, the children's ability to view themselves from an external perspective Tomasello discusses clearly requires more sophisticated cognitive capacities than those identified by Reddy. I propose thus to see Tomasello's and Reddy's accounts as complementary rather than contradictory, that is, to consider the basic (dyadic) mutual attention Reddy identifies as grounding the more complex instances of (triadic) mutual attention discussed by Tomasello. However, a more systematic integration of their insights falls beyond the scope of this study.

98 Hutto claims that folk psychology is quite a sophisticated skill, which has to meet at least the following prerequisites: (1) a practical understanding of propositional attitudes (e.g., beliefs and desires); (2) a capacity to represent the objects that these attitudes take—propositional contents as specified by that-clauses (e.g., x in "I believe that x"; y in "I fear that y," etc.); (3) an understanding of the "principles" governing the interaction of the attitudes, both with one another and with other key psychological players, such as perception and emotion; and (4) an ability to apply all the above sensitively, that is, adjusting for relevant differences in particular cases by making allowances for different variables such as a person's character, circumstances, and so on (Hutto 2007: 48). For a more elaborate discussion of folk psychology and its relation to narrative competency and practices in terms of evolution and development, see Hutto (2008).

99 "When things 'are as they should be,' the narratives of folk psychology are unnecessary" (Bruner 1990: 40; cited in Gallagher and Hutto 2008: 30). For a more detailed discussion of the dynamics between canonicity and breach lying at the heart of narrative practices, see Bruner (1990: 33–98).

100 "Episodic memory" is a term first introduced by Tulving (1972). Hoerl and McCormack describe it as involving the exercise of a particular form of attention—attention to specific past events (2005: 264). Episodic recall, in their view, is not only dependent on the availability of information retained from the past, but also on the subject him/herself having a particular kind of active influence on the way that information is processed. In other words, it "is a matter of a subject's using her own memory to pursue certain kinds of questions about the past; for an answer to come forward, however, the subject's pursuing the relevant question must have a causal influence on the way information retained from past experience is being processed" (267). (NB: this way of describing attention to the past as an *active* process is highly similar to Gallagher's conceptualization of attention in terms of action dispositions in current environments).

101 In their opinion, based on empirical psychological research, a thorough understanding of causality emerges only after five years of age (Hoerl and McCormack 2005: 270–73).

102 For various concrete examples of how adults work on improving children's causal understanding in contexts of joint reminiscing, see Hoerl and McCormack (2005: 273–77).

103 For example, Davies (2007), Edwards (2007), Greenberg (2007), Randall (2007), Ryan (2007), Palmer (2009), Phelan (2009), Carbonell (2010), Green (2011), and Ramin and Marandi (2012).

104 In this aspect, it clearly resembles *H*.

105 For further reflections on the uses of storytelling in the sciences, philosophy, and literature, see Nash (1990).

106 Although contemporary philosophers and cognitive scientists acknowledge and discuss the fundamental role narrative sense-making plays in

human interaction, what still remains to be studied in a systematic way is how *traumatic* events both desperately need, and, paradoxically, almost unavoidably escape narrativization.

107 For the crucial importance of generic framing for the epistemological, aesthetic and ethical impact of narratives, see Korthals Altes (2013) and Spolsky (2015a).

108 Yet, another reason their interaction fails could be the fact that, whereas there in no shared concern between Joe and Logan, due to their different experiences of fatherhood (or lack thereof, in Joe's case), it seems that Clarissa *is* able to empathize with Logan. As Joe himself acknowledges, "in John Logan she saw a man prepared to die to prevent the kind of loss she felt herself to have sustained. The boy was not his own, but he was a father and he understood. His kind of love pierced Clarissa's defenses" (*EL*: 32).

Chapter 4

1 However, as I made clear through my brief discussion of *Sabbath's Theater* and *Solar*, paralysis can also manifest itself as a blockage within ways of sense-making pertaining to, for example, primary intersubjectivity in instances in which other forms of intersubjectivity are necessary.

2 Studies of psychopathologies such as Fuchs's (2010, 2015) admit the crucial importance of phenomenology for understanding and describing mental illness. See also Zahavi (2000) for a collection of articles exploring the self and its pathologies from a combination of philosophical, psychopathological, and phenomenological frameworks.

3 Husserl's works on intersubjectivity are collected in the three volumes of *Husserliana* (13, 14, 15) published in 1973. Heidegger's *Being and Time* (1927) remains the key entry point into his reflections on ontological categories such as "Being-with" (*Mitsein*) and "Being-with-one-another" (*Miteinundandersein*). As for Merleau-Ponty, his *Phenomenology of Perception* (1945) contains deep analyses of intersubjectivity too (especially part 2, chapter 4).

4 See Thompson (2007), Gallagher and Zahavi (2008), Gallagher (2012), and Zahavi (2014) for surveys of the attempts to integrate the insights of these phenomenologists into contemporary cognitive science.

5 As Spolsky argues, "Cognitive psychologists, perhaps because in framing their hypotheses about normal brains they regularly depend on the empirical evidence provided by traumatized or diseased brains, regard failures as pathological, and thus, as not at all ordinary. In the familiar belief that they are thereby avoiding the contaminations of fictions, they overlook the very real evidence of human behavior that fictional characters in their interactions provide. Their empirical studies, however, like the short scenarios philosophers call thought experiments, are vastly oversimplified

stand-ins for the complexity of human responsiveness" (2015a: 130–31). J.L. Austin (1962), H.P. Grice (1975), Stanley Cavell (1988, 1994, 2005), Jacques Derrida (1988) and Spolsky herself (1990, 1993, 2001, 2011, 2015a), though, from their different perspectives (speech act theory, philosophy, and cognitive literary studies), have addressed in great detail the ubiquity of failures of understanding characterizing various types of social interactions.

6   In my view, Sartre's numerous examples of problematic social encounters from *Being and Nothingness* (1943) could also provide rich sources for further reflections on these issues.

7   Systematic investigations of the reflections on intersubjectivity of other phenomenologists such as Schütz, Gurwitsch, Scheler, or Stein could also prove extremely valuable for clarifying the philosophical status of paralysis and invasion. For first attempts to integrate these philosophers' insights into contemporary cognitive science, see, for example, Zahavi (2014), and Szanto and Moran (2016).

8   Here, another instantiation of the "believing is seeing" metaphor underlying Joe's paralysis in *EL* is obvious.

9   His "theory" (as he repeatedly calls it; for example, *At*: 229, 233) is that Briony's infatuation with him and her subsequent jealousy made Briony lie. As I argued though, her behavior is better understood in terms of misunderstanding and self-deception caused by her paralysis, rather than as structured by conscious deception.

10 "She took her daughter in her arms, onto her lap—ah, that hot smooth little body she remembered from her infancy, and still not gone from her, not quite yet—and said that the play was 'stupendous,' and agreed instantly, murmuring into the tight whorl of the girl's ear, that this word could be quoted on the poster which was to be on an easel in the entrance hall by the ticket booth" (*At*: 4).

11 Once the reader realizes that Briony was the narrator of the novel, the previously postulated omniscience of this narrator becomes, of course, highly problematic. In contrast, unreliability and limited perspective seem now to characterize this voice.

12 For discussions of the hermeneutic process as a complex form of joint attention between readers and authors/narrators, see Herman (2008), Currie (2007, 2010), Caracciolo (2012), and Popova (2015).

13 For interesting discussions of the metafictional/meta-mimetic/meta-narrative elements of *Atonement*, see Finney (2004), O'Hara (2010), and Spiridon (2010).

14 Furthermore, since the old Briony in the Coda is diagnosed with vascular dementia—a neurological disorder characterized by "loss of memory, short- and long-term, the disappearance of single words . . . then language itself, along with balance, and soon after, all motor control, and finally the autonomous nervous system" (*At*: 354–55)—her unreliability as a narrator increases even more. For analyses of memory and forgetfulness in connection with *Atonement*, see Hidalgo (2005) and De Azevedo (2010).

15 As I argued in the previous chapter, Joe's *scientific* discovery of his paralysis does not offer such possibilities.

16 As I made clear in the introduction of this thesis, similar views regarding the therapeutic power of literature are also shared by cognitive literary scholars working with functional approaches to literature.

17 For example, Dewey (1934), McLuhan (1964), Derrida (1992), Felski (2008), and Attridge (2004, 2015).

18 Dewey, for example, makes the following crucial claim in *Art as Experience*: "The sense of increase of understanding, of a deepened intelligibility on the part of objects and nature and man, resulting from esthetic experience has led philosophic theorists to treat art as a mode of knowledge.... But there is a great difference between the transformation of knowledge that is effected in imaginative and emotional vision.... In both production and enjoyed perception of works of art, knowledge is transformed; it becomes something more than knowledge because it is merged with non-intellectual elements to form an experience worthwhile as an experience" (Dewey 1958 [1934]: 288–90).

19 In *The Singularity of Literature*, Attridge criticizes "the dualisms of the aesthetic tradition," that is, "the opposition of form and content, which sets formal properties aside from any connection the work has to ethical, historical, and social issues" (2004: 108). In his opinion, "Instead of being opposed to content ... form includes the mobilization of meanings, or rather of the events of meaning: their sequentiality, interplay, and changing intensity, their patterns of expectation and satisfaction or tension and release, their precision or diffuseness. It does not include any extractable sense, information, image, or referent that the work lays before the reader. Through this mobilization of meanings, the work's linguistic operations such as referentiality, metaphoricity, intentionality, and ethicity are staged" (109).

20 Part of his PhD dissertation on McEwan, *Mimesis and the Imaginable Other: Metafictional Narrative Ethics in Ian McEwan's "Black Dogs" and "Atonement"* (2010).

21 For example, Lévinas (1948, 1961, 1972, 1982, 1991), Bauman (1995), Ricoeur (1984, 1985, 1988, 1990), and Kearney (1998, 1999, 2002).

Bibliography

Abbott, H. P. (2001), "Humanists, Scientists, and the Cultural Surplus," *SubStance*, 30(1–2): 203–19.

Abbott, H. P. (2008), "Unreadable Minds and the Captive Reader," *Style*, 42 (4): 448–67.

Adamson, L. B. and C. Russell (1999), "Emotion Regulation and the Emergence of Joint Attention," in P. Rochat (ed.), *Early Social Cognition: Understanding Others in the First Months of Life*, 281–97, Mahwah, NJ: Lawrence Erlbaum Associates Inc.

Adamson, L. B. and D. McArthur (1995), "Joint Attention, Affect, and Culture," in C. Moore and P. J. Dunham (eds.), *Joint Attention: Its Origins and Development*, 205–22, Mahwah, NJ: Lawrence Erlbaum Associates, Inc.

Adler, H. and S. Gross (2002), "Adjusting the Frame: Comments on Cognitivism and Literature," *Poetics Today*, 23 (2): 195–220.

Alber, J. (2009), "Impossible Storyworlds – And What to Do with Them," *Storyworlds*, 1: 79–96.

Alber, J. and R. Heinze (2011), *Unnatural Narratives, Unnatural Narratology*, Berlin: De Gruyter.

Alber, J., S. Iversen, H. S. Nielsen and B. Richardson (2010), "Unnatural Narratives, Unnatural Narratology: Beyond Mimetic Models," *Narrative*, 18 (2): 113–36.

Aldama, F. L. (ed.) (2010), *Toward a Cognitive Theory of Narrative Acts*, Austin: University of Texas Press.

Alexander, R. D. (1975), "The Search for a General Theory of Behavior," *Behavioral Sciences*, 20: 77–100.

Alexander, R. D. (1979), *Darwinism and Human Affairs*, Seattle: University of Washington Press.

Allyn, D. (2000), *Make Love Not War: The Sexual Revolution an Unfettered History*, Boston: Little, Brown.

Ammaniti, M. and V. Gallese (2014), *The Birth of Intersubjectivity: Psychodynamics, Neurobiology, and the Self*, New York: Norton.

Andresen, J. (2001), *Religion in Mind: Cognitive Perspectives on Religious Belief*, Cambridge: Cambridge University Press.

Aristotle (2006 [c. 335 BC]), *Poetics*, trans. J. Sachs, Newburyport, MA: Focus Publishing.

Atran, S. (2004), *In Gods We Trust: The Evolutionary Landscape of Religion*, Oxford: Oxford University Press.

Attridge, D. (2004), *The Singularity of Literature*, London and New York: Routledge.

Attridge, D. (2015), *The Work of Literature*, Oxford: Oxford University Press.

Austin, J. L. (1962), *How to Do Things with Words*, Oxford: Oxford University Press.

Bakhtin, M. (1981), *The Dialogic Imagination: Four Essays*, Austin: University of Texas Press.

Barkow, J. H., L. Cosmides, and J. Tooby (eds.) (1992), *The Adapted Mind: Evolutionary Psychology and the Generation of Culture*, Oxford: Oxford University Press.

Baron-Cohen, S. (1995), *Mindblindness: An Essay on Autism and Theory of Mind*, Cambridge, MA: MIT Press.

Baron-Cohen, S., A. Leslie, and U. Frith (1985), "Does the Autistic Child Have a 'Theory of Mind'?," *Cognition*, 21: 37–46.

Bateson, M. C. (1979), "The Epigenesis of Conversational Interaction: A Personal Account of Research Development," in M. Bullowa (ed.), *Before Speech: The Beginning of Human Communication*, 63–77, London: Cambridge University Press.

Bauman, Z. (1993), *Postmodern Ethics*, Oxford: Blackwell.

Beebe, B., S. Knoblauch, J. Rustin, and D. Sorter (2003), "A Comparison of Meltzoff, Trevarthen, and Stern," *Psychoanalytic Dialogues*, 13(6): 809–36.

Beer, G. (1983), *Darwin's Plots: Evolutionary Narrative in Darwin, George Elliot, and Nineteenth Century Fiction*, London: Routledge and Kegan Paul.

Bernaerts, L., D. De Geest, L. Herman, and B. Vervaeck (2013), *Stories and Minds: Cognitive Approaches to Literary Narrative*, Lincoln: University of Nebraska Press.

Bleuler, E. (1911), "Dementia Praecox oder Gruppe der Schizophrenien," in G. Aschaffenburg (ed.), *Handbuch der Psychiatrie, division 4.1*, Leipzig: Franz Deuticke.

Boden, M. (2006). *Mind as Machine: A History of Cognitive Science* (vol. 2). Oxford: Oxford University Press.

Bortolussi, M. and P. Dixon (2002), *Psychonarratology*, Cambridge: Cambridge University Press.

Bowlby, J. (1969), *Attachment and Loss. Vol. 1: Attachment*, New York: Basic Books.

Boyd, B. (1998), "Jane, Meet Charles: Literature, Evolution, and Human Nature," *Philosophy and Literature*, 22: 1–30.

Boyer, P. (2001), *Religion Explained: The Evolutionary Origins of Religious Thought*, London: Basic Books.

Böckler, A. and N. Sebanz (2013), "Linking Joint Attention and Joint Action," in J. Metcalfe and H. S. Terrace (eds.), *Agency and Joint Attention*, 206–15, Oxford: Oxford University Press.

Bradley, A. and A. Tate (2010), *The New Atheist Novel: Fiction, Philosophy, and Polemic after 9/11*, London and New York: Continuum.

Bråten, S. (2002), "Altercentric Perception by Infants and Adults in Dialogue: Ego's Virtual Participation in Alter's Complementary Act," in M. Stamenov and V. Gallese (eds.), *Mirror Neurons and the Evolution of Brain and*

Language, 273–94, Amsterdam and Philadelphia: John Benjamins Publishing Company.

Bråten, S. (2009), *The Intersubjective Mirror in Infant Learning and Evolution of Speech*, Amsterdam and Philadelphia: John Benjamins Publishing Company.

Bråten, S. and C. Trevarthen (2007), "Prologue: From Infant Intersubjectivity and Participant Movements to Simulation and Conversation in Cultural Common Sense," in S. Bråten (ed.), *On Being Moved: From Mirror Neurons to Empathy*, 21–34, Amsterdam and Philadelphia: John Benjamins Publishing Company.

Bratman, M. E. (2007), *Structures of Agency*, Oxford: Oxford University Press.

Broughton, L. (1991), "Portrait of the Subject as a Young Man: The Construction of Masculinity Ironized in 'Male' Fiction," in P. Shaw and P. Stockwell (eds.), *Subjectivity and Literature from the Romantics to the Present Day*, 135–45, London: Pinter.

Bruhn, M. and Wehrs, D. (eds.) (2013), *Cognition, Literature, and History*, New York: Routledge.

Bruner, J. (1990), *Acts of Meaning*, Cambridge, MA and London: Harvard University Press.

Burke, M. and E. Troscianko (2016), *Cognitive Literary Science: Dialogues Between Literature and Cognition*, Oxford: Oxford University Press.

Buss, D. M. (1994), *The Evolution of Desire: Strategies of Human Mating*, New York: Basic Books.

Butler, J. (1990), *Gender Trouble: Feminism and the Subversion of Identity*, New York: Routledge.

Butler, J. (2004), *Undoing Gender*, New York: Routledge.

Byrnes, B. C. (2009), *Ian McEwan's On Chesil Beach: The Transmutation of a "Secret,"* Nottingham: Paupers' Press.

Campbell, J. (2005), "Joint Attention and Common Knowledge," in N. Eilan, C. Hoerl, T. McCormack, and J. Roessler (eds.), *Joint Attention: Communication and Other Minds*, 287–97, Oxford: Oxford University Press.

Caracciolo, M. (2012), "On the Experientiality of Stories: A Follow-Up on David Herman's 'Narrative Theory and the Intentional Stance,'" *Partial Answers: Journal of Literature and the History of Ideas*, 10 (2): 197–221.

Caracciolo, M. (2014a), "Beyond Other Minds: Fictional Characters, Mental Simulation, and 'Unnatural' Experiences," *Journal of Narrative Theory*, 44 (1): 29–53.

Caracciolo, M. (2014b), *The Experientiality of Narrative: An Enactive Approach*, Berlin: De Gruyter.

Caracciolo, M. (2016), "Cognitive Literary Studies and the Status of Interpretation: An Attempt at Conceptual Mapping," *New Literary History*, 47: 187–208.

Carbonell, C. D. (2010), "A Consilient Science and Humanities in McEwan's *Enduring Love*," *Comparative Literature and Culture*, 12 (3). Available at http://docs.lib.purdue.edu/clcweb/vol12/iss3/12 (accessed 1 April 2019).

Carroll, J. (1995), *Evolution and Literary Theory*, Columbia: University of Missouri Press.

Carroll, J. (2004), *Literary Darwinism: Literature and the Human Animal*, New York: Routledge.

Carroll, J. (2008), "An Evolutionary Paradigm for Literary Study," *Style* 42 (2–3): 103–35.

Carruthers, P. (2005), *Consciousness: Essays from a Higher-Order Perspective*, Oxford: Oxford University Press.

Cassirer, E. (1955 [1925]), *The Philosophy of Symbolic Forms, Volume 2: Mythical Thought*, New Haven: Yale University Press.

Cavell, S. (1988), *In Quest of the Ordinary: Lines of Skepticism and Romanticism*, Chicago: University of Chicago Press.

Cavell, S. (1994), *A Pitch of Philosophy: Autobiographical Exercises*, Harvard: Harvard University Press.

Cavell, S. (2005), *Philosophy the Day after Tomorrow*, Cambridge, MA: Harvard University Press.

Childs, P. (ed.) (2006), *The Fiction of Ian McEwan*, Houndmills and New York: Palgrave Macmillan.

Childs, P. (2007a), "Believing Is Seeing: The Eye of the Beholder," in P. Childs (ed.), *Ian McEwan's Enduring Love*, 107–22, London and New York: Routledge.

Childs, P. (ed.) (2007b), *Ian McEwan's Enduring Love*, London and New York: Routledge.

Childs, P. (2009), "Contemporary McEwan and Anosognosia," in P. Nicklas (ed.), *Ian McEwan: Art and Politics*, 23–38. Heidelberg: Universitätsverlag Winter.

Colombetti, G. (2014), *The Feeling Body: Affective Science Meets the Enactive Mind*, Cambridge, MA: The MIT Press.

Costantini, M. and C. Sinigaglia (2011), "Grasping Affordances: A Window into Social Cognition," in A. Seemann (ed.), *Joint Attention: New Developments in Psychology, Philosophy of Mind, and Social Neuroscience*, 431–60, Cambridge, MA: MIT Press.

Crane, M. and A. Richardson (1999), "Literary Studies and Cognitive Science: Toward a New Interdisciplinarity," *Mosaic*, 32(2): 123–40.

Crooks, R. L. and K. Bauer (2013), *Our Sexuality*, Belmont: Wadsworth.

Currie, G. (2007), "Framing Narratives," in D. D. Hutto (ed.), *Narrative and Understanding Persons*, 17–42, Cambridge: Cambridge University Press.

Currie, G. (2010), *Narratives and Narrators: A Philosophy of Stories*, Oxford: Oxford University Press.

Dalewski, H. M. (1965), *The Forked Flame: A Study of D.H. Lawrence*, London: Faber and Faber.

Davies, R. (2007), "Enduring McEwan," in P. Childs (ed.), *Ian McEwan's Enduring Love*, 66–75, London and New York: Routledge.

De Azevedo, M. (2010), "Memory and Forgetfulness in Ian McEwan's *Atonement*," *Signotica*, 23: 165–78.

De Clérambault, G. G. (1942 [1921]), "Les Psychoses Passionelles," in *Oeuvres psychiatriques*, 315–22, Paris: Presses Universitaires.

De Jaegher, H. and E. Di Paulo (2007), "Participatory Sense-Making: An Enactive Approach to Social Cognition," *Phenomenology and the Cognitive Sciences*, 6 (4): 485–507.

Dennett, D. (1991), *Consciousness Explained*, London: Penguin.

Dennett, D. (2013), *Intuition Pumps and Other Tools for Thinking*, New York: W.W. Norton Company.

Derrida, J. (1988), *Limited Inc.*, Evanston: Northwestern University Press.

Derrida, J. (1992), *Acts of Literature*, ed. D. Attridge, New York and London: Routledge.

Desrochers, S., P. Morissette, and M. Ricard (1995), "Two Perspectives on Pointing in Infancy," in C. Moore and P. J. Dunham (eds.), *Joint Attention: Its Origins and Development*, 85–102, Mahwah, NJ: Lawrence Erlbaum Associates, Inc.

De Waal, F. (2009), *The Age of Empathy: Nature's Lessons for a Kinder Society*, New York: Three Rivers Press.

Dewey, J. (1958 [1934]), *Art as Experience*, New York: G.P. Putnam's Sons.

Diels, H. (ed.) (1903), *Die Fragmente der Vorsokratiker*, Berlin.

Disannayake, E. (2000), *Art and Intimacy: How the Arts Began*, Seattle: University of Washington Press.

Doherty, G. (1996), "'Ars Erotica' or 'Scientia Sexualis'?: Narrative Vicissitudes in D. H. Lawrence's *Women in Love*," *The Journal of Narrative Technique*, 26 (2): 137–57.

Doherty, G. (2001), *Oriental Lawrence: The Quest for the Secrets of Sex*, New York: Peter Lang.

Donald, M. (1991), *The Origins of the Modern Mind: Three Stages in the Evolution of Culture and Cognition*, Cambridge, MA: Harvard University Press.

Dupuy, J.-P. (2009), *On the Origins of Cognitive Science: The Mechanization of the Mind*, Cambridge, MA: The MIT Press.

Eco, U. (1979), *The Role of the Reader: Explorations in the Semiotics of Texts*, Bloomington: Indiana University Press.

Eco, U. (1992), *Interpretation and Overinterpretation*, Cambridge: Cambridge University Press.

Edwards, P. (2007), "Solipsism, Narrative, and Love in *Enduring Love*," in P. Childs (ed.), *Ian McEwan's Enduring Love*, 77–90, London and New York: Routledge.

Egan, K. (1997), *The Educated Mind: How Cognitive Tools Shape Our Understanding*, Chicago: University of Chicago Press.

Eilan, N., C. Hoerl, T. McCormack, and J. Roessler (eds.) (2005), *Joint Attention: Communication and Other Minds*, Oxford: Oxford University Press.

Ekman, P. (1999), "Basic Emotions," in T. Dalgleish and M. J. Power (eds.), *Handbook of Cognition and Emotion*, 45–60, Sussex: John Wiley and Sons.

Eliade, M. (1957), *The Sacred and the Profane: The Nature of Religion*, New York: Harcourt.

Empson, W. (1995 [1930]), *Seven Types of Ambiguity*, London: Penguin Books.

Felman, S. (1977), "Turning the Screw of Interpretation," *Yale French Studies*, 55/56: 94–207.

Felski, R. (2008), *Uses of Literature*, Malden, MA: Blackwell.

Field, T. M., R. Woodson, R. Greenberg, and D. Cohen (1982), "Discrimination and Imitation of Facial Expressions by Neonates," *Science*, 218: 179–82.

Finney, B. (2004), "Briony's Stand against Oblivion: The Making of Fiction in Ian McEwan's *Atonement*," *Journal of Modern Literature*, 27 (3): 68–82.

Flanagan, O. (2007), *The Really Hard Problem: Meaning in a Material World*, Cambridge, MA and London: The MIT Press.

Flavell, J. H. (1963), *The Developmental Psychology of Jean Piaget*, New York: Van Nostrand.

Forster, E. M. (1962 [1927]), *Aspects of the Novel*, Harmondsworth: Penguin.

Foucault, M. (1978 [1976]), *The History of Sexuality, Vol.1: An Introduction*, New York: Random House.

Foucault, M. (1989 [1961]), *Madness and Civilization*, London: Routledge.

Franco, F. (2005), "Infant Pointing: Harlequin, Servant of Two Masters," in N. Eilan, C. Hoerl, T. McCormack, and J. Roessler (eds.), *Joint Attention: Communication and Other Minds*, 129–64, Oxford: Oxford University Press.

Franco, F. (2013), "Embodied Attention in Infant Pointing," in J. Metcalfe and H. S. Terrace (eds.), *Agency and Joint Attention*, 152–64, Oxford: Oxford University Press.

Freud, S. (1957 [1915]), "Thoughts for the Times of War and Death," in J. Strachey (ed.), *The Standard Edition of the Complete Psychological Works of Sigmund Freud, Vol. 14*, 273–302, London, UK: Hogarth Press.

Fuchs, T. (2010), "The Psychopathology of Hyperreflexivity," *Journal of Speculative Philosophy*, 24 (3): 239–55.

Fuchs, T. (2012), "The Phenomenology and Development of Social Perspectives," *Phenomenology and the Cognitive Sciences*, 12: 655–83.

Fuchs, T. (2015), "Pathologies of Intersubjectivity in Autism and Schizophrenia," *Journal of Consciousness Studies*, 22 (1–2): 191–214.

Fuchs, T. (2018), *Ecology of the Brain: The Phenomenology and Biology of the Embodied Mind*, Oxford: Oxford University Press.

Fuchs, T. and H. De Jaegher (2009), "Enactive Intersubjectivity: Participatory Sense-Making and Mutual Incorporation," *Phenomenology and the Cognitive Sciences*, 8: 465–86.

Fuchs, T. and S. C. Koch (2014), "Embodied Affectivity: On Moving and Being Moved," *Frontiers of Psychology*, 5: 1–12.

Gallagher, S. (2001), "The Practice of Mind: Theory, Simulation, or Interaction?," *Journal of Consciousness Studies*, 8 (5–7): 83–107.

Gallagher, S. (2004), "Understanding Interpersonal Problems in Autism: Interaction Theory as an Alternative to Theory of Mind," *Philosophy, Psychiatry, and Psychology*, 11 (3): 199–217.

Gallagher, S. (2008), "Inference or Interaction: Social Cognition without Precursors," *Philosophical Explorations*, 11 (3): 163–73.

Gallagher, S. (2011a), "Interactive Coordination in Joint Attention," in A. Seeman (ed.), *Joint Attention: New Developments in Psychology, Philosophy of Mind, and Social Neuroscience*, 293–306, Cambridge, MA: MIT Press.

Gallagher, S. (2011b), "Narrative Competency and the Massive Hermeneutical Background," in P. Fairfield (ed.), *Hermeneutics in Education*, 21–38, New York: Continuum.

Gallagher, S. (2012), *Phenomenology*, Basingstoke: Palgrave Macmillan.

Gallagher, S. and D. D. Hutto (2008), "Understanding Others through Primary Interaction and Narrative Practice," in J. Zlatev, T. P. Racine, C. Sinha and E. Itkonen (eds.), *The Shared Mind: Perspectives on Intersubjectivity*, 17–38, Amsterdam and Philadelphia: John Benjamins Publishing Company.

Gallagher, S. and D. Zahavi (2008), *The Phenomenological Mind. An Introduction to Philosophy of Mind and Cognitive Science*, London: Routledge.

Gallagher, S. and R. S. Jacobson (2012), "Heidegger and Social Cognition," in J. Kiverstein and M. Wheeler (eds.), *Heidegger and Cognitive Science*, 213–45, New York: Palgrave Macmillan.

Gallese, V. L. (2001), "The 'Shared Manifold' Hypothesis: From Mirror Neurons to Empathy," *Journal of Consciousness Studies*, 8: 33–50.

Gallese, V. L. (2005), "'Being Like Me': Self-Other Identity, Mirror Neurons and Empathy," in S. Hurley and N. Chater (eds.), *Perspectives on Imitation II*, 101–18, Cambridge, MA: MIT Press.

Garton, S. (2004), *Histories of Sexuality: Antiquity to Sexual Revolution*, London: Equinox.

Gauthier, T. (2013), "'Selective in Your Mercies': Privilege, Vulnerability, and the Limits of Empathy in Ian McEwan's *Saturday*," *College Literature: A Journal of Critical Literary Studies*, 40 (2): 7–30.

Gibbs, R. (2005), *Embodiment and Cognitive Science*, New York: Cambridge University Press.

Gibson, J. J. (1986), *The Ecological Approach to Visual Perception*, Hillsdale, NJ: Lawrence Erlbaum Associates Inc.

Gilbert, A. (2008), *What the Nose Knows: The Science of Scent in Everyday Life*, New York: Crown Publishers.

Gilbert, M. (1990), "Walking Together: A Paradigmatic Social Phenomenon," *Midwest Studies*, 15: 1–14.

Glendinning, S. (1998), *On Being with Others: Heidegger-Derrida-Wittgenstein*, London: Routledge.

Gold, N. (ed.) (2005), *Teamwork: Multi-Disciplinary Perspectives*, New York: Palgrave Macmillan.

Goldman, A. (2005), "Imitation, Mind Reading, and Simulation," in S. Hurley and N. Chater, *Perspectives on Imitation II*, 79–94, Cambridge, MA: MIT Press.

Gomez, J.-C. (2005), "Joint Attention and the Notion of Subject: Insights from Apes, Normal Children, and Children with Autism," in N. Eilan, C. Hoerl,

T. McCormack, and J. Roessler (eds.), *Joint Attention: Communication and Other Minds*, 5–84, Oxford: Oxford University Press.

Good, K. P. and L. Kopala (2006), "Sex Differences and Olfactory Function," in W. J. Brewer, D. Castle, and C. Pantelis (eds.), *Olfaction and the Brain*, 183–202, Cambridge: Cambridge University Press.

Goodheart, E. (2008), "Do We Need Literary Darwinism?," *Style*, 42 (2–3): 181–85.

Gordon, R. M. (2005), "Intentional Agents Like Myself," in S. Hurley and N. Chater (eds.), *Perspectives on Imitation I.*, 95–106, Cambridge, MA: MIT Press.

Green, S. (2011), "'Up There with Black Holes and Darwin, Almost Bigger than Dinosaurs:' The Mind and McEwan's *Enduring Love*," *Style*, 45 (3): 441–63.

Greenberg, J. (2007), "Why Can't Biologists Read Poetry?: Ian McEwan's 'Enduring Love'," *Twentieth Century Literature*, 53 (2): 93–124.

Grice, H. P. (1975), "Logic and Conversation," in P. Cole and J. Morgan (eds.), *Syntax and Semantics*, Vol. 3 (*Speech Acts*), 41–58, New York: Academic Press.

Gurwitsch, A. (1979), *Human Encounters in the Social World*, Pittsburgh, PA: Duquesne University Press.

Hadot, P. (2006 [2004]), *The Veil of Isis. An Essay on the History of the Idea of Nature*, Cambridge, MA: The Belknap Press of Harvard University Press.

Hakemulder, J. (2000), *The Moral Laboratory: Experiments Examining the Effects of Reading Literature on Social Perception and Moral Self-Concept*, Amsterdam and Philadelphia: John Benjamins Publishing Company.

Hart, E. (2001), "The Epistemology of Cognitive Literary Studies," *Philosophy and Literature*, 25 (2): 314–34.

Hatfield, R. W. (1994), "Touch and Human Sexuality," in V. L. Bullough, B. Bullough and A. M. Stein (eds.), *Human Sexuality: An Introduction*, 581–85, New York: Garland Publishing.

Head, D. (2007), *Ian McEwan*, Manchester and New York: Manchester University Press.

Head, D. (2013), "On Chesil Beach: *Another 'Overrated' Novella?*" in S. Groes (ed.), *Ian McEwan: Contemporary Critical Perspectives*, 2nd ed., 115–22. London [etc.]: Bloomsbury.

Heidegger, M. (1962 [1927]), *Being and Time*, trans. J. Macquarrie and E. Robinson, New York: Harper & Row.

Herman, D. (2003), "Stories as a Tool for Thinking," in D. Herman (ed.), *Narrative Theory and the Cognitive Sciences*, Stanford: CSLI Publications.

Herman, D. (2008), "Narrative Theory and the Intentional Stance," *Partial Answers: Journal of Literature and the History of Ideas*, 6 (2): 233–60.

Herman, D. (2011a), "Re-Minding Modernism," in D. Herman (ed.), *The Emergence of Mind: Representations of Consciousness in Narrative Discourse in English*, 243–72, Lincoln and London: University of Nebraska Press.

Herman, D. (ed.) (2011b), *The Emergence of Mind: Representations of Consciousness in Narrative Discourse in English*, Lincoln and London: University of Nebraska Press.

Hidalgo, P. (2005), "Memory and Storytelling in Ian McEwan's *Atonement*," *Critique*, 46 (2): 82–91.

Hobson, P. (1993), *Autism and the Development of Mind*, Hillsdale, NJ: Lawrence Erlbaum Associates.

Hobson, P. (2005), "What Puts Jointness into Joint Attention," in N. Eilan, C. Hoerl, T. McCormack and J. Roessler (eds.), *Joint Attention: Communication and Other Minds*, 185–204, Oxford: Oxford University Press.

Hobson, P. and J. Hobson (2011), "Joint Attention or Joint Engagement? Insights from Autism," in A. Seemann (ed.), *Joint Attention: New Developments in Psychology, Philosophy of Mind, and Social Neuroscience*, 115–36, Cambridge, MA: MIT Press.

Hoerl, C. and T. McCormack (2005), "Joint Reminiscing as Joint Attention to the Past," in N. Eilan, C. Hoerl, T. McCormack, and J. Roessler (eds.), *Joint Attention: Communication and Other Minds*, 260–86, Oxford: Oxford University Press.

Hurley, S. L. (1998), *Consciousness in Action*, Cambridge, MA: Harvard University Press.

Hurley, S. and N. Chater (eds.) (2005), *Perspectives on Imitation* (2 vols.), Cambridge, MA: MIT Press.

Husserl, E. (1973a), Zur Phänomenologie der Intersubjektivität. *Texte aus dem Nachlass. Erster Teil*: 1905–1920 *(Husserliana 13)*, I. Kern (ed.), The Hague: Martinus Nijhoff.

Husserl, E. (1973b), Zur Phänomenologie der Intersubjektivität. *Texte aus dem Nachlass. Zweiter Teil*: 1921–1928 *(Husserliana 14)*, I. Kern (ed.), The Hague: Martinus Nijhoff.

Husserl, E. (1973c), Zur Phänomenologie der Intersubjektivität. *Texte aus dem Nachlass. Dritter Teil*: 1929–1935 *(Husserliana 15)*, I. Kern (ed.), The Hague: Martinus Nijhoff.

Hutto, D. D. (2007), "The Narrative Practice Hypothesis: Origins and Applications of Folk Psychology," in D. D. Hutto (ed.), *Narrative and Understanding Persons*, 43–68, Cambridge: Cambridge University Press.

Hutto, D. D. (2008), *Folk Psychological Narratives: The Sociocultural Basis of Understanding Reasons*, Cambridge, MA: MIT Press.

Hutto, D. D. and M. Ratcliffe (eds.) (2007), *Folk Psychology Re-assessed*, Dordrecht: Springer.

Ionescu, A. (2017), "Narrative Strategies of Representing the Environmental Crisis in Ian McEwan's *Solar*," in C. Sandten, C. Gualtieri and R. Pedretti (eds.), *Crisis, Risks and New Regionalisms in Europe: Emergency Diasporas and Borderlands*, 287–304, Trier: WVT.

Iser, W. (1974), *The Implied Reader: Patterns of Communication in Prose Fiction from Bunyan to Beckett*, Baltimore: Johns Hopkins University Press.

Iser, W. (1978), *The Act of Reading: A Theory of Aesthetic Response*, Baltimore: Johns Hopkins University Press.

Jackendoff, R. (1987), *Consciousness and the Computational Mind*, Cambridge, MA: The MIT Press.

Jackson, T. (2000), "Questioning Interdisciplinarity: Cognitive Science, Evolutionary Psychology, and Literary Criticism," *Poetics Today*, 21: 319–47.

Jackson, T. (2002), "Issues and Problems in the Blending of Cognitive Science, Evolutionary Psychology, and Literary Study," *Poetics Today*, 23 (1): 161–79.

Jackson, T. (2003), "'Literary Interpretation' and Cognitive Literary Studies," *Poetics Today*, 24 (2): 191–205.

Jaén, I. and S. J. Jacques (eds.) (2012), *Cognitive Literary Studies: Current Themes and New Directions*, Austin: University of Texas Press.

James, W. (1884), "What Is an Emotion?," *Mind*, 9: 188–205.

James, W. (1890), *The Principles of Psychology*, New York: Henry Holt and Company.

Jaus, H. R. (1982), *Toward an Aesthetics of Reception*, Minneapolis: University of Minnesota Press.

Kearney, R. (1998), *The Wake of Imagination*, London: Routledge.

Kearney, R. (1999), *Poetics of Modernity: Toward a Hermeneutic Imagination*, Amherst, MA: Prometheus.

Kearney, R. (2002), *On Stories*, London: Routledge.

Kelly, M. G. E. (2013), *Foucault's History of Sexuality Volume 1, The Will to Knowledge: An Edinburgh Philosophical Guide*, Edinburgh: Edinburgh University Press.

Kermode, F. (1973), *Lawrence*, Bungay: Fontana.

Kermode, F. (1979), *The Genesis of Secrecy: On the Interpretation of Narrative*, Cambridge, MA and London: Harvard University Press.

Kidd, D. C. and E. Castano (2013), "Reading Literary Fiction Improves Theory of Mind," *Science*, 342 (6156): 377–80.

Korthals Altes, L. (2009), "The End of Literature as a Basis for a Renewed Disciplinarity," in S. Winko, J. Fotis and G. Lauer (eds.), *Grenzen der Literatur. Zum Begriff und Phänomen des Literarischen (Revisionen. Grundbegriffe der Literaturtheorie; No. 2)*, 403–21, Berlin and New York: De Gruyter Mouton.

Korthals Altes, L. (2013), *Ethos and Narrative Interpretation: The Negotiation of Values in Fiction*, Lincoln: University of Nebraska Press.

Kuiken, D., D. Miall, and S. Sikora (2004), "Forms of Self-Implication in Literary Reading," *Poetics Today*, 25 (2): 171–203.

Kuzmičová, A. (2012), "Presence in the Reading of Literary Narrative: A Case for Motor Enactment," *Semiotica*, 189 (1/4): 23–48.

Lakoff, G. (1987), *Women, Fire, and Dangerous Things: What Categories Reveal about the Mind*, Chicago: University of Chicago Press.

Lakoff, G. and M. Johnson (1999), *Philosophy in the Flesh: The Embodied Mind and Its Challenge to Western Thought*, New York: Basic Books.

Lamarque, P. (2004), "On Not Expecting Too Much from Narrative," *Mind and Language*, 19: 393–408.

Lawrence D. H. (1923), *Studies in Classic American Literature*, New York: Thomas Seltzer, Inc.

Lawrence, D. H. (1959), *Lady Chatterley's Lover*, New York: Grove Press.

Lawrence, D. H. (1981 [1915]), *The Collected Letters of D.H. Lawrence*, Kingswood: The Windmill Press Ltd.

Lawrence, D. H. (1995 [1915]), *The Rainbow*, London: Penguin Books.

Leslie, A. M. (1987), "Children's Understanding of the Mental World," in R. L. Gregory (ed.), *The Oxford Companion to the Mind*, 139–42, Oxford: Oxford University Press.

Leverage, P., H. Mancing, R. Schweickert and J. M. William (eds.) (2010), *Theory of Mind and Literature*, West Lafayette, IN: Purdue University Press.

Lévinas, E. (1969 [1961]), *Totality and Infinity*, Pittsburgh, PA: Duquesne University Press.

Lévinas, E. (1985 [1982]), *Ethics and Infinity. Conversations with Philippe Nemo*, Pittsburgh, PA: Duquesne University Press.

Lévinas, E. (1987 [1948]), *Time and the Other*, Pittsburg, Pennsylvania: Duquesne University Press.

Lévinas, E. (1998 [1991]), *Entre Nous: On Thinking-of-the-Other*, New York: Columbia University Press.

Lévinas, E. (2003 [1972]), *Humanism of the Other*, Chicago: University of Illinois Press.

Lodder, P., M. Rotteveel, and M. van Elk (2015), "Enactivism and Neonatal Imitation: Conceptual and Empirical Considerations and Clarifications," *Frontiers of Psychology*, 5: 29–39.

Lyons, W. (1980), *Emotion*, Cambridge: Cambridge University Press.

Mar, R., K. Oakley, J. Hirsh, J. dela Paz, and J. B. Peterson (2006), "Bookworms Versus Nerds: Exposure to Fiction Versus Non-Fiction, Divergent Associations with Social Ability, and the Simulation of Fictional Social Worlds," *Journal of Research in Personality*, 40 (5): 694–712.

Marcus, S. (1966), *The Other Victorians: A Study of Sexuality and Pornography in Mid-Nineteenth Century England*, New York: Basic Books.

Mathews, P. (2012), "After the Victorians: The Historical Turning Point in McEwan's *On Chesil Beach*," *Critique*, 53: 82–91.

Matthews, S. (2007), "Seven Types of Unreliability," in P. Childs (ed.), *Ian McEwan's Enduring Love*, 107–22, London and New York: Routledge.

McEwan, I. (1982 [1981]), *The Imitation Game: Three Plays for Television*, London: Picador.

McEwan, I. (1992 [1987]), *The Child in Time*, London: Vintage.

McEwan, I. (1998a [1992]), *Black Dogs*, London: Vintage.

McEwan, I. (1998b), "Interview with Ian McEwan," *Bold Type*.

McEwan, I. (2006a [1975]), "Homemade," in *First Love, Last Rites*, 23–44, London: Vintage.

McEwan, I. (2006b [1975]), "Solid Geometry," in *First Love, Last Rites*, 1–23, London: Vintage.

McEwan, I. (2006 [1997]), *Enduring Love*, London: Vintage.

McEwan, I. (2006 [2005]), *Saturday*, London: Vintage.

McEwan, I. (2007 [2001]), *Atonement*, London: Vintage.

McEwan, I. (2007), "The Ghost in My Family" (interview), *The Sunday Times*, March 21.

McEwan, I. (2008 [2007]), *On Chesil Beach*, London: Vintage.

McEwan, I. (2011 [2010]), *Solar*, London: Vintage.

McEwan, I. (2014), *The Children Act*, London: Jonathan Cape.

McEwan, I. and D. Remnick (2010 [2007]), "Naming What Is There" (interview), in R. Roberts (ed.), *Conversations with Ian McEwan*, 156–75, Jackson: University Press of Mississippi.

McEwan, I. and I. Hamilton (2010 [1978]), "Points of Departure" (interview), in R. Roberts (ed.), *Conversations with Ian McEwan*, 3–18, Jackson: University Press of Mississippi.

McEwan, I. and M. D'Ancona (2007), "The Magus of Fitzrovia" (inteview), *The Spectator*, April 4.

McLaren, A. (1999), *Twentieth-Century Sexuality: A History*, Oxford: Basil Blackwell.

McLuhan, M. (1964), *Understanding Media: The Extensions of Man*, New York: McGraw-Hill.

Meltzoff, A. N. and M. K. Moore (1977), "Imitation of Facial and Manual Gestures by Human Neonates," *Science*, 198: 75–8.

Meltzoff, A. N. and R. Brooks (2013), "Gaze Following and Agency in Human Infancy," in J. Metcalfe and H. S. Terrace (eds.), *Agency and Joint* Attention, 125–38, Oxford: Oxford University Press.

Merleau-Ponty, M. (1960), *Signes*, Paris: Gallimard.

Merleau-Ponty, M. (1962 [1945]), *Phenomenology of Perception*, London: Routledge & Kegan Paul.

Merleau-Ponty, M. (1964), *The Primacy of Perception*, Evanston: Northwestern University Press.

Metcalfe, J. and H. S. Terrace (eds.) (2013), *Agency and Joint Attention*, Oxford: Oxford University Press.

Miall, D. (2006), *Literary Reading: Empirical and Theoretical Studies*, New York: Peter Lang.

Michael, J. (2011), "Shared Emotions and Joint Action," *Review of Philosophical Psychology*, 2 (2): 355–73.

Mill, J. S. (1867), *An Examination of Sir William Hamilton's Philosophy*, 3rd edn, Longmans: London.

Miller, G. (2000), *The Mating Mind: How Sexual Choice Shaped the Evolution of Human Nature*, New York: Anchor.

Möller, S. (2011), *Coming to Terms with Crisis: Disorientation and Reorientation in the Novels of Ian McEwan*, Heidelberg: Universitätsverlag Winter.

Moore, C. and P. J. Dunham (eds.) (1995), *Joint Attention: Its Origins and Role in Development*, Mahwah, NJ: Lawrence Erlbaum Associates, Inc.

Moore, P. A. (2016), *The Hidden Power of Smell: How Chemicals Influence Our Lives and Behavior*, Heidelberg, New York, Dordrecht, London: Springer International Publishing.

Nash, C. (1990), *Narrative in Culture: The Uses of Storytelling in the Sciences, Philosophy, and Literature*, London and New York: Routledge.

Naugle, D. (2002), *Worldview: The History of a Concept*, Grand Rapids, MI: Eerdmans.

Nelson, K. (1996), *Language in Cognitive Development: Emergence of the Mediated Mind*, Cambridge: Cambridge University Press.

Nelson, K. (2003), "Narrative and the Emergence of a Consciousness of Self," in G. Fireman, T. E. McVay Jr., and O. J. Flanagan (eds.), *Narrative and Consciousness: Literature, Psychology, and the Brain*, 17–36, Oxford: Oxford University Press.

Nelson, K. (2005), "Emerging Levels of Consciousness in Early Human Development," in H. S. Terrace and J. Metcalfe (eds.), *The Missing Link in Cognition: Origins of Self-Reflective Consciousness*, 116–41, Oxford: Oxford University Press.

Nelson, K. (2007), *Young Minds in Social Worlds: Experience, Meaning, and Memory*, London and Cambridge, MA: Harvard University Press.

Nesse, R. M. and A. T. Lloyd (1992), "The Evolution of Psychodynamic Mechanisms," in J. H. Barkow, L. Cosmides, and J. Tooby (eds.), *The Adapted Mind: Evolutionary Psychology and the Generation of Culture*, 601–24, Oxford: Oxford University Press.

Newen, A., L. de Bruin, and S. Gallagher (2018), *The Oxford Handbook of 4E Cognition*, Oxford: Oxford University Press.

Noë, A. (2004), *Action in Perception*, Cambridge, MA: The MIT Press.

Norris, C. (2015), "Ectopiques," *In/Stead* 4. Available at http://www.insteadjo urnal.com/article/ectopiques/ (accessed 2 April 2019).

Nussbaum, M. (2001), *Upheavals of Thought: The Intelligence of Emotions*, Cambridge: Cambridge University Press.

Nygren, A. (1953), *Agape and Eros*, Philadelphia: The Westminster Press.

O'Hara, D. K. (2010), "Briony's Being-For: Metafictional Narrative Ethics in Ian McEwan's *Atonement*," *Critique: Studies in Contemporary Fiction*, 52 (1): 74–100.

Owen, I. R. (2017), *On Attachment: The View from Developmental Psychology*, London: Karnac Books Ltd.

Pacherie, E. and J. Dokic (2006), "From Mirror Neurons to Joint Action," *Cognitive Systems Research*, 7: 101–12.

Palmer, A. (2004), *Fictional Minds*, Lincoln: University of Nebraska Press.

Palmer, A. (2009), "Attributions of Madness in Ian McEwan's *Enduring Love*," *Style*, 43 (3): 291–308.

Palmer, A. (2010), *Social Minds in the Novel*, Columbus: The Ohio State University Press.

Parnas, J. (2003), "Self and Schizophrenia: A Phenomenological Perspective," in T. Kircher and A. David (eds.), *The Self in Neuroscience and Psychiatry*, 217–41. Cambridge: Cambridge University Press.

Paterson, M. (2007), *The Senses of Touch: Haptics, Affects and Technology*, Oxford and New York: Berg.

Pearsall, R. (1969), *The Worm in the Bud: The World of Victorian Sexuality*, London: Weidenfeld & Nicolson.

Pelosi, P. (2016), *On the Scent: A Journey through the Science of Smell*, Oxford: Oxford University Press.

Phelan, J. (2009), "Cognitive Narratology, Rhetorical Narratology, and Interpretive Disagreement: A Response to Alan Palmer's Analysis of *Enduring Love*," *Style*, 43 (3): 309–21.

Piaget, J. (1928 [1926]), *The Child's Conception of the World*, London: Routledge and Kegan Paul.

Piaget, J. (1952 [1936]), *The Origins of Intelligence in Children*, New York: International University Press.

Popova, Y. (2015), *Stories, Meaning, and Experience: Narrativity and Enaction*, New York and London: Routledge.

Pynchon, T. (1967 [1965]), *The Crying of Lot 49*, London: Jonathan Cape.

Rako, S. and J. Friebely (2004), "Pheromonal Influences on Sociosexual Behavior in Postmenopausal Women," *Journal of Sex Research*, 41: 372–380.

Ramin, Z. and S. M. Marandi (2012), "Unraveling Identity in Ian McEwan's *Enduring Love*," *Studies in Literature and Language*, 4 (1): 78–85.

Randall, M. (2007), "'I Don't Want Your Story:' Open and Fixed Narratives in *Enduring Love*," in P. Childs (ed.), *Ian McEwan's Enduring Love*, 44–54, London and New York: Routledge.

Ratcliffe, M. (2007), *Rethinking Commonsense Psychology: A Critique of Folk Psychology, Theory of Mind and Simulation*, Basingstoke, UK: Palgrave Macmillan.

Reddy, V. (2005), "Before the 'Third Element': Understanding Attention to Self," in N. Eilan, C. Hoerl, T. McCormack, and J. Roessler (ed.), *Joint Attention: Communication and Other Minds*, 85–109, Oxford: Oxford University Press.

Reddy, V. (2008), *How Infants Know Minds*, Cambridge, MA: Harvard University Press.

Reddy, V. (2011), "A Gaze at Grips with Me," in A. Seemann (ed.), *Joint Attention: New Developments in Psychology, Philosophy of Mind, and Social Neuroscience*, 137–58, Cambridge, MA: MIT Press.

Reddy, V. (2013), "Joining Intentions in Infancy," *Journal of Consciousness Studies*, 22 (1–2): 24–44.

Richardson, A. (2004), "Studies in Literature and Cognition: A Field Map," in A. Richardson and E. Spolsky (eds.), *The Work of Fiction: Cognition, Culture, and Complexity*, 1–29, Aldershot: Ashgate.

Ricoeur, P. (1970 [1965]), *Freud and Philosophy*, New Haven: Yale University Press.

Ricoeur, P. (1984, 1985, 1988 [1983, 1984, 1985]), *Time and Narrative*, Chicago: University of Chicago Press.

Ricoeur, P. (1992 [1990]), *Oneself as Another*, Chicago: University of Chicago Press.

Bibliography

Ricoeur, P. (1994), "Wonder, Eroticism and Enigma," in J. Nelson and S. Longfellow (eds.), *Sexuality and the Sacred: Sources for Theological Reflection*, Louisville, KY: John Knox Press.

Ridley, M. (1993), *The Red Queen: Sex and the Evolution of Human Nature*, London: Viking.

Rizzolatti, G. and C. Sinigaglia (2008), *Mirrors in the Brain. How Our Minds Share Actions and Emotions*, New York: Oxford University Press.

Rochat, P. (2009), *Others in Mind: Social Origins of Self-Consciousness*, Cambridge: Cambridge University Press.

Rochat, P. and C. Passos-Ferreira (2009), "From Imitation to Reciprocation and Mutual Recognition," in J. A. Pineda (ed.), *Mirror Neuron System: The Role of Mirroring Processes in Social Cognition*, 191–212, New York: Humana Press.

Rochat, P., C. Passos-Ferreira, and P. Salem (2009), "Three Levels of Intersubjectivity in Early Development," in A. Carassa, F. Morganti, and G. Riva (eds.), *The Proceedings of the International Workshop Enacting Intersubjectivity*, 173–90, Como: Larioprint.

Roessler, J. (2005), "Joint Attention and the Problem of Other Minds," in N. Eilan, C. Hoerl, T. McCormack, and J. Roessler (ed.), *Joint Attention: Communication and Other Minds*, 230–59, Oxford: Oxford University Press.

Roth, P. (2007 [1995]), *Sabbath's Theater*, London: Vintage.

Rushdie, S. (2013), *Joseph Anton: A Memoir*, London: Random House.

Ryan, K. (1994), *Ian McEwan*, Tavistock: Northcote House Publishers.

Ryan, K. (2007), "After the Fall," in P. Childs (ed.), *Ian McEwan's Enduring Love*, 44–54, London and New York: Routledge.

Sacks, O. (1995), *An Anthropologist on Mars: Seven Paradoxical Tales*, New York: Alfred Knopf.

Sander, D. and K. Scherer (eds.) (2009), *The Oxford Companion to Emotion and the Affective Sciences*, Oxford: Oxford University Press.

Sanford, A. and C. Emmott (2012), *Mind, Brain and Narrative*, Cambridge: Cambridge University Press.

Sartre, J.-P. (1956 [1943]), *Being and Nothingness*, New York: Philosophical Library.

Schmid, H.-B. (2009), *Plural Action: Essays in Philosophy and Social Science*, Dordrecht: Springer.

Schneider, R. (2001), "Towards a Cognitive Theory of Literary Character: The Dynamics of Mental-Model Construction," *Style* 35(4): 607–40.

Scholl, B. J. and P. D. Tremoulet (2000), "Perceptual Causality and Animacy," *Trends in Cognitive Sciences*, 4/8: 299–309.

Schore, A. (2019), *The Development of the Unconscious Mind*, New York and London: W.W. Norton, Inc.

Schreier, M. (2009), "Belief Change through Fiction: How Fictional Narratives Affect Real Readers," in S. Winko, J. Fotis, and G. Lauer (eds.), *Grenzen der Literatur. Zum Begriff und Phänomen des Literarischen (Revisionen. Grundbegriffe der Literaturtheorie; No. 2)*, 315–37, Berlin and New York: De Gruyter Mouton.

Schütz, A. (1945), "On Multiple Realities," *Philosophy and Phenomenological Research*, 5 (4): 533–76.

Sebanz, N., G. Knoblich, and W. Prinz (2005), "How Two Share a Task: Corepresenting Stimulus–Response Mappings," *Journal of Experimental Psychology. Human Perception and Performance*, 31 (6): 1234–46.

Seemann, A. (ed.) (2011), *Joint Attention: New Developments in Psychology, Philosophy of Mind, and Social Neuroscience*, Cambridge, MA: MIT Press.

Seemann, A. (2011), "Joint Attention: Towards a Relational Account," in A. Seemann (ed.), *Joint Attention: New Developments in Psychology, Philosophy of Mind, and Social Neuroscience*, 183–202, Cambridge, MA: MIT Press.

Shaffer, D. R. and K. Kipp (2014), *Developmental Psychology. Childhood and Adolescence* (9th ed.), Belmont: Wadsworth.

Sheveland, J. N. (2008), "Divine Love in Christianity," in Y. R. Greenberg (ed.), *Encyclopedia of Love in World Religions Vol. 1*, 161–62, Santa Barbara: ABC CLIO.

Sigman, M. and C. Kasari (1995), "Joint Attention Across Contexts in Normal and Autistic Children," in C. Moore and P. J. Dunham (eds.), *Joint Attention: Its Origins and Development*, 189–204, Mahwah, NJ: Lawrence Erlbaum Associates, Inc.

Sistani, R. R., R. S. Hashim, and S. I. Hamdan (2014), "A Perpetual Search for the Idealized Lost Love Object: An Object-Relations Reading of Ian McEwan's *Enduring Love*," *Review of European Studies*, 6 (3): 142–52.

Slay, J. (1996), *Ian McEwan*, New York: Twayne Publishers.

Solomon, R. (1976), *The Passions*, New York: Anchor/Doubleday.

Sontag, S. (1966), *Against Interpretation and Other Essays*, London: Picador.

Spiridon, M. (2010), "The (Meta)narrative Paratext: Coda as a Cunning Fictional Device," *Neohelicon*, 37: 53–62.

Spolsky, E. (1990), "The Uses of Adversity: The Literary Text and the Audience That Doesn't Understand," in E. Spolsky (ed.), *The Uses of Adversity: Failure and Accommodation in Reader Response*, 17–35, Lewisburg: Bucknell University Press.

Spolsky, E. (1993), *Gaps in Nature: Literary Interpretation and the Modular Mind*, Albany: State University of New York Press.

Spolsky, E. (1994), "Doubting Thomas and the Senses of Knowing," *Common Knowledge*, 3 (2): 111–29.

Spolsky, E. (2001), *Satisfying Skepticism: Embodied Knowledge in the Early Modern World*, Aldershot, Hampshire: Ashgate.

Spolsky, E. (2003), "Cognitive Literary Historicism: A Response to Adler and Gross," *Poetics Today*, 24 (2): 161–83.

Spolsky, E. (2011), "An Embodied View of Misunderstanding in *Macbeth*," *Poetics Today*, 32: 489–520.

Spolsky, E. (2015a), *The Contracts of Fiction: Cognition, Culture, Community*, Oxford: Oxford University Press.

Spolsky, E. (2015b), "The Biology of Failure, the Forms of Rage, and the Equity of Revenge," in L. Zunshine (ed.), *The Oxford Handbook of Cognitive Literary Studies*, 34–54, Oxford: Oxford University Press.

Stern, D. N. (1985), *The Interpersonal World of the Infant: A View from Psychoanalysis and Developmental Psychology*, New York: Basic Books.
Stern, D. N. (2000 [1985]), *The Interpersonal World of the Infant: A View from Psychoanalysis and Developmental Psychology* (Revised ed.), New York: Basic Books.
Sternberg, M. (2003a), "Universals of Narrative and Their Cognitivist Fortunes (I)," *Poetics Today*, 24 (2): 297–395.
Sternberg, M. (2003b), "Universals of Narrative and Their Cognitivist Fortunes (II)," *Poetics Today*, 24 (3): 517–638.
Storey, R. (1996), *Mimesis and the Human Animal: On the Biogenetic Foundations of Literary Representation*, Evanston: Northwestern University Press.
Strachey, L. (1918), *Eminent Victorians*, Harmondsworth: Penguin.
Strachey, L. (1921), *Queen Victoria*, Harmondsworth: Penguin.
Suleiman, S. and I. Crosman (eds.) (1980), *The Reader in the Text: Essays on Audience and Interpretation*, Princeton: Princeton University Press.
Summers-Bremner, E. (2014), *Ian McEwan: Sex, Death and History*, Amherst: Cambria Press.
Szanto, T. and D. Moran (eds.) (2016), *"The Phenomenology of Sociality: Discovering the 'We,"* London and New York: Routledge.
Szreter, S. and K. Fisher (2010), *Sex Before the Sexual Revolution: Intimate Life in England 1918–1963*, Cambridge: Cambridge University Press.
Taylor, C. (1989), *Sources of the Self: The Making of Modern Identity*, Cambridge, Mass.: Harvard University Press.
Thagard, P. (2014), "Cognitive Science," in E. N. Zalta, *The Stanford Encyclopedia of Philosophy*. Available at http://plato.stanford.edu/archives/fall2014/entries/cognitive-science/ (accessed 2 April 2019).
Thompson, E. (2007), *Mind in Life: Biology, Phenomenology, and the Sciences of the Mind*, Cambridge, MA: The Belknap Press of Harvard University Press.
Tollefsen, D. (2005), "Let's Pretend! Joint Action and Young Children," *Philosophy of the Social Sciences*, 35: 75–97.
Tomasello, M. (1995), "Joint Attention as Social Cognition," in C. Moore and P. J. Dunham (eds.), *Joint Attention: Its Origins and Development*, 103–30, Mahwah, NJ: Lawrence Erlbaum Associates, Inc.
Tomasello, M. (1999), *The Cultural Origins of Human Cognition*, Cambridge, MA [etc.]: Harvard University Press.
Tomasello, M. (2008), *Origins of Human Communication*, Cambridge, MA: MIT Press.
Tomasello, M. (2009), *Why We Cooperate*, Cambridge, MA: The MIT Press.
Tompkins, J. P. (ed.) (1980), *Reader-Response Criticism: From Formalism to Post-Structuralism*, Baltimore: Johns Hopkins University Press.
Trevarthen, C. (1979), "Communication and Cooperation in Early Infancy: A Description of Primary Intersubjectivity," in M. Bullowa (ed.), *Before Speech: The Beginning of Interpersonal Communication*, 99–136, Cambridge: Cambridge University Press.

Trevarthen, C. (1980), "The Foundations of Intersubjectivity: Development of Interpersonal and Cooperative Understanding of Infants," in D. Olson (ed.), *The Social Foundation of Language and Thought: Essays in Honor of Jerome S. Bruner*, 316–41, New York: Norton.

Trevarthen, C. (2006), "The Concepts and Foundations of Intersubjectivity," in S. Bråten (ed.), *Intersubjective Communication and Emotion in Early Ontogeny*, 15–46, Cambridge: Cambridge University Press.

Trevarthen, C. (2011), "The Generation of Human Meaning: How Shared Experience Grows in Infancy," in A. Seemann (ed.), *Joint Attention: New Developments in Psychology, Philosophy of Mind, and Social Neuroscience*, 73–114, Cambridge, MA: MIT Press.

Trevarthen, C. and P. Hubley (1978), "Secondary Intersubjectivity: Confidence, Confiding and Acts of Meaning in the First Year," in A. Lock (ed.), *Action, Gesture and Symbol: The Emergence of Language*, 183–229, London: Academic Press.

Trivers, R. L. (1976), "Foreword," in R. Dawkins, *The Selfish Gene*, New York: Oxford University Press.

Trivers, R. L. (1985), *Social Evolution*, Menlo Park, CA: Benjamin/Cummings.

Tronick, E., Als, H., Adamson, L., Wise, S., and T. B. Brazelton, "The Infant's Response to Entrapment between Contradictory Messages in Face-to-Face Interaction," *Journal of the American Academy of Child and Adolescent Psychiatry*, 17: 1–13.

Trudgill, E. (1976), *Madonnas and Magdalens: The Origins and Development of Victorian Sexual Attitudes*, London: Heinemann.

Tulving, E. (1972), "Episodic and Semantic Memory," in E. Tulving and W. Donaldson (eds.), *Organization of Memory*, 381–403, New York: Academic Press.

Tuomela, R. (2007), *Philosophy of Sociality: The Shared Point of View*, New York: Oxford University Press.

Underhill, J. W. (2011), *Creating Worldviews: Metaphor, Ideology and Language*, Edinburgh: Edinburgh University Press.

Van Gennep, A. (2004 [1960]), *The Rites of Passage*, London: Routledge.

Varela, F., E. Thompson and E. Rosch (1991), *The Embodied Mind: Cognitive Science and Human Experience*, Cambridge, MA: The MIT Press.

Vermeule, B. (2010), *Why Do We Care about Literary Characters?*, Baltimore and London: Johns Hopkins University Press.

Vesper, C., S. Butterfill, N. Sebanz, and G. Knoblich (2010), "A Minimal Architecture for Joint Action," *Neural Networks*, 23(8/9): 998–1003.

Vygotsky, L. (1986), *Thought and Language*, Cambridge, MA: The MIT Press.

Wally, J. (2012), "Ian McEwan's *Saturday* as a New Atheist Novel? A Claim Revisited," *Anglia - Zeitschrift für englische Philologie*, 130 (1): 95–119.

Weeks, J. (1989 [1981]), *Sex, Politics, and Society: The Regulation of Sexuality since 1800*, Longman: Harlow.

Weeks, J. (2010), *Sexuality*, 3rd ed., London and New York: Routledge.

Wellman, H. M., D. Cross, and J. Watson (2001), "Meta-Analysis of Theory-of-Mind Development: The Truth About False Belief," *Child Development*, 72: 655–84.

Wells, L. (2010), *Ian McEwan*, Houndmills: Palgrave Macmillan.

Wilson, D. A. and R. J. Stevenson (2006), *Learning to Smell: Olfactory Perception from Neurobiology to Behavior*, Baltimore: The Johns Hopkins University Press.

Wittgenstein, L. (1980), *Remarks on the Philosophy of Psychology II*, Oxford: Blackwell.

Wittgenstein, L. (1992), *Last Writings on the Philosophy of Psychology; Volume II*, Oxford: Blackwell.

Woolf, V. (1996 [1925]), *Mrs. Dalloway*, London: Penguin Books.

Wright, R. (1994), *The Moral Animal: Why We Are the Way We Are. The New Science of Evolutionary Psychology*, London: Vintage.

Wyatt, T. D. (2003), *Pheromones and Animal Behavior: Communication by Smell and Taste*, Cambridge: Cambridge University Press.

Wyschogrod, E. (1981), "Empathy and Sympathy as Tactile Encounter," *Journal of Medicine and Philosophy*, 6: 25–43.

Zahavi, D. (ed.) (2000), *Exploring the Self: Philosophical and Psychopathological Perspectives on Self-Experience*, Amsterdam/Philadelphia: John Benjamins Publishing Company.

Zahavi, D. (2003), *Husserl's Phenomenology*, Stanford: Stanford University Press.

Zahavi, D. (2008), "Simulation, Projection and Empathy," *Consciousness and Cognition*, 17: 514–22.

Zahavi, D. (2014), *Self and Other: Exploring Subjectivity, Empathy, and Shame*, Oxford: Oxford University Press.

Zahavi, D. and P. Rochat (2015), "Empathy ≠ Sharing: Perspectives from Phenomenology and Developmental Psychology," *Consciousness and Cognition*, 36: 5443–553.

Zunshine, L. (2006), *Why We Read Fiction: Theory of Mind and the Novel*, Columbus: Ohio State University Press.

Zunshine, L. (ed.) (2015), *The Oxford Handbook of Cognitive Literary Studies*, Oxford: Oxford University Press.

Index of Names

Index of Subjects

www.ingramcontent.com/pod-product-compliance
Lightning Source LLC
Chambersburg PA
CBHW050438280326
41932CB00013BA/2160